THE INSURANCE DICTIONARY

THE A TO Z OF LIFE & HEALTH

THE
INSURANCE
DICTIONARY

THE A TO Z OF LIFE & HEALTH

THIRD EDITION

JOHN R. INGRISANO, CLU
& CORINNE M. INGRISANO

Dearborn
Financial Publishing, Inc.

While a great deal of care has been taken to provide accurate and current information, the ideas, suggestions, general principles and conclusions presented in this book are subject to local, state and federal laws and regulations, court cases and any revisions of same. The reader is thus urged to consult legal counsel regarding any points of law—this publication should not be used as a substitute for competent legal advice.

Executive Editor: Kathleen A. Welton
Acquisitions Editor: Wendy Lochner
Project Editor: Ronald J. Liszkowski
Copy Editor: Ellen Allen
Interior Design: Sara Shelton
Cover Design: Bob Post

Published by Dearborn Financial Publishing, Inc.

Printed in the United States of America.
90 91 92 10 9 8 7 6 5 4 3 2

Library of Congress Cataloging-in-Publication Data

Ingrisano, John R., 1950–
    The insurance dictionary : the A to Z of life & health / John Ingrisano, Corinne M. Ingrisano. -- 3rd ed.
        p.   cm.
    ISBN 0-88462-864-7
    1. Insurance, Life--Dictionaries. 2. Insurance, Health--Dictionaries. I. Ingrisano, Corinne M. II. Title.
HG8759.I54   1989
368.3'003--dc20   89-12545
                                                                CIP

Introduction

THE INSURANCE DICTIONARY is a handy reference tool for all who work directly in or indirectly with the insurance industry. It is the most comprehensive and informative compilation of life and health insurance terms on the market today.

Definitions cover not only basic life and health insurance terms, but also a wide range of related subjects, including agent training and agency building concepts, retirement and estate planning, investments and securities, government benefit programs, taxation, etc. Also included are the names and descriptions of organizations and government agencies that have a direct or related bearing on life and health fields. A separate listing of pertinent abbreviations is provided at the back of the book.

It should be noted, however, that the definitions appearing in this dictionary are not intended to be legal or contract definitions, and they should not be used or relied upon as such. Their sole purpose is to help the reader arrive at a clear and practiced understanding of the general meanings of these words and phrases as they are commonly used in the life and health insurance business.

Considering the unprecedented scope of this undertaking, some terms may have been inadvertently omitted, and readers may disagree over the wording of some definitions. Also, ongoing developments in the industry will continue to bring new terminology and changes in the meaning of existing terms. We welcome readers' suggestions on these matters so that future editions of THE INSURANCE DICTIONARY will be even better and will continue to meet the needs of the insurance community.

A

A & H policy: A policy that provides benefits for loss resulting from either an accident or sickness. Also called health policy.

abandonment: The relinquishment or surrender of rights, interests or property by one person or party to another, either expressly or by implication.

abatement: The diminishing or the entire doing away of anything, as in an abatement of taxes.

absolute: A complete or final ruling or order, without conditions.

absolute assignment: A policy assignment under which the assignee receives full control over the policy and full rights to its benefits. As a general rule, when a policy is assigned to secure a debt, the insured retains all rights in the policy in excess of such debt, even though the assignment is absolute in form. (*See also: assignment* and *collateral assignment.*)

absolute beneficiary: (*See: irrevocable beneficiary.*)

absolute ownership: The insured has full legal rights and control of property (selection of beneficiaries, settlement options, etc.) in a policy. The interest of explicit right of possession is so free from limitations, qualifications or restrictions that it cannot be taken away without that person's consent.

abstract, insurance: A brief of a record, listing particular accounting, statistical or reference data submitted to the home office or district offices for a specific situation.

accelerated endowment: (*See: accelerated paid-up or endowment.*)

1

accelerated option: A provision whereby a policyowner applies accumulated dividends to mature a policy more rapidly than would otherwise take place.

accelerated paid-up or endowment: The fully paid date of an ordinary life or limited payment life policy, or the maturity date of an endowment policy may be advanced or accelerated under certain conditions by using dividend accumulation values to provide the amount necessary to make the desired change.

accelerative endowment: An option whereby life insurance policy dividends may be used to accelerate the cash accumulation process and mature a policy as an endowment before the regular maturity date.

acceptance: (*See: offer and acceptance.*)

accepted reinsurance: (*See: assumed reinsurance.*)

accident: In the context of situations covered by accident and health insurance, an unintended, unforeseen and unexpected event which generally results in injury and/or loss.

accidental bodily injury: Unforeseen and unintended bodily injury resulting from an accident. Generally considered a more liberal term or definition in accident insurance policies, as distinguished from a technical interpretation of the term accidental means. (*See also: accidental means.*)

accidental death: Death as the result of accidental bodily injury; that is, injury which is unintended, unexpected and unusual. Contrasted with death by accidental means, which means that the cause of the accident itself must be accidental (slipping off a ladder, etc.). Thus, a broken neck as a result of an intended safe dive into a swimming pool is accidental death, but not accidental means.

accidental death and dismemberment benefit: A policy provision that pays a stated benefit in case of death or the loss of limbs or sight as a result of an accident.

accidental death benefit: A payment for loss of life due to an accident that was the direct cause of death. A provision added to a life insurance policy for payment of an additional benefit, related to the face amount of the basic policy, when death occurs by accidental means as defined in the policy. This is often called double indemnity when the additional benefit equals the face of the policy. (*See also: capital sum* and *double indemnity.*)

accidental death insurance: A form of insurance that provides payment if the death of the insured results from accident. Accidental death insurance is often combined with dismemberment insurance in a form called accidental death and dismemberment. (*See also: double indemnity.*)

accidental dismemberment: Often defined as "the severance of limbs at or above the wrists or ankle joints, or the entire irrevocable loss of sight." Loss of use, in itself, is not usually considered to be dismemberment.

accidental means: An unforeseen, unexpected, unintended cause of an accident. The means that causes the mishap must be accidental for any claim to be payable.

accidental means death benefit: An optionally available benefit providing for the payment of a multiple (usually double) of the face amount of the policy in case of death by accidental means. The benefit usually covers death resulting from bodily injury effected solely through external, violent and accidental means, independently and exclusively of all other causes, and within 90 days after such injury.

accidental means, death by: Death resulting from a cause that is accidental, so that both the cause and the result are accidental.

accident and health insurance: Insurance under which benefits are payable in case of disease, accidental injury, or accidental death. Also called health insurance, personal health insurance, sickness and accident insurance, A & H insurance.

accident and sickness insurance: (*See: accident and health insurance.*)

accident frequency: Rate of occurrence of accidents.

accident frequency rate: The total number of disabling injuries suffered by employees per 1,000,000 employee-hours of work on an annual basis.

accident industrial: An unforeseen, unintended accident that has occurred as a result of one's employment or occupation.

accident insurance: Replaces a part of earned income that has been lost due to disability caused by accidental injury. May also pay medical expenses caused by accidental injury, as well as an indemnity for death or loss of sight or limbs suffered through accident. (*See also: accident and health insurance.*)

accident policy: One which provides indemnities for loss resulting from accidental bodily injuries.

accident severity rate: The number of days lost from disability injuries or death per 1,000 employee-hours of work, with 6,000 days charged for death.

accommodation: An obligation assumed gratis.

accommodation line: Business accepted from an agent or broker that would ordinarily be rejected on a strict underwriting basis; insurance that by itself would not be acceptable to an insurer, written as an accommodation where the possibility of securing other desirable business seems to justify it and because of the overall profitability of the agent's or customer's account.

account: Refers to the individual cash-value investment funds in a variable life insurance product. Also, a term commonly used to mean to subtract or list as an expense or debt obligation. (*See also: debit.*)

account and risk: Regarding finances, this is the understanding between a broker and client upon which all securities transactions are based. The broker, acting as agent in the transaction, will execute orders for the account and risk of the client, who acts as principal.

account current: A monthly financial statement—showing premiums written, cancellations, endorsements and commissions—provided by the insurer to the agent.

account payable: A debt owed by an enterprise and arising out of the normal course of business dealings.

account receivable: A debt owed to an enterprise, arising out of the normal course of business dealings.

accrual basis of accounting: A method of accounting which attempts to match revenues with expenses by recognizing revenue when a service is rendered and expense when the liability is incurred irrespective of the receipt or disbursement of cash.

accrue: To accumulate. When a right is vested in a person, that right is said to accrue to the benefit of that person.

accrued benefit: The amount of retirement benefit that has been accumulated on behalf of a participating employee. In the case of a defined benefit plan, an employee's accrued benefit would be expressed as the amount he or she could expect to receive at normal retirement if no future funds were contributed to the plan. In the case of a money-purchase plan or profit-sharing plan, a participant's accrued benefit means the balance presently accrued in his or her individual account.

accrued benefit cost method: A method of determining pension benefit costs under which the actuarial costs are based directly upon benefits accrued to the date of cost determination. Such benefits are determined either by the terms of the plan or by some assumed allocation of total prospective benefits to years of service. When the annual cost of the plan for a given year is calculated, the method assumes that a precisely determinable unit of benefit is associated with that year of a participant's credited service.

accrued future service benefit: That portion of a participant's pension retirement benefit that relates to his or her period of credited service after the effective date of the plan but before a specified current date.

accrued interest: The pro rata portion of interest that has been earned, or is due, at time of accounting.

accrued liability: That amount of money needed to offset the participant's accumulated benefits under a retirement plan. A plan's accrued liability is equal to the difference between the present value of future benefits and the present value of future contributions. A plan is considered fully funded when the funds held under the plan equal the plan's accrued liability. Conversely, when the assets of a plan are less than its accrued liability, the plan is deemed to have an unfunded accrued liability.

accumulated dividends: Policy dividends left with the life insurance company to accumulate at interest.

accumulated earnings penalty tax: (*See: accumulated earnings tax.*)

accumulated earnings tax: A penalty tax imposed on the retained earnings of a corporation when they are retained "for the purpose of avoiding the income tax with respect to its shareholders ...by permitting earnings and profits to accumulate instead of being divided or distributed." This tax does not fall on earnings that are "accumulated for the reasonable needs of the business."

accumulated funding deficiency: In a funding standard account in a pension plan subject to the funding standards plan, an excess of the charges to the account over the credits. (*See also: funding standard account.*)

accumulated interest: Interest payments that are past due and unpaid.

accumulated surplus: A surplus accumulated by a corporation from its profits. (*See also: surplus* and *surplus account.*)

accumulation: Percentage addition to policy benefits as a reward to the insured for continuous renewal.

accumulation benefit: Percentage addition to, and increase of, policy benefits provided by a health insurer as a reward for the timely and continuous renewal of the contract by the insured.

accumulation clause: Provides for a slight increase in policy benefits when policy premiums have been paid. It rewards persistency.

accumulation period: In retirement and annuity plans, the period when funds are accumulated for later disbursement. This is in contrast to the income period, when the accumulated funds are disbursed in the form of annuity or pension benefits.

accumulation, policy: A percentage increase in policy benefits as a reward to the insured for continuous renewal.

acquisition cost: The cost to a company of selling new policies, including commissions paid to agents and brokers, clerical costs, medical and inspection fees, and, in some companies, field supervision costs.

actions: When used in a policy, the term refers to legal actions or proceedings in court. Actions under the policy for claims against the insuring company are ordinarily restricted by the policy.

active life reserve: Policy reserve accumulated by insurers from premium payments and interest earnings under noncancellable and guaranteed renewable life insurance contracts in amounts that, together with future net premiums and future interest earnings, will be sufficient to pay claims arising beyond the current policy years of contracts currently in force. The reserve is necessary in a level premium policy to cover a claim cost that increases with age. The excess of new level premiums over annual claim costs in the early years is accumulated with interest and then dissipated in later years to provide for the excess of claim costs over net premiums

actively employed: A requirement placed on full-time employees for participation in a retirement or medical plan. It is a protective underwriting measure that presumes that if employees are healthy enough to be on the job, they are healthy enough to be covered.

active trust: One that imposes upon the trustee the duty of taking active measures in the execution of trust, such as where property is conveyed to the trustee with directions to sell and distribute the proceeds among creditors of the grantor. (*For contrast, see: dry trust.*)

activities of daily living (ADL): Getting out of bed, bathing, dressing and moving around indoors. A measure for rating an individual's level of disability and for predicting long term care utilization.

act of God: An accident or event, resulting from natural causes and beyond human control or influence, such as flood, lightning, earthquake, or hurricane.

actuarial assumptions: The assumptions about uncertain future events or experiences used in actuarial calculations, such as future claim rates, expenses and earnings. (*See also: actuarial present value.*)

actuarial cost: A cost derived through the use of actuarial present values.

actuarial cost method: In pension plans, a technique for establishing the amount and incidence of normal costs, supplemental costs, and actuarial liabilities pertaining to benefits and expenses. Actuarial cost methods involve valuation techniques used to determine the proper charges against annual operating techniques and to measure the liabilities of the pension plan at any given date. (*See also: accrued benefit cost method* and *projected benefit cost method.*)

actuarial equivalent: The mathematical equal of something else. Amount of annuity or pension which can be provided at the same cost as a specified annuity of a different type payable at the same age or as an annuity of the same or a different type payable at a different age.

actuarial experience gains or losses: In pensions, the effects on actuarially calculated costs of deviations between actual prior experience and the actuarial assumptions used.

actuarial liability: Under a pension plan, the excess of the present value of total prospective benefits of the plan (plus administrative expenses, if included in the normal cost) over the present value of future normal cost accruals determined by the actuarial cost method in use.

actuarially reduced annuity: An annuity payable to an employee who retires before normal retirement age. The amount is less than would have been payable at normal retirement age, since contributions will have been paid and interest accumulated for a shorter period. Starting the payments at an earlier age will increase the probable number of annuity payments. (*See also: actuarial equivalent.*)

actuarially sound: A pension fund is considered to be actuarially sound when the amount of money in the fund and the current level of contributions to the fund are sufficient (on the basis of assumptions on interest, mortality, and employee turnover) to meet the liabilities that have accrued and that are accruing on a current basis.

actuarial present value: The current worth of an amount payable or receivable in the future, where each such amount is discounted at an assumed rate of interest and adjusted for the probability of its payment or receipt.

actuarial report: A report containing certain required actuarial information about a retirement plan and provided by an actuary. The actuarial report must contain information on number of participants, contributions received, normal costs, accrued liabilities, current value of assets and liabilities, and certificate of the contributions necessary to provide the benefits.

actuarial revaluation gains or losses: In pension plans, the effects on actuarially calculated costs of changes in actuarial assumptions as to future events or the adoption of a different actuarial cost method.

actuarial valuation: An examination of a pension plan to determine if it is actuarially sound. A plan is actuarially sound if funds are accumulating at a rate sufficient to provide the promised pension benefits when due. This involves a determination as to composition of the work force, earnings levels, turnover, interest earned, mortality and any other factors affecting cost, to determine if they are consistent with the assumptions on the basis of which the plan was established. Generally used in connection with self-administered, trustee, split-funded or deposited administration plans, since under group annuity plans the insurance carrier guarantees the payment of all benefits.

actuary: A professional person trained in mathematics, statistics, and accounting and the principles of operation of insurance, annuities, and retirement plans. The actuary determines, on the basis of existing experience, the estimated costs of future losses.

addition: (*See: paid-up additions.*)

additional death benefit: A life insurance policy provision or term now used by some insurers in lieu of double indemnity. (*See also: double indemnity* and *accidental death benefit.*)

additional insurance: Insurance that is added to an existing policy. Unless it is agreed to by the company or its duly-authorized agent, the insurance is void.

additional insured: An individual other than the one identified as the insured in the policy, such as the insured's spouse, who is protected under the terms of the contract.

additional optional policy: Similar to the alternative optional policy, with the exception that the policy as issued has a separate number; either one or both policies may be placed. (*See also: alternative optional policy.*)

additional premium: In universal and variable life policies, the amount of gross premium in excess of the recommended or target premium for the policy.

additional provisions: Provisions in addition to the insuring and benefit provisions and to the uniform provisions that define and limit the coverage. Also called general provisions.

additional reserve for guaranteed renewable policies: The excess of net level premiums over annual claim costs of life and guaranteed renewable and noncancellable health policies, accumulated with interest, in the early years. This additional reserve is then dissipated in the later years to provide for the excess of claim costs over the premiums. The total reserve is variously referred to as the active life reserve, the level premium reserve, or the policy reserve.

adequate consideration: The generally recognized market value of an asset. In the case of a security, it may be either the prevailing price of a security on a nationally recognized exchange or, if the security is not traded on such an exchange, a value not less favorable than the current bid and asked price quoted by people other than the issuer of the security. In the case of an asset other than a security, the fair market value of the asset as determined in good faith by the trustees or named fiduciary of the plan in accordance with regulations. In a legal sense, an adequate consideration is one that is equal, or reasonably proportional, to the value of that for which it is given.

adhesion: A contract in which the buyers must adhere to, or accept, the established, preexisting terms of a standard contract. With a contract of adhesion the buyer has no opportunity to bargain for terms, rates, values, etc. Life insurance is a contract of adhesion.

adjustable death benefit: Refers to the policyowner's right to increase or decrease the specific amount within a variable life policy. Also describes the general feature of death benefit flexibility in interest-sensitive products.

adjustable life insurance: Insurance that combines features of both term and whole life coverage, whereby the insured may obtain the amount of insurance desired for the premium he or she can best afford, the length of coverage and amount of accumulated cash value being the variable factors.

adjustable premium: The contractual right of the company to modify premium payments under certain specified conditions. It also refers to the policyowner's right to change scheduled premiums in certain interest-sensitive products.

adjusted earnings: Net earnings from an insurer's operations, plus the estimated value of additional insurance in force or of the growth in premiums written.

adjusted gross estate: Gross estate less debts, funeral costs and administration expenses. The marital deduction, federal estate and gift taxes are not used to calculate the adjusted gross estate; instead, they are dependent upon the adjusted gross estate figure for their computation.

adjusted net gain from operations: Referring to an insurer, the net gain from operations, plus the estimated value of increases in the amount of insurance in force and/or the growth in premiums during the year.

adjusted net worth: The worth of an insurance or other company, consisting of capital and surplus, plus an estimated value for the business on the company's books.

adjusted premium method: The procedure for determining statutory minimum nonforfeiture values under the standard nonforfeiture law. The adjusted premium method is based on the amortization over the premium paying period of a specified allowance for additional expenses incurred during the first policy year.

adjusted taxable gifts: Total amount of post-1976 taxable gifts other than those included in the gross estate.

adjustment income: An added, step-down income, over and beyond that required to cover the family's minimum needs, to help the surviving family members adjust to the shock of lower income following the insured's death. Also called readjustment income.

adjustment period: An estimated period of time, as much as two years, for a family to recover and adjust to the loss of income after the death of its principal wage earner.

administration bond: A bond that must be given by a person or company to guarantee the matters of administration. Commonly used in wills to guarantee the fidelity of the executor or administrator of the estate.

administration expenses: An estate shrinkage factor. Includes probate costs, executor's or administrator's fee, attorney fees, etc.

administrator: The person appointed by the probate court to manage and settle the estate of a person who died with no will. (*See also: executor.*)

administrator, pension plan: Any person or institution designated as administrator in a pension plan instrument; or if an administrator is not so designated, the plan sponsor; or in the case of a plan in which an administrator is not designated and the plan sponsor cannot be identified, any person who the secretary of labor may prescribe by regulation.

administrator's deed: The legal instrument conveying title to property (generally, real estate), provided by a person who is legally vested with the right of administration of an estate, especially an estate of a minor, an incompetent, or of a testator having no competent executor.

admitted assets: In the case of an insurance company, all assets that are approved by the state insurance department as existing property in the ownership of the company. Such assets include all funds, securities, property, equipment, rights of action, or resources of any kind owned by the company or held in trust for others.

admitted company: An insurance company licensed to do business in a particular state or states. Also called an authorized company or a licensed company.

adult: A legal determination referring to one who has reached maturity; a person who has reached the age of legal capacity.

adult day care: An environment that offers daytime companionship, supervision and support for people who live at home.

ad valorem: Designates a percentage charge (generally an assessment of taxes) against the value of property. Literally, according to the value.

advance discounting for mortality: Calculation of the number of people covered by a plan of insurance (such as pension or retirement plan) who will die before reaching the age that benefits start.

advance discounting for severance: In group pension plan funding, consideration of the number of employees who will end employment before retirement, thus permitting lower contributions to the plan by the employer.

advanced life underwriter: A life insurance agent who sells and services insurance to satisfy such needs, as those for estate planning, retirement planning and business insurance. He or she must be well versed in the uses of life insurance, disability coverages and employee benefits in their more complex forms to solve financial problems facing individuals, families, estates, small businesses and corporations. (*See also: advanced life underwriting.*)

advanced life underwriting: In general, this term refers to the marketing of life insurance products in the more complex areas of personal and business insurance, estate planning and qualified retirement planning, according to tax and estate planning requirements.

advanced underwriter: (*See: advanced life underwriter.*)

advanced underwriting: (*See: advanced life underwriting.*)

advance funding: The pre-retirement funding of pension plans. The term may be applied to any arrangement under which sums intended for the payment of retirement benefits are set aside under proper legal safeguards in advance of the date of actual retirement. It does not necessarily imply full funding, since the initial accrued liability may be frozen. The advance funding approach is the conventional funding method used in pension plans today.

advancement: In a legal sense, a gift made during lifetime by one who dies without a will. The advancement must be taken into account as a reduction of the share of inheritance.

advance payments: Any payments made to the insured by the insurance company before the settlement date. The term given to the amount of money or the number of weeks or months paid in advance of the current period on weekly premium monthly debit policies. In ordinary insurance, the amount of money that applicants tender with their applications for insurance.

advance premium: Any premiums paid before their due date.

adventure clause: Phrase in a policy describing a particular trip or voyage which is to be undertaken.

adverse claimants: Persons claiming or asserting rights in opposition to each other.

adverse possession: An actual and visible possession under a claim of right not consistent with the right of the true owner.

adverse selection: Selection against the company. The tendency of less favorable insurance risks to seek or continue insurance to a greater extent than other risks. Also, the tendency of policyowners to take advantage of favorable options in insurance contracts.

advisory insurance organizations: Rating and information bureaus that advise insurers, yet do not require members to follow recommendations.

aero insurance: Specifically provides coverage against the risks of flying.

affidavit of claim: A written, signed statement required when a claim is filed with an insurer and containing the facts on which the claim is based.

affiliated companies: Insurers associated under common stock ownership or interlocking directorates.

age: For life and health insurance purposes, the age in years of an applicant, insured or beneficiary. Some companies use the age at the last birthday. Other companies use the age at the nearest birthday (last or next).

age-adjusted death rate: Death rates standardized for age in order to make comparisons between different populations or within the same population at various intervals of time.

age-adjusted mortality rate: (*See: age-adjusted death rate.*)

age at issue: For insurance purposes, the age of an insurance applicant or an insured at the time coverage goes into effect. In some companies, the issue age is the age at last birthday. In others, it is the age at the nearest birthday.

age change: In insurance, the date on which a person becomes one year older. Depending upon the individual insurance company, a person's age may change as of the last birthday or the nearest birthday (six months after last birthday).

age last birthday: One method of insurance rating that rates people at their age as of the last birthday, with such rating held until the next birthday. Thus, until a person actually celebrates a birth date anniversary, he or she is rated as of the usual calendar age.

age limits: Minimum or maximum set age limits for the insuring of new applicants or for the renewal of policies.

agency: A situation wherein one party (an agent) has the power to act for another (an insurance company) in dealing with third parties. Also, a sales office under the direction of either a general agent, a special agent, or a branch manager. Also, an insurance office operated by an independent agent who has an agent's contract with at least one insurance company.

agency agreement or contract: A legal document containing the terms of the contract between the agent and company, signed by both parties. Also, agent's contract or general agent's contract or agreement.

agency builder: A term used to describe a life and/or health insurance general agent or agency manager, usually pertaining to some measure of growth in production or gross sales, and usually pertaining to the type of operation where new agents are recruited and contracted regularly.

agency department: The home office department of an insurance company responsible for the appointment and servicing of the agency organization. The agency department is most often responsible for policy sales, conservation of old business, service to policyowners and various marketing services.

agency development: The ongoing building of a life and/or health agency by a general agent or manager through recruitment of new agents and the continued development of the existing personnel.

agency director: Company director in charge of supervising a territorial division's agencies on a particular type of sales or market.

agency plant: The total force of agents representing an insurance company. Can also mean the physical facilities of an agency.

agency superintendent: An officer or other executive of a company in charge of supervising agencies, either of a territorial division or of the entire company—usually reporting directly to the agency vice president. Also called superintendent of agencies.

agency system: A method of marketing and selling insurance. Entails sales and service by commissioned insurance agents, most often supervised by general agents or agency managers, in contrast to sales by salaried employees or by mail.

age nearest birthday: A method used by insurance companies to compute age as that nearest the insured's closest birthday. Thus, if the insured has passed six months after the last birthday, he or she is considered to be one year older. (*See also: age last birthday.*)

agent: Anyone who solicits insurance or aids in the placing of risks, delivery of policies, or collection of premiums on behalf of an insurance company. The acts of agents are binding upon the company only to the extent specified in their contracts or otherwise authorized. They cannot bind the company by any statement contrary to the provisions of the application or policy. Agents cannot delegate their rights or powers unless expressly authorized. In most states, insurance solicitors are regarded as agents of the insurance company and not of the insured.

agent authority: The rights and powers granted in the agency contract and/or the authority which the public may reasonably expect the agent to have. It almost never includes authority to change or waive the provisions of a policy, to alter an application, or to make an amendment or add a rider to the contract.

agent, general: The company representative in a given territory who is entrusted with the task of supervising the company's business within that territory. The general agent is an independent contractor compensated on a commission basis, usually paying all expenses from commissions, although some general agents' contracts contain provisions for company paid expenses usually associated with managerial contracts.

agent, independent: An independent business person who represents insurance companies (usually property/casualty, but sometimes also life and health) under contract in a sales and service capacity and is paid on a commission basis. Sometimes referred to as a local agent.

agent license: (*See: license.*)

agent, local: An insurance agent (usually property/casualty, but sometimes also life and/or health), who, as an independent contractor, represents insurance companies in a sales and service capacity and is paid on a commission basis and licensed by the state in which he or she operates. The powers are limited by the terms of the agency contract and by the state laws. An agent to whom a small territory is assigned and to whom limited authority is usually given.

agent of record: The agent writing the initial policy application and who is entitled to any and all commissions on the issued insurance contract, or the agent assigned by the agency or home office to service a particular policy owner. Also, an agent given written authorization by a present policyowner to seek out and negotiate insurance contracts with companies other than his or her own. Similar to a broker, the agent of record represents the interests of the client in dealings with other insurance companies' agents.

The agent of record usually receives a percentage of the commission earned on the new policy.

agent qualification laws: Educational, experiential and other requirements established by state laws for persons desiring to be licensed as agents.

agent, resident: An agent who is licensed by the state in which he or she lives.

agent's authority of power: (*See: agent authority.*)

agent's balance: A periodic statement issued by the company of the sums owed to or by an agent.

agent's certificate: A report submitted by the agent with the application, telling the company what the agent knows about the applicant, for example, habits, financial worth, morals, general appearance, etc.

agent's commission: The payment of a percentage of the premium generated from an insurance policy to the agent by a company.

agent's letter of record: Written authorization by a policyowner granting the agent authority to act on his or her behalf in negotiating an insurance contract with an insurer other than the agent's own company. (*See also: agent of record.*)

agent, surveying: A local agent who submits business by means of applications but does not actually write policies.

age 100: In mortality tables, the maximum age that any individual may be expected to live. In whole life policies, age 100 is the age of endowment.

age-specific mortality rate: (*See: mortality rate, age specific.*)

age-specified death rate: Within a specific age group, the ratio of deaths to the population of the same age group during a given period of time.

aggregate amount: The maximum dollar amount that can be collected under any policy for any claim, during the policy duration.

aggregate funding method: A method of accumulating money for future payments of pensions, whereby the present value of all future benefit payments is actuarially determined; from this amount is deducted whatever funds may be on hand with the trustee or insurance company. The balance is then distributed as a cost over the future.

aggregate indemnities: The sum total that can be collected under all health insurance policies applicable to the covered loss.

aggregate indemnity: A maximum dollar amount that may be collected for any disability, period of disability, or under the terms of the policy.

aggregate limit clause: Under this clause (used in noncancellable policies), the company promises to pay up to a total of 15 months, two years, five years, or even ten years for an aggregate of all disabilities. When the total payments for all of the insured's disabilities reach the aggregate limit, the policy expires.

aggregate method: The aggregate subcategory of projected benefit cost methods assumes that the excess of total present value of projected benefits over the sum of plan assets (including assets held by funding agencies and reserves held by the employer as represented by pension liabilities shown on the firm's balance sheet) and the unfunded part of any supplemental liability, will be distributed over future years as a level amount or percentage of total earnings in respect of all covered employees, without identifying any part of such future cost accruals with the projected benefits of specific individuals.

aggregate mortality table: A mortality table based on life insurance experience in which the rates of mortality at any age are based on all insurance in force at that age, without reference to the duration of insurance. (*See also: select mortality table* and *ultimate mortality table.*)

aggregate projected benefit cost method: (*See: aggregate method.*)

aggregate reserve: A company figure specifying reserves for losses for which premiums have been received but which are not yet due for payment.

agreement: Mutual understanding and consent between the parties to a contract. Also, the written document that stipulates the terms of such understanding.

air insurance: (*See: aero insurance.*)

aleatory: That which depends on an uncertain event.

aleatory contract: A contract in which both parties realize that one party may obtain far greater value under the agreement than the other, and in which payment depends upon an unforeseen event. An insurance contract is an aleatory contract in that it may or may not provide more in benefits than premiums paid.

alien carrier: An insurer whose domicile is a foreign country. (*See also: alien company.*)

alien company: A company incorporated or organized under the laws of any foreign nation, province or territory.

all lines agency: An insurance agency that sells and services all major types of insurance, including life, health and property/casualty.

all lines insurance: An all-in-one concept of insurance that includes life, health, property and liability insurance in a single contract.

allocated benefits: Payments under the provisions of some policies for specified services, limited to maximum specified amounts.

allocated funding instruments: In pension plans, the contractual arrangements under which funds are allocated to purchase insurance or annuities for individual participants.

allocation: In a pension plan, an accounting method for spreading income or expense, but not necessarily on a *time* basis. For example, allocation of an expenditure between current expense and capital accounts.

allocation formula: As used in a profit-sharing trust, the formula used to credit the employer's contributions to employees.

alterations: Changes in the meaning or language of a policy. An alteration cannot be made without the written consent of the insurance company.

alternate beneficiary: (*See: contingent beneficiary.*)

alternate valuation date: Under most circumstances, valuation of a decedent's estate for tax purposes is made as of the date of death. However, the executor may elect to value all property in the estate as of its value six months from the date of death.

alternative optional policy: An additional policy issued under the same policy number, but differing from the original policy in amount, plan or benefit. Only one policy may be placed.

ambiguity: Language in the insurance policy that can be subject to different interpretations. Any ambiguity in a policy is always construed against the insurance company.

ambulatory: Movable, revocable, subject to change. Customarily used in discussing wills to denote the power a testator has to change his or her will at any time so desired.

American Academy of Actuaries: A society organized to advance knowledge of actuarial science and concerned with the development of education in the field and the support of high standards within the actuarial profession.

American agency system: (*See: agency system.*)

American College: An education institution located in Bryn Mawr, Pennsylvania, which confers the Chartered Life Underwriter (CLU) and the Chartered Financial Consultant (ChFC) designations and a Master of Science in Financial Services degree. Concerned with continuing agent training, research and publication in areas related to the life insurance and financial planning business. Formerly known as the American College of Life Underwriters.

American College of Life Underwriters: The former name of the American College (*See also: American College.*)

American Council of Life Insurance: An organization representing the life insurance industry in legislative and regulatory areas at federal, state and local levels of government. Provides the public with information about the purposes and uses of life insurance, maintains research facilities to record the performance of the industry and measures attitudes of the public on relative issues. Located in Washington, D.C.

American Experience Table of Mortality: The mortality table published in 1861 by Sheppard Homans, an actuary with the Mutual Life Insurance Company of New York. It was widely used for the calculation of life insurance premiums and reserves and was the basis for the issuing of a large amount of insurance over many years. It has now been replaced in the United States by the CSO Table.

American Life Convention: An association of life insurance companies concerned with legislative matters, intercompany communication and the exchange of information in the areas of investments, management and taxation.

American Men's Mortality Table, The: A mortality table constructed from the mortality table furnished by American and Canadian companies for the period 1900–1915. Never widely adopted because of legal technicalities.

American Society of Chartered Life Underwriters: A professional association for those who hold the CLU or associate degree from the American College, created to provide continuing education and to promote the exchange of ideas among CLUs and public information about the importance of the role of the CLU in insuring human life values.

amicus curiae: A friend of the court.

amortization: The act or process of extinguishing a debt or other liability, usually by equal payments made at regular intervals that will reduce the outstanding debt to zero at the end of a given period of time.

amortization fund: A sum of money accumulated periodically and held aside for the payment of a debt.

amortization quota: The amount of funds removed from income in order to provide for amortization.

amount at risk: The difference between the face value of a policy and its accrued cash value at a given time. In other words, the amount over and above what the member has contributed in the way of cash value toward the payment of his or her own claim. Since the value increases each year, the net amount at risk decreases and finally reaches zero when the cash value becomes the face value. At that time, the policy is said to mature or endow.

amount of coverage: (*See: face amount.*)

ancillary: Designating or pertaining to a document, proceeding, officer, or office, etc., that is subordinate to, or in aid of, another primary or principal one; an ancillary attachment, bill, or suit presupposes the existence of another principal proceeding.

ancillary benefits: Secondary benefits provided in a contract providing insurance coverage, such as benefits provided for miscellaneous hospital charges in a basic room and board hospitalization policy.

anniversary date: The annual recurrence of the policy date of issue.

annual actuarial cost: The sum of the normal cost and annual supplemental cost and, if separate, an adjustment for actuarial gains or losses.

annual exclusion: *(See: taxable gift.)*

annual financial statement (convention form):   *(See: convention.)*

annual payment annuity: An annuity purchased by the payment of annual premiums over a period of years.

annual pension cost: *(See: annual actuarial cost.)*

annual premium: The total premium amount due on an annual basis to meet the contractual requirements of a policy and to keep it in force.

annual premium annuity: *(See: annual payment annuity.)*

annual premium deferred annuity: *(See: retirement annuity.)*

annual renewable term insurance: *(See: yearly renewable term insurance.)*

annual renewal agreement: A policy clause stating that the insurance company agrees to renew the policy under stated conditions.

annual report: An insurer's published statement to its policyowners giving pertinent financial information and reviewing the year's activities and results.

annual report summary: A summary of assets and liabilities, receipts and disbursements, current value assets, present value of vested benefits, and any other financial information about a retirement plan, which must be provided annually to participants.

annual return: An IRS form required yearly of every employer who maintains a pension, annuity or profit-sharing plan, including a Keogh plan, that contains information with respect to the qualification, financial conditions and operations of the plan.

annual statement: A company's yearly financial report that is required by the various state insurance departments. The report covers the calendar year period and is presented in a form agreed upon by the National Association of Insurance Commissioners. This form is also known as the Annual Convention Blank.

annual supplemental cost: Under a pension plan, that portion of the supplemental cost and/or interest allocated for a given year. *(See also: supplemental cost.)*

annuitant: One to whom an annuity is payable or a person who receives an annuity for life or for a specified period.

annuity: A stipulated sum payable at certain regular intervals during the lifetime of one or more persons or payable for just a specified period; also, the contract providing such an arrangement.

annuity age change: The date of the last birthday.

annuity, cash refund: An annuity contract that provides the annuitant with income for life, with a death benefit equal to the premiums paid, less annuity payments already received. (*For contrast, see: annuity, installment refund.*)

annuity certain: A contract providing income for a definite and specified period of time, with payment going to a designated beneficiary if the annuitant dies.

annuity certain, life: An annuity payable for a specified number of years and after that period for as long as the annuitant lives. A combination of annuity certain and a life annuity.

annuity consideration: The single payment, or periodic payments, that must be made to purchase an annuity.

annuity, contingent: (*See: annuity, joint and survivor.*)

annuity, deferred: An annuity under which the first payment is not made to the annuitant until the expiration of a fixed number of years or until the annuitant attains a specific age; often used to provide retirement income.

annuity due: An annuity under which the payments are made at the beginning of each period (i.e., monthly, quarterly, yearly, et al.)

annuity, endowment: Provides for a payment to the named beneficiary if the insured dies prior to the maturity date. If the insured lives to the maturity date, he or she may elect to receive either a monthly income for life or a lump-sum settlement. The contract is, in fact, a deferred annuity coupled with decreasing term insurance running to maturity.

annuity, equity: (*See: variable annuity.*)

annuity, five or ten years certain: Annuity guaranteed for a specified number of payments. Should the annuitant die before receiving all the payments, the balance is continued to his or her beneficiary.

annuity, fixed: (*See: fixed annuity.*)

annuity, flexible premium: A deferred annuity under which premiums may vary from year to year within stipulated limits. Often used to fund IRAs.

annuity, group: An arrangement providing annuities at retirement to a group of persons covered under a master contract. It is usually issued to an employer to fund a pension plan for the benefit of employees. The individual members of the group hold certificates as evidence of their coverage.

annuity, immediate: An annuity under which the first payment falls due one month, three months, six months, or 12 months after the payment of the purchase price, as desired by the annuitant.

annuity, individual: An annuity agreement in which an insurer agrees to pay an individual a specified annuity. (*For contrast see: annuity, group.*)

annuity, installment refund: A life annuity incorporating an agreement that, upon the death of the annuitant the insurer will continue payments to a beneficiary until the total payments equal the consideration paid to the insurer. (*For contrast see: annuity, cash refund.*)

annuity, joint and survivor: A life annuity with two or more annuitants. The insurer will make payments throughout the annuitants' lifetimes. Also called a contingent annuity.

annuity, joint life: An annuity payable for as long as two or more persons shall live, but terminating upon the death of the first.

annuity, last survivor: (*See: annuity, joint and survivor.*)

annuity, life: An annuity contract that agrees to pay a guaranteed income for life, but makes no provision for the return of the unused premium after death.

annuity, modified refund: An arrangement commonly used under a contributory pension plan. If an employee dies after retirement, the beneficiary or estate receives a sum equal to the accumulated value of the employee's own contributions to the pension fund (with or without interest up to the retirement date), less the total retirement benefits received prior to death.

annuity mortality table: (*See: mortality table.*)

annuity plan, group: *(See: group annuity plan.)*

annuity, private: Annuity issued by an individual or organization other than a company regularly engaged in annuity sales.

annuity purchase rate: The guaranteed premium rate at which annuities are purchased at retirement—as used in a deposit administration contract.

annuity, qualified: An annuity used to fund and/or distribute a qualified retirement plan. Employees of certain nonprofit Section 501(c)(3) organizations and public school systems may arrange with their employers for the purchase of tax-deferred annuity plans. Contributions and increments in value are not taxed presently to the employee. Also refers to tax-deferred annuities used to fund the retirement benefits in an HR-10, IRA, pension or profit-sharing plan.

annuity, refund: An annuity that provides that upon the death of the annuitant the company will continue to make payments to a designated beneficiary until the total amount paid equals the purchase price.

annuity, retirement: *(See: retirement annuity, pension annuity, income bond, retirement policy.)*

annuity, reversionary: *(See: annuity, survivorship.)*

annuity risk: The risk borne by the insurer that an annuitant will outlive his or her accumulated annuity benefits.

annuity, single payment: *(See: single payment annuity.)*

annuity, straight life: *(See: annuity, life.)*

annuity, survivorship: A life annuity beginning at the death of one person (the insured) and continuing through the lifetime of another person (the annuitant).

annuity table: A table developed to measure life expectancy; it shows how long people at a given age can be expected to live.

Annuity Table for 1949: A scaled mortality table with projection factors and taking into consideration reduction in mortality rates.

annuity, temporary: A life annuity terminating at the end of a number of years or at the death of the annuitant, whichever occurs first.

annuity, variable: *(See: variable annuity.)*

annuity with minimum period: (*See: annuity certain.*)

answering objections: An anticipated phase of the sales process. Specific techniques may be employed by an agent, both in attempting to secure an interview, and to overcome objections raised by the prospect during the interview itself.

anti-coercion law: A provision contained in state codes declaring use of coercion to be an unfair practice and, hence, a violation of insurance law. (*See also: unfair competition and practices law.*)

anti-compact laws: Antitrust laws that limit agreements to prevent competition.

anti-discriminatory laws: Laws prohibiting companies from offering preferential rates not warranted by the standard rating of the risk.

anti-rebate laws: State laws that prohibit an agent or company from giving part of the premium back to the insured as an inducement to buy insurance coverage.

anti-selection: (*See: adverse selection.*)

apparent authority: The power that is logical for the public to assume an agent has, whether he or she actually has been granted that power by contract or not. An agent can bind the company by acting under apparent authority as well as under actual authority insofar as commitments to the public go. An agent who knowingly commits his or her company under the power of apparent authority is open to a possible civil suit from the company to recover damages.

applicant: An individual applying for an insurance policy either on his or her own life or health or on that of another; one who fills out and signs a written application for insurance.

application: A form supplied by the life insurance company and usually filled out by the agent and medical examiner (if applicable) on the basis of information on the life and/or health of the proposed insured received from the applicant. The form is signed by the applicant and becomes part of the insurance contract if a policy is issued. This form gives information to the home office underwriting department so it may consider whether the requested insurance policy will be issued and, if so, in what classification and at what premium rate.

appointment: The authorization of an agent to represent a company. Also, a time agreed upon for an interview with a prospect.

appointment papers: Documents that the agent compiles and returns to his or her company. These documents are connected with the agent's appointment.

apportionable annuity: One which provides for a pro rata proportionate payment covering the period from the date of the last regular premium payment to the date of death.

apportionment: (*See: pro rata.*)

approach: The part of a sales presentation designed to open the discussion with the prospective insured. The approach may be made either by telephone or in person.

approval: Acceptance of an application for an insurance policy as meeting the underwriting standards of a company.

arbitrary rule: A provision under Section 401(a)(3)(A) of the Internal Revenue Code that a pension plan must cover 70 percent or more of all employees, not including short service, seasonal and part-time employees, or that 70 percent or more of the employees similarly defined must be eligible for coverage under the plan, and at least 80 percent of those eligible must actually participate.

arbitration clause: A clause within a policy providing that if the policyowner and the insurer fail to agree on the settlement amount of a claim, they select a neutral arbitrator with the authority to bind both parties to the settlement.

Armstrong Investigation: An investigation of a large number of insurance companies in the United States in 1905 which led to the enactment of stricter state supervision and insurance requirements.

arrears: The status of a policy on which the premium has not been paid, but which may still be in force due to the grace period.

arrears and advances: In reference to home service insurance, arrears are the total of premiums due up to and including the current week or month. Advances are the total premiums paid in advance of the current week or month.

assessed value: The monetary worth of property established by a governmental agency for the purpose of assessing taxes.

assessment: An additional amount charged to the insured by the insurance company to meet losses greater than those anticipated in the premium charged.

assessment clause: A statement included in some policies that allows the company to charge (assess) the policyowner additional premiums.

assessment company or society: An insurer that makes assessment on members' losses rather than operating on a fixed premium basis. Such organizations often operate on a minimum stated premium and reserve, with the right to make additional assessments any time the premium is insufficient to cover obligations and expenses.

assessment insurance: A plan of insurance by which either the amount of insurance or the number and amount of the assessments are variable. Assessment insurance is offered by assessment associations, sometimes called natural premium, flexible premium or stipulated premium companies. They usually contain a "safety clause" that provides for the levying of additional assessments, the increasing of rates or the scaling down of benefits when collections prove inadequate to pay claims.

assessment insurer: *(See: assessment company or society.)*

assessment society: *(See: assessment company or society.)*

assessor: The designated public official who makes an official estimate of value.

asset: Anything of value that is owned.

assets, current: *(See: current assets.)*

assets, insurance company: Those assets that include all funds, property, goods, securities, rights or resources of any kind, less such items as are declared nonadmissible by state laws. Nonadmissible items consist mainly of deferred or overdue premiums.

asset share: A theoretical year by year accumulation of funds out of premiums. The asset share is the amount available for providing nonforfeiture benefits and dividends, setting up contingency reserves and for providing ultimate profit for the insurer.

asset share values: *(See: valuation.)*

asset valuation: *(See: valuation, asset.)*

assign: To transfer, as in a right or risk.

assigned risk: A risk not ordinarily acceptable to insurers, but for which coverage is required by law and which is, therefore, assigned to insurers participating in an assigned risk pool.

assignee: The person or business to whom a right or rights under an insurance policy are transferred by means of an assignment.

assignment: The legal transfer by a policyowner of benefits of a policy to another party. If the company is given due notice of the assignment, all or certain policy benefits will accrue to the person named as assignee.

assignment, absolute: *(See: absolute assignment.)*

assignment, collateral: *(See: collateral assignment.)*

assignment, conditional: *(See: conditional assignment.)*

assignment of benefits: In health insurance the policyowner's authorization to have the insurer pay benefits directly to someone else, usually a physician or hospital under a medical expense policy, or to a legal guardian under a disability income policy.

assignment, voluntary: *(See: voluntary assignment.)*

assignor: A person or business who transfers rights under an insurance policy to another by means of an assignment.

assigns: The parties to whom an assignment has been made. Assignments of life insurance generally are not valid until approved in writing by the company. The assigns have no right or title to a policy's benefits until such transfer has been consented to by the company.

Associated Medical Care Plan: The formal name for Blue Shield. *(See also: Blue Shield.)*

association A & H policy: Individual accident and health policies written to cover a member of a trade or professional association. Also called association insurance.

Association for Advanced Life Underwriting: A conference of the National Association of Life Underwriters with headquarters in Washington, DC. Membership is limited to insurance professionals with advanced underwriting sales experience. The organization issues periodic bulletins to its members on advanced underwriting topics.

association group: Trade or professional association members insured jointly under a group policy. Insurance provided to a trade, business or professional association whereby all members are protected under one contract.

association insurance: Insurance provided through individual policies issued to members of an association.

Association of Life Insurance Counsel: Professional organization of attorneys of life insurance companies.

Association of Life Insurance Medical Directors: An organization of doctors and medical directors of insurance companies.

Association of Superintendents of Insurance of the Provinces of Canada: The corresponding Canadian organization to the National Association of Insurance Commissioners in the United States.

assume: To accept all or part of a company's insurance or reinsurance on a risk.

assumed interest rate: The rate of interest used by an insurance company to calculate its reserves. Historically, this rate is usually rather low—2 percent to 3 percent—for sake of safety.

assumed reinsurance: Business accepted for reinsurance from another insurance company. (*See also: reinsurance.*)

assumption of risk: The accepting of a risk by an insurance company. Also refers to a condition whereby insureds place themselves knowingly in high-risk situations.

assumption reinsurance: A procedure whereby, in exchange for the assets underlying the liabilities and the right to receive future premiums, one insurer assumes the policy liabilities of another insurer.

assurance—insurance: Synonymous terms. Assurance is used more commonly in England than in the United States. (*See also: insurance.*)

assured: (*See: insured.*)

assurer: (*See: insurer.*)

at occupation: An underwriting designation for an occupational accident.

attained age: The age an insured has reached on a specific date. For life insurance, the age is based on either the nearest or the last birthday, depending upon the practices of the individual insurance company.

attending physician's report: A statement from the applicant's physician providing the specifics of an accident or sickness, the treatment and prognosis. This is privileged information and is given in confidence to the medical directors of the insuring company.

attestation clause: The clause of an insurance policy to which the officers of the insurance company sign their names to complete the contract. Sometimes used at the end of an application to attest to the truth and completeness of the statements made by an applicant for insurance. Also, that clause in a will in which witnesses certify that the will was signed in their presence by the maker of the will and that it was properly executed.

attorney in fact: The authority granted to an individual to legally act for another. (*See also: power of attorney.*)

audit: A legally required review of a company's, agency's or individual's financial records.

auditor: Individual who makes a formal examination and verification of financial and other records.

authorization: The amount of insurance an underwriter says he or she will accept on a given risk.

authorized company: A company duly authorized by the state insurance department to operate in that state. Also called admitted company.

authorized insurer: (*See: authorized company.*)

automatic cost-of-living increases: Under Social Security, a feature stating that whenever prescribed conditions exist and Congress has not made an automatic increase in Social Security benefits in over a year, cost-of-living increase in benefits and taxable wage base for future years will be made. The purpose of this provision is to prevent Social Security incomes from falling behind during periods of inflation.

automatic coverage: A policy provided in many forms of insurance, that comes into existence or adjusts the amount of coverage to provide protection for increasing risks and changing interests of the insured's property.

automatic paid-up: A provision whereby a policy becomes paid-up for a specified amount if or when premium payments are discontinued. This occurs automatically and without any action on the insured's part.

automatic premium loan provision: An option which will automatically pay any premium in default at the end of the grace period. The amount is charged against the cash value as a policy loan, provided the premium is not in excess of the policy's cash surrender value on the due date of the premium (computed on the assumption that such premium had been paid.)

automatic reinsurance treaty: (*See: reinsurance treaty.*)

auxiliary fund: That portion of contributions to a funded pension plan that is not invested in insurance policies or annuities. This fund, together with the guaranteed values of the insurance policies or annuities, will provide the retirement benefit for the employee upon retirement. (*See also: funded pension plan.*)

avails (of a contract):   The benefit derived from a contract, including death benefit, dividends, waiver of premium, etc.

average earnings clause: An optional provision in a disability income policy that permits the company to limit the monthly income disability benefits to the amount of his or her average earnings for the 24 months prior to the disability. Generally found only in guaranteed renewable and noncancellable policies. (*See also: relation of earnings to insurance.*)

average indexed monthly earnings (AIME):   The basis utilized for calculating the primary insurance amount (PIA) for Social Security benefits.

average monthly wage: The average wage base for computing virtually all Social Security benefits prior to 1979, and after that, when eligibility for the benefits first commences.

average net cost: In life insurance, the average net cost of participating policies is determined by adding 20 years of premiums, subtracting from that total the total of 20 years of dividends and the 20th year cash value. The remainder arrived at is divided by 20 and is the average 20-year net cost. For a nonparticipating policy, the 20th year cash value is subtracted from the total of 20 years' premiums. That result is divided by 20 to achieve the average net cost for 20 years.

average pay plan: Pension plan wherein benefits received are based upon the individual's pay averaged over the years of participation in the plan.

average risk: The basis of all insurance. A risk in accordance with the conditions called for in the establishment of the basic rate of an insurance company.

average weekly benefits: Usually called weekly compensation in workers' compensation insurance. The amount payable per week for disability or death as prescribed by law. This is usually a percentage of the average weekly wage, subject to a minimum and maximum amount.

average weekly wage: The average rate of remuneration per week, computed as prescribed by law.

aviation clause: *(See: aviation exclusion.)*

aviation exclusion: A provision in the policy, either attached by rider or included in standard policy language that excepts from coverage deaths due to aviation unless the insured was a passenger on a regularly scheduled airline.

aviation hazard: The increased danger or risk of accidental death or injury resulting from participation in flying.

B

back-end load: A surrender charge deducted from the cash value in some variable life insurance products before the remaining cash value is paid to the policyowner when the policy is surrendered. Most such policies have a decreasing back-end load that generally disappears completely after a certain number of years.

bailout provision: (*See: ten-day free look provision.*)

balance: In insurance, the residual amount of money due a company from its agent after all credits and charges are calculated.

balanced security: A concept used in needs analysis to determine the amount of income a family would require should the chief wage earner die or become disabled. It is based on the accounting concept of income versus expenses.

balance sheet: One of the three major kinds of financial statements used by businesses. It is primarily a status report that shows the financial condition of a business or organization as of a particular date—usually the end of the year. (*See also: income statement* and *statement of changes in financial position.*)

balance sheet reserve: Amount expressed as a liability on the insurance company's balance sheet for benefits owed to policyowners.

balance sheet reserve plan: A funding plan that sets up a bookkeeping entry acknowledging some or all of the liability incurred for the payment of benefits and taking this liability into account in determining profits and the stockholders' equity.

banding: Based on the principle of economy of size, premiums are often banded, so that larger size policies are charged a more favorable rate than smaller policies.

bank check plan: A simplified method of monthly premium payment. With the prearranged consent of the insured, the insurance company automatically deducts the monthly premium due from the insured's checking account.

bank loan insurance: *(See: financed insurance.)*

bankrupt: Unable to pay debts. A debtor whose estate is vested in a trustee for division among creditors pursuant to an order of the court.

bankruptcy: A legal proceeding ordering the distribution of an insolvent person's property among creditors, thus relieving this individual of all liability to these creditors, even though this payment may be less than the full obligation to them.

bank trusteed retirement plan: A qualified retirement plan administered by a bank.

base pay: An individual's basic earned wage or salary, excluding overtime, bonuses and unearned income.

basic hospitalization policy: A medical expense health plan that provides payment for hospital expenses only. Pays first-dollar benefits, but has relatively low limits. *(See also: hospitalization policy.)*

basic premium: A percentage of the standard premium used to determine the premium for a workers' compensation risk, utilizing the retrospective rating plan that permits adjustment of the final premium for a risk on the basis of the loss experience of the insured during the period of protection, subject to maximum and minimum limits.

basic rate: The manual or experience rate from which are taken discounts or to which are added charges to compensate for the individual circumstances of risk.

basic split-dollar plan: A plan to purchase life insurance that enables a more financially able relative, employer or associate to pay a substantial portion of another individual's insurance premiums. Under the basic plan, the insured pays the excess, if any, of the premium due over the annual increase in the cash value of the policy.

before-tax earnings: A person's gross income from salary, commissions, fees, etc., before deductions for federal, state or other income taxes.

beneficial interest: A financial or other valuable interest arising from an insurance policy.

beneficiary: The person to whom the proceeds of a life or health insurance policy are payable when the insured dies. There are three types of beneficiaries: Primary beneficiaries are those first entitled to the proceeds; secondary beneficiaries are entitled to proceeds only if no primary beneficiary is living when the insured dies; tertiary beneficiaries are those entitled to proceeds if no primary or secondary beneficiaries are alive when the insured dies. Secondary and tertiary beneficiaries are also referred to as alternate or contingent beneficiaries, since their claims are contingent on the deaths of the primary beneficiaries.

beneficiary, absolute: *(See: irrevocable beneficiary.)*

beneficiary change: The replacement of one beneficiary in a policy with another. The beneficiary may be changed only if the policy gives such right to the policyowner and if the law permits.

beneficiary, contingent: *(See: contingent beneficiary.)*

beneficiary, irrevocable: *(See: irrevocable beneficiary.)*

beneficiary, primary: The principal beneficiary who is first entitled to the proceeds of a policy upon the death of the insured. *(For contrast see: contingent beneficiary.)*

beneficiary, revocable: *(See: revocable beneficiary.)*

benefit: Monetary sums payable to a recipient, contingent upon the occurrence of the conditions set out in the policy. Not synonymous with indemnity. *(See also: indemnity.)*

benefit clause: A provision in health policies that describes the payments and the services provided under the contract.

benefit, flat dollar: In a pension plan, a monthly benefit that is the same for all employees, regardless of length of service or standard of living. In a health plan, a fixed amount payable for a specified medical service or procedure.

benefit, flat percentage: A monthly pension benefit that is determined by a fixed percentage of compensation. Although recognizing the employee's standard of living, it ignores length of service.

benefit for child of retired worker: Under Social Security, a monthly benefit provided for a natural or adopted child or step-child or, in some cases, for a grandchild of a person receiving old-age benefits. The benefit is paid until the child is 18 (or be-yond, if the child is totally and permanently disabled)—or until 22, if he or she is a full-time student in a public or accredited school or college—unless the child marries.

benefit for disabled child of deceased, disabled, or retired worker: Under Social Security, a monthly benefit provided for an eligible disabled child or grandchild (although over 18) of a deceased, disabled, or retired worker.

benefit for disabled widow or widower—age 50–62: Under Social Security, a monthly benefit paid to an eligible disabled widow or widower of a covered worker; in some cases, paid as early as age 50. The amount of the benefit depends on the Primary Insurance Amount (PIA) of the deceased covered worker and the widow's or widower's age when benefits begin.

benefit of selection: The desirable advantage employed by an insurance company through the careful selection of insurance risks.

benefit period: In reference to health insurance, the maximum length of time benefits will be paid for any one accident, illness or hospital stay.

benefit planning: The analysis of what one wishes to accomplish with insurance proceeds and other policy benefits regarding personal, family or business arrangements. This is normally an integral part of one's overall estate or business planning.

benefit, retirement: The amount payable to a life insurance or annuity policyowner or beneficiary, or a participant in a retirement plan, or to his or her beneficiary, at retirement age.

benefits department: The home office department in a life insurance company that processes all claims under life, health, group or disability benefit policies. It handles the distributions of benefits of the company's policies.

bequest: The transfer of an individual's property by will at his or her death. Bequests may be either charitable or taxable.

"Big I, The": *(See: National Association of Insurance Agents.)*

bilateral contract: One in which both parties have enforceable commitments. For instance, in a contract of sale, one party promises to deliver the item sold and the other party promises to pay the stated price. Insurance contracts are not bilateral. They are unilateral because only one party, the insurer, makes an enforceable promise to pay; the insured cannot be required to pay the premium. *(See also: unilateral contract.)*

binder: *(See: binding receipt.)*

binding receipt: The receipt for payment of the first premium that assures the applicant that if he or she dies before receiving the policy, the company will pay the full claim if the policy is issued (or would have been issued) as applied for.

birth rate: The number of births related to the total population in a given group during a given period of time.

blackout period: The period of years during which no Social Security benefit is payable to the surviving spouse of a deceased, fully insured worker, between the time the youngest child of the worker (in the spouse's case) attains the age of 18 and the spouse's age 60.

blackout period income: Income to help meet expenses during the blackout period. *(See: blackout period.)*

blanket accident medical expense: A reimbursement health policy that entitles the insured who suffers an accidental bodily injury to collect up to the maximum policy benefits for all hospital and medical expenses incurred, without any limitations on individual types of medical expenses. Some included expenses are: treatment by doctors, surgeons, nurses, hospital room and board, drugs, x-rays, lab fees.

blanket expense policy: One that pays all charges or costs for a designated illness or injury, up to a maximum figure, as compared to a policy that pays only specified amounts for designated allowable charges or costs.

blanket insurance: A group health insurance policy covering a number of individuals who are not individually named but are exposed to the same hazards, such as members of an athletic team, company officials who are passengers in the same company plane, etc.

blanket medical expense: A provision in a health policy providing for payment of virtually all hospital and medical expenses up to a maximum amount.

Blue Cross: An independent membership association operating on a service basis and providing protection against the costs of hospital care. Benefit payments are made directly to the hospital. Benefits vary among various Blue Cross associations. Blue Cross plans are usually established on a group basis. However, individual enrollment is sometimes permitted, and plans of community enrollment are undertaken in some localities. Blue Cross plans are usually (but not always) organized under special state legislation.

Blue Cross Commission: The national Blue Cross organization that coordinates the various local and state Blue Cross plans, but has no authority except to establish standards and provide guidance to any hospital service plan it recognizes.

Blue Plans: Generic term referring to those insurers authorized to use the designation Blue Cross or Blue Shield and the insignia of either. (*See also: Blue Cross* and *Blue Shield.*)

Blue Shield: The familiar title for the Associated Medical Care Plans, an independent membership association cooperating with Blue Cross and providing protection against the costs of surgery, doctors, and other items of medical care. Benefit payments are made directly to the doctor, not to the policyowner.

bodily injury: Refers to injury to the body of a person and is usually specifically defined in the policy. There are varying definitions in use.

bond, fiduciary: A bond executed on behalf of a person appointed by a court to a position of trust; it guarantees performance of statutory duties and proper accounting.

bonus funding: (*See: salary funding.*)

book value: (*See: net worth.*)

borderline risk: In insurance, one that is questionable and on the border between being acceptable and unacceptable to the insurer. (*See also: accommodation line.*)

branch manager: A life and/or health insurance company employee who manages one of the company's branch offices. The branch manager is in charge of all activities of the branch office and is responsible for hiring and training agents. Identical to a life and/or health insurance general agent, except that the branch manager is an employee of the insurer and usually salaried, rather than an independent contractor on commission.

branch office: A life and/or health insurance company field office established to supervise business within a certain territory. It is the sole representative agency of the company in a given area. Essentially, it is an agency under the management of a salaried branch manager employed by the insurer.

branch office system: A system of providing insurance services through branch offices of the insurer. As compared to the general agency system. (*See also: general agency system.*)

breach of contract: The violation of, or failure to perform, the terms of a contract. The breaking of a legally binding agreement. An insurance policy is a legal contract, and failure to comply with the terms or conditions incorporated in the policy constitutes a breach of contract. Because insurance-policies are unilateral contracts, only the insurer can be held liable for breach of contract.

breach of warranty: When used in reference to an insurance applicant or policyowner, the result of making fraudulent statements or withholding information that causes an insurance company to assume a risk it would not otherwise insure. Misrepresentation by the policyowner as to a condition precedent to the issuance of the policy. (*See also: condition precedent.*) This act voids the policy. (*See also: warranty.*)

break in service: For purposes of pension plans, a 12-month period during which an employee works 500 or fewer hours.

broad form policies: In insurance, policies that offer broad protection with few limitations. (*For contrast see: limited policies.*)

broker: One who places business with more than one insurance company and who has no exclusive contract requiring that all his or her business first be offered to a single company. The broker legally represents the customer whereas the agent is the legal representative of the company who has appointed him or her as an agent.

brokerage agency: In insurance, a private business operated by a broker, who conducts business on behalf of clients seeking to purchase personal or property insurance. It may also be a life or health insurance general agency servicing business of agents other than full-time (career) agents of the company represented by the agency. (*See also: brokerage business.*)

brokerage business: Business a company receives from insurance brokers. Also business directed to the company by full-time (career) agents of other companies.

brokerage department: The department of an insurance company designated to assist agents in handling insurance outside of their territory and to help brokers place insurance. Also, that arm of a life insurance company that services the business of agents of other companies.

broker-agent: An individual who represents one or more insurers but may also serve as a broker by searching the market to place an applicant's policy to maximize protection and minimize cost.

broker-dealer: A business entity licensed and registered with the Securities and Exchange Commission (SEC) and therefore possessing the legal right to offer securities products to the public. An agent selling variable life products and related securities (such as mutual funds) must be registered with a broker-dealer.

brother-sister group: A group of two or more companies in which the same person or persons owns more than a 50 percent interest in each organization in the group.

bucking arrears: Applying advance payments of one policyowner to another policyowner's arrears. It is a falsification of records and a form of embezzlement.

budget plan: A plan whereby large policies of insurance are divided into smaller policies, to expire and be renewed on consecutive years, the policies being written at pro rata of the long-term rates so that the premium payment is spread over several years.

burial insurance: A slang term usually referring to a small policy of life insurance ($1,000 to $5,000) intended to pay the funeral costs of the deceased insured.

business: In insurance, a term designating the volume of premiums or, in life insurance, the face amount of insurance written.

business continuation insurance: Generally refers to life or health insurance used to fund a business continuation plan. (*See also: buy-sell agreement.*)

business continuation plan: (*See: buy-sell agreement.*)

business expediency concept: A term describing an action or activity wherein the primary motivation is to benefit directly or otherwise the business owner. For example, establishing a pension plan or other employee benefit plan. Employees expect employers to provide such plans, therefore, an employer without a pension plan may be unable to hire and retain suitable workers.

business health insurance: Health insurance coverage issued primarily to indemnify a business for the loss of services of a key employee or a partner or an active close corporation stockholder; or, in a partnership or close corporation, to buy out the interest of a partner or stockholder who becomes permanently disabled.

business in force: The total dollar amount of coverage an insurance company is carrying and for which it is at risk.

business insurance: In life and/or health insurance, coverage concerned primarily with the protection of an insured's business or vocation. Business insurance protects a business against the loss of its key executives and/or key employees; stabilizes the business through the establishment of better credit relations; and provides a practical plan for the retirement of business interests in the event of the death of one of the owners.

business insurance, contingent: *(See: contingent business insurance.)*

business life insurance trust: An agreement whereby a trustee agrees to collect and distribute the proceeds of a policy of business life insurance. Used when partners or shareowners agree to buy out the interest of a deceased partner or shareowner.

business overhead expense insurance: A form of disability income coverage designed expressly to pay necessary overhead expenses to help a business operate during total disability of the owner.

business under common control: For purposes of Keogh plans, if a person has a controlling interest in an unincorporated business and in other unincorporated and/or incorporated businesses, then all such businesses must be treated as one business as far as pension plans are concerned. These businesses are called businesses under common control. A business under common control may be either a parent-subsidiary group, a brother-sister group or a combined group. *(See also: parent-subsidiary group, brother-sister group and combined group.)* The term is not limited to unincorporated businesses, but may refer to corporations in appropriate contexts. *(See also: controlled business.)*

buyer's guide: In life insurance, a booklet or brochure based on the model developed by the NAIC, explaining different kinds of life insurance, insurance terms, and cost indexes to assist consumers. Their distribution by insurers to prospective buyers is required in some states.

buy-sell agreement: An agreement between the owners of a business that provides that the shares owned by any one of them who dies shall be sold to and will be purchased by the surviving co-owners or by the business at a value or formula previously agreed upon by the parties and stipulated in the agreement. Also applies to buyout arrangements between owners and key employees.

buy term and invest the difference: A controversial concept whereby an individual purchases term insurance in the amount of protection desired, then places the difference between the premium paid and what would have been paid for the same whole life coverage in other investments. This concept has been incorporated into flexible feature products such as variable and universal life insurance products. (*See also: variable universal life.*)

C

calendar year experience: With respect to insurance, a measurement or evaluation of the loss occurring during the 12 calendar months beginning January 1, within an insured group. (*See also: experience.*)

calendar year major medical plan: A major medical insurance plan that provides reimbursement of covered expenses, with a deductible amount to be applied only once during the period from January 1 of any year through December 31 of the same year.

call: To the life and/or health insurance agent, any bona fide effort made to contact a prospect to arrange an insurance sales interview.

Canada Pension Plan: A Canadian federally operated (except in Quebec) Social Security plan. Provides a monthly pension, usually from age 65, for contributors to the plan. With few exceptions, all persons between ages 18 and 70 are covered. Employees and employers each pay a percentage of earnings into the plan. Contributions are deductible and benefits reportable for income tax purposes.

cancellable contract: In health insurance, a contract that may be terminated by the insurer at any time. Usually, all that is required for cancellation is five day notice by the insurance company to the policyowner's last known mailing address.

cancellation: In insurance, the termination of a contract by either the insured or the insurer prior to the end of the policy period. In life and noncancellable health insurance, the company generally may not cancel a policy except for nonpayment of premiums.

cancellation provision: A provision in a health policy that allows the insurance company to cancel the contract at any time, providing the insured is notified in writing.

canvassing account: In insurance, an account initially created without any premiums transferred to it from other accounts; it therefore creates its own account by the issue of new business.

capacity: A term referring to the maximum amount of coverage an insurance company will issue on a single risk. Legal capacity refers to one's mental competence to manage his or her own legal affairs.

capital: The total worth of an individual, a partnership, or all the shares of stock of a corporation. Assets or principal, as contrasted with income (which may or may not result from ownership and/or use of those assets or that principal).

capital asset: An item not ordinarily bought and sold in the course of one's business, but having monetary value and often the source of income or used in the production thereof.

capital budget: For a life insurance company, a period-by-period statement of beginning capital assets, planned acquisitions and disposals, and the resultant ending capital assets, together with the sources and disposition of funds so involved—a complete accounting of capital investments and transactions.

capital charges: The funds necessary to cover interest upon and amortization of monies invested in an enterprise. The costs of borrowed money, business or personal.

capital conservation method: A method of determining the amount of money needed to satisfy projected income needs that employs only the earnings on principal (not the principal itself) to satisfy those needs. (*See also: capital need analysis.*)

capital expenditures: Outlays of cash or other property or the creation of liability in exchange for property to remain permanently in the business; usually land, buildings, machinery and equipment.

capital gain (or loss): The gain (or loss) resulting from the sale of a capital asset in relation to its purchase price or value at the time of acquisition. (*See also: capital asset.*)

capital gains tax: A provision in the federal income tax law that previously subjected profits from the sale of capital assets to less tax than would be required for ordinary income.

capital goods: The means of production, such as factory buildings, equipment, etc., used to produce wealth. Also goods used in the production of other goods.

capital, gross working: (*See: current assets.*)

capitalization: The act or process of converting (obtaining the present worth of) future incomes into current equivalent capital value.

capitalization of interest: The process of automatically adding the unpaid interest to the principal of a policy loan.

capitalization of policy loans: The process of increasing the policy loan principal in order to take into account the unpaid loan interest.

capitalization rate: The rate of interest or return used in the process of capitalization, ordinarily assumed to reflect the factor or risk to capital so invested.

capitalized value: The money valuation of a business, arrived at by dividing the annual profits by an assumed rate of earning that is usually the current capitalization rate for similar risks.

capital loss: (*See: capital gain (or loss).*)

capital market: The market for long-term investment funds, involving primarily investment bankers, savings banks, insurance companies, pension funds, and trust companies.

capital needs analysis: A capital conservation method of total needs selling, showing how future financial needs can be met from the economic value and income-producing capabilities of current and future assets.

capital net worth: A business's total assets, less its liabilities.

capital stock: The shares of ownership in a corporation.

capital stock insurance company: An insurance company owned by its stockholders, much as any other corporation, contrasted with a mutual insurance company that is owned by its policyowners and operated for their own benefit. (*See also: mutual company.*)

capital sum: In health insurance, the amount provided for the loss of life, or of two bodily members (such as arms or legs), or the sight of both eyes, or the loss of any two members and/or eyes. Indemnities for loss of one member of the sight of one eye are usually percentages of the capital sum. Often used interchangeably with principal sum or accidental death benefit.

capital utilization method: A method of determining the amount of money needed to satisfy future income needs, based on the projection that both the earnings and principal will be spent at the end of the period during which the income will be needed.

captive agent: In insurance, an agent who has agreed to sell insurance for only one company or group.

career agency: A life insurance general agency or branch office in which there is a management commitment to the ongoing recruiting and development of career agents.

career agent: In life insurance, an agent who is under contract to represent one company and/or agency of that company, and who frequently receives some form of subsidy or financing early in his or her career, subject to the fulfilment of certain production and training requirements.

career average: A method of determining pension benefits that provides each employee with an annual credit. The amount of retirement benefit is the sum of all accumulated credits.

career average formula: The method of determining pension benefits by which the unit of benefit credited during any particular year of employment is based upon the employee's compensation during that year.

career path: A step-by-step systematized approach to the continuing development of an insurance agent's education and career training.

career presentations: In life insurance recruiting, that step in which a prospective agent is given detailed information about the career being considered.

carrier: In insurance, another term for insurer, used because the insurance company assumes or carries the risk for its policyowners.

carryback period for employer contributions: A retirement plan provision providing that an employer's contribution to a plan for a particular taxable year may be paid any time prior to the pertinent tax filing date, with extensions, and be counted for that taxable year. This means the funding standard account should have a zero balance just prior to the tax filing date. (*See also: funding standard account.*)

carryback (carryforward) provision: Provision in the Internal Revenue Code that allows a working spouse to determine his or her compensation for a taxable year and to make a contribution to an IRA up to the tax-filing date for the previous year. IRS provision permitting operating losses or capital losses to be carried back or forward to preceding or following years in order to offset the business's other years' profits or capital gains.

carryover basis: A term from the 1976 Tax Reform Act concerning the cost basis (for capital gains income tax purposes) of property passing from a decedent equal to whatever basis the property had in the decedent's hands at death. Code Section 1023 prescribing carryover basis was repealed by P.L. 96-223 effective for decedents dying after December 31, 1976.

carryover, contribution: (*See: contribution carryover.*)

carryover credit: (*See: credit carryover.*)

case management: The professional arrangement and coordination of health services through assessment, service plan development and monitoring.

cash account: The agent's account on a cash basis; that is, one on which the page numbers, premiums, arrears and/or advances are not listed.

cash accumulation policy: A life insurance policy that builds significant cash value or equity. Whole life policies and endowment policies were previously the two primary types of cash accumulation policies. Today, universal life and the various variable products must also be considered cash accumulation policies.

cash assets: Assets consisting of cash or cash equivalents that can be quickly converted to cash.

cash basis of accounting: A method of accounting that recognizes revenue only when cash is actually received and expenses only when they are paid.

cash equivalents: Assets that can be readily converted into cash.

cash refund annuity: An annuity that provides that, upon the death of the annuitant, before payments totaling the full purchase price have been made, the excess of the amount paid by the purchaser over the total annuity payments received will be paid in one sum to designated beneficiaries.

cash surrender value: *(See: cash value.)*

cash value: The equity amount available to the policy owner when a life insurance policy is surrendered to the company, or the amount upon which the total available for a policy loan is determined. During the early policy years in a traditional whole life policy, the cash value is the reserve less a surrender charge; in the later policy years, the cash surrender value usually equals or closely approximates the reserve value.

cash value, guaranteed: *(See: guaranteed cash value.)*

cash value policy: *(See: permanent life insurance policy.)*

Casualty Actuarial Society: A professional actuarial association dedicated to advancing actuarial knowledge in insurance fields other than life.

Casualty Index: A service provided by the Hooper-Holmes Bureau, Inc. that protects insurance company subscribers against fraudulent insurance practices that might be attempted by policyowners. Member companies report protective information to the information center on a daily basis and subscribers, in turn, make inquiry regarding each of their applicants.

casualty insurance: Most insurance except life (including personal accident), marine and, sometimes, fire. It is principally concerned with insurance against loss due to legal liability to third persons. Accident and sickness insurance was originally considered a part of casualty insurance and is still so classified by many states.

catastrophe: A sudden, unexpected, unavoidable and severe calamity or disaster. With respect to insurance, an event that causes a loss of extraordinary amount.

catastrophe hazard: The hazard of loss as a result of a simultaneous peril to which all insured in a particular group, or a large number of insureds, are subject.

catastrophe insurance: *(See: comprehensive major medical insurance and major medical expense insurance.)*

catastrophe reinsurance: An agreement whereby a reinsuring company assumes defined losses above a stated aggregate amount that may result from a catastrophe.

cause specific mortality rate: (*See: mortality rate, cause specific.*)

cede: To transfer to a reinsurer all or part of the insurance or reinsurance written by an insurance company. (*See also: reinsurance.*)

ceding company: The insurance company that transfers all or part of the insurance or reinsurance it has written to another insurer, that is, to a reinsuring company.

center of influence: In insurance prospecting, an individual with outstanding prestige or influence within a group, who can provide the agent with qualified referrals and may be helpful in the agent's dealings with those prospects.

certificate, group: (*See: group certificate.*)

certificate of authority: In insurance, a document detailing the powers an insurance company grants to a particular agent. Also, the legal certificate issued by a state insurance department granting an insurer the legal power and right to sell insurance in that state.

certificate of convenience: In insurance, a term referring to a temporary license or permit empowering a person to act as an agent, even though he or she is not fully licensed: such as an agent studying for a licensing examination; or a relative, administrator or executor who must engage in certain practices of an agent while settling the estate of a fully licensed agent or during the disability or absence (usually on military duty) of a licensed agent.

certificate of insurance: In group insurance a document, issued to a group member that describes the benefits provided under the master contract.

Certified Employee Benefit Specialist: A professional designation available to people who work with employee benefit plans if they pass certain examinations. Directed by the Wharton School of the University of Pennsylvania, the program covers the legal, financial and organizational framework within which employee benefit plans must function.

Certified Financial Planner (CFP):   A professional designation awarded by the International Board of Standards and Practices for Certified Financial Planners, Inc. (IBCFP), to persons who have passed a series of examinations on tax management, insurance, retirement and estate planning.

cession: In insurance, the act of yielding property or right under a reinsurance agreement. An amount ceded as reinsurance. (*See also: reinsurance.*)

cestui que trust: The person for whose benefit a trust is created or who is to receive the income or the benefits of a trust.

cestui que vie: The person whose life measures the duration of an estate.

change of beneficiary provision: A life and health insurance provision giving a policyowner the right to change the beneficiary at any time he or she chooses unless the beneficiary has been designated on an irrevocable basis.

change of occupation provision: An optional health insurance provision that states that if the insured changes occupations, the insurance company must be notified so that premium rates can be adjusted. If the insured fails to notify the company, coverage on a claim will be based on what the insured's premium payment would have purchased under the current occupation classification.

change of plan provision: Policy provision whereby the policyowner may change a policy to some other plan of insurance. If the change is to a lower premium plan, a medical examination is usually required.

charitable bequest: Any gift of property, including life insurance proceeds, transferred by will to a nonprofit organization. Such gifts are deductible for purposes of computing the estate tax, provided the donee organization is one specified by law.

charitable gift: Voluntary and complete transfer of property by an individual to a qualified charitable or civic organization for less than adequate and full consideration. Not a bona fide business transaction.

charitable giving through life insurance: (*See: life insurance for charitable giving.*)

charitable trust: A trust designed for the benefit of a class or the public generally. It is different from a private trust in that the beneficiaries are not designated individually.

charter: The granting of rights from a state to a business corporation, as in the right to incorporate and transact business.

Chartered Financial Analyst: A member of the Institute of Chartered Financial Analysts. Members are practicing financial analysts with at least five years of experience. They have passed a series of three examinations dealing with a broad range of subjects from basic accounting to domestic and international economics.

Chartered Financial Consultant (ChFC): A designation awarded by the American College to financial services professionals who complete ten fundamental financial planning courses. This program answers the growing needs of individuals seeking proficient help in their personal financial planning process.

Chartered Life Underwriter (CLU): A designation conferred on an individual by The American College in recognition of the attainment of certain standards of education and proficiency in the art and science of life underwriting. The right to the designation is open to any person involved in the field of life insurance who meets the preliminary requirements and who passes a series of ten examinations.

charter policy: *(See: guaranteed dividend policy.)*

cheap takeover: The purchase of a deceased stockholder's interest in a company at less than fair market value price.

Chicago plan: *(See: financed insurance.)*

child's benefit: In reference to Social Security, a benefit payable to an unmarried child of a retired, disabled or deceased worker until the child's age 18 (or until age 22 if a full-time student, or indefinitely if totally disabled) in an amount equal to a portion of the worker's Primary Insurance Amount.

claim: A policyowner's request or demand on the insurance company for payment of benefits according to the provisions of a policy.

claim agent: In insurance, an individual authorized by an insurance company to pay a loss.

claimant: In insurance, one who submits a claim for payment of benefits for a suffered loss, according to the provision of a policy.

claim department: *(See: benefits department.)*

claims forms provision: In health insurance policies, a provision that requires the insurance company to provide claim forms to a policyowner within 15 days after the insurer receives notice of a claim.

claims reserve: Within an insurance company, those amounts set aside to cover future payments or claims already incurred.

claims reserve, group life insurance: (*See: group life insurance, claims reserve.*)

class: A group of insureds with the same general characteristics and exposure to a peril, who are grouped together for rating purposes.

classification: In insurance, the systematic arrangement of defined classes or risks. The grouping of persons for the purpose of determining an underwriting or rating group into which a particular risk must be placed.

classified insurance: In life or health insurance, coverage on impaired risks (*See: substandard.*)

classified risk: In life and health insurance policies, the scaling of premiums to compensate for substandard health or other risks. More commonly called substandard. (*See also: substandard risk.*)

class rate: The insurance premium rate applicable to a specified class or risk.

clause: A specific section of an insurance policy (or rider attached to it) dealing with a particular subject in that policy. Also called a provision.

clean-up fund: A reserve intended to cover the medical costs of a last illness, burial expenses, probate charges, miscellaneous outstanding bills, etc.

clearance fund: (*See: clean-up fund.*)

client: In insurance, a person or company on whose behalf the agent or broker acts. The term usually infers that a well-developed business relationship exists between the insured and the agent or broker, with more than one purchase of insurance having been made or contemplated.

close: That part of a sales interview designed to motivate the prospect to arrive at a buying decision regarding the plan being presented by the agent. A trial close is an attempt by the agent to move a prospect closer to a decision-making position.

close corporation: A corporate business that has substantially identical ownership and management interests. Generally, a small group of individuals owns the company as shareholders, controls it as directors and operates it as officers.

close corporation insurance: (*See: business insurance.*)

closed contract of insurance: An insurance contract wherein rates and policy provisions cannot be changed. Fraternal insurance companies are not permitted to write this type of insurance.

closed-end mutual fund: (*See: mutual fund.*)

closely held company: Same as close corporation, except the company need not be incorporated, and owner-operators may be partners.

cloud on title: Anything blocking clear title to property. Claims outstanding against real estate by people other than the apparent owner.

CLU: (*See: Chartered Life Underwriter.*)

COB (coordination of benefits):   (*See: nonduplication of benefits.*)

codicil: An addendum or supplementary document making an addition to or change in a will. It is subject to the same legal formalities of execution (e.g., witnesses) as the will.

cognitor: An agent appointed to act for another in an action.

coinsurance (percentage participation):   A health insurance principle under which the company insures only part of the potential loss, with the insured paying the other part. For instance, in a major medical policy, the company may agree to pay 75 percent of the insured's expenses, the insured to pay the other 25 percent. Most commonly used as synonymous with risk-sharing or loss-sharing. The coinsurance provision states that the insurance company and the policyowner will share covered losses.

coinsurer: One who shares the risk under an insurance policy or policies.

cold calling: (*See: cold canvassing.*)

cold canvassing: A prospecting method whereby an insurance agent, without any prior introduction, contacts prospects about whom he or she has little or no qualifying information.

collateral assignee: The person to whom a collateral assignment is made.

collateral assignment: The assignment of an insurance policy to a creditor as security for a debt. Under a collateral assignment, the creditor is entitled to be reimbursed out of policy proceeds for the amount owed in the event of the insured's death. (*For comparison, see: absolute assignment.*) The beneficiary is entitled to any excess of policy proceeds over the amount due the creditor.

collateral assignment plan: A variation of the basic split-dollar plan, whereby the insured initially applies for and owns the policy, names the beneficiary and then collaterally assigns the policy to someone else as security for annual loans equaling the annual increase in the policy's cash value. The insured remits the full premium, including any difference between the premium due and the amount borrowed.

collateral bond: Additional security or collateral for a loan.

collateral loan: A loan guaranteed by the pledge of specific property as collateral.

collection book: The home service insurance agent's running account of the amount of premium collected on each policy, the week of collection, or date paid, and the policy period covered by the payment.

collection fee: With home service insurance, the agent's fee, usually computed as a percentage of premium collections, for making ordinary premium collections for which he or she is not paid a first-year or renewal commission. Also, the fee, a percentage of the premium paid to an agent, for his or her insurance collections.

College of Insurance, The: An academic institution endorsed and supported by insurance business leaders and life insurance companies, providing a complete curriculum leading to a Bachelor of Business Administration (B.B.A.) degree. Various certificate courses are offered, as well as preparation for licenses, designations and fellowship examinations.

College Retirement Equities Fund (CREF):   The organization that introduced the variable annuity, selling fixed and variable annuities to college faculty and staff members only. CREF is a separate body under the Teachers Insurance and Annuity Association.

collegia: Group or associations in ancient Rome that were influential in the development of life insurance and pensions. Forerunners of mutual benefit societies.

collusion: A secret agreement between two or more parties for fraudulent or illegal purposes.

combination agency: One that sells both home service and ordinary life policies.

combination agent: An authorized insurance company representative who sells and services both home service and ordinary insurance policies. More commonly known today as a home service agent. In some companies, collection of premiums is part of the combination agent's job.

combination company: A life insurance company whose agents sell both weekly or monthly premium home service and ordinary life insurance.

combination funding plan: (*See: combination plan.*)

combination life and annuity contract: Single-premium life insurance and single-premium non-refund annuity contracts issued in combination, either in one policy or concurrently in two. These were popular in the 1930s, required no evidence of insurability, and the combined single-premium equaled 105 to 110 percent of the sum payable at death.

combination plan: A pension plan that combines a life insurance contract with an unallocated, auxiliary fund or side fund, in order to increase the future pension amount.

combination policy: A life insurance policy that incorporates term, whole life, and/or endowment provisions in a single contract. Also one or more insurance policies printed on one joined sheet and providing coverage against several hazards under the one document.

Combined Annuity Mortality Table: A mortality table published in 1928 for use with group annuities that used a four-year setback for female annuitants.

combined group: Two or more companies, each a member of either a parent-subsidiary group or a brother-sister group and at least one being a common parent of the parent-subsidiary group and a member of the brother-sister group.

commercial health insurance: (*See: commercial insurance.*)

commercial inspection report: The investigation report made by an organization that specializes in obtaining information regarding persons who desire insurance, employment, credit, etc.

commercial insurance: The most prevalent form of life and health insurance coverage, of which the most distinguishing features are that the insurer need not accept the premium and renew the coverage from one premium due date to the next, and that rates may be adjusted at the company's option. (*See also: optional renewable.*)

commercial partnership: A partnership—either general or limited—that usually has some substantial inventory and/or fixed assets representing the capital investment of the partners.

commercial policy: (*See: commercial insurance.*)

commercial report: (*See: commercial inspection report.*)

commission: The percentage of the premium paid to an insurance agent or broker by the insurer as compensation for completing the sales.

commission, contingent: A commission, the amount of which is dependent upon the profitableness or some other characteristic of the business written by an insurance agent or reinsurer.

commissioner: The head of a state insurance department. The public officer charged with the supervision of the insurance business in the state and the administration of insurance laws. Called superintendent or director in some jurisdictions.

Commissioners Disability Table: A table of morbidity approved in 1964 by the National Association of Insurance Commissioners.

Commissioners Industrial Extended Term Mortality Table, 1961: A companion table to the 1961 CSI Table, used for valuation and computation of extended term insurance benefits only in case additional mortality margins are deemed to be necessary.

Commissioners Standard Industrial Mortality Table, 1961: Approved by the National Association of Insurance Commissioners as a standard for valuation and for computing nonforfeiture values and rates for industrial life insurance policies.

Commissioners Standard Ordinary Mortality Table (CSO): A standard mortality table prepared by the National Association of Insurance Commissioners used in the life insurance rate calculations.

commissioners values: A list of securities published by the National Association of Insurance Commissioners each year. Those listed are the ones that may be reported by insurance companies on their balance sheets.

commission of authority: A document detailing the delegated powers granted by the insurance company to an agent.

commissions, graded: In insurance, the commission concept that pays a larger commission to the agent or broker during the first policy year than in renewal years. In group insurance, a decremental scale of commissions applied to the group insurance premium, the commission percentage varying in inverse proportion to the size of the premium.

commissions, level: In insurance selling, the concept whereby the agent receives commission payments of equal amounts over a several year period.

commitments: A guarantee by an insurance company to accept certain risks.

common accident provision: An optional provision in a life insurance contract that states that the primary beneficiary must outlive the insured a specified amount of time (usually 30 or 60 days) in order to receive policy proceeds. Otherwise, the contingent beneficiary receives the proceeds. This provision protects the interests of the contingent beneficiary in the event that the insured and the primary beneficiary die as a result of the same accident (or within a certain period of time, regardless of the causes).

common disaster clause: (*See: common accident provision.*)

common interest group: (*See: association group.*)

common-law employee: An employee who is not a self-employed person; one who is employed by a company.

common trust funds: Assets held by a bank or other financial institution in its capacity as trustee, executor, administrator or guardian that are pooled in large sums for investment purposes.

community property law: Provides that husband and wife are each entitled to one-half of the total earnings and property acquired after marriage.

community property state: A state in which community property law determines ownership of property held by a husband and wife. (*See also: community property law.*)

community rating: In medical insurance plans, the evaluation method used to determine premiums charged by service-plan insurers by averaging the charge for the insurance among all insureds according to hospital and medical costs in the community, without differentiation among insureds in terms of the individual risk assumed by the insurer. The communitywide rate is a flat sum, varying only with the amount of benefits, regardless of age, sex, occupation or condition of health. (*See also: Blue Cross.*)

commutation rights: In life insurance, the right of the beneficiary to receive in one lump sum the cash value of the remaining payments under an option selected by the insured of a life insurance policy.

commutative contract: A contract under which each of the contracting parties gives and receives relatively equivalent values.

commute: To establish, as of a given date, the single-sum value equivalent to a series of amounts due at various dates, with allowance for interest or for interest and mortality combined. Also, to pay the commuted value.

commuted value: The single sum that represents the present worth, or equivalent value, of a stipulated number of install ments payable at fixed future dates. The commuted value is computed on the basis of a given rate of interest. Often called discounted value.

compensation: In general, payment. For pension purposes, benefits are generally paid upon base pay, or salary only without overtime, premium pay or bonuses. For purposes of taxation and private pension plans, compensation means wages, salaries, professional fees and other amounts received for personal services actually rendered, including, but not limited to, commissions paid to salespeople, compensation for services on the basis of a percentage of profits, commissions on insurance premiums, tips and bonuses.

compensation, current: (*See: current compensation.*)

competency or competent party: A person being of legal age and sound mind and under no legal handicap. The fitness or ability to enter into a legally binding contract.

competitive state fund: In insurance, a state fund writing coverage in competition with private insurers.

components: The parts that make up a whole, as in the modular components of an agent training and development program.

compos mentis: Legally sane.

compound interest: Interest earned on interest. Interest earned on principal over a given period that is then added to the original principal to become the new principal upon which interest is earned during the new period, and so on, from period to period.

comprehensive coverage: Protection under one insurance agreement that covers all hazards within the general scope of the contract, except those specifically excluded.

comprehensive health insurance: A health insurance policy that incorporates the coverages of major medical and basic medical expense policies into one policy.

comprehensive major medical insurance: A medical expense policy designed to give the protection offered by both a basic and a major medical policy. It is characterized by a high maximum benefit, a coinsurance clause and a corridor deductible. Also sometimes known as catastrophe insurance or major medical expense insurance. (*See also: corridor deductible.*)

compulsory health insurance: Plans of insurance under the supervision of a state or federal government, providing protection for medical, hospital, surgical, and disability benefits to all who qualify.

compulsory insurance: Any form of insurance required by law.

compulsory membership: In reference to pension plans, a requirement that eligible employees must, as a condition of employment, join a contributory plan. Compulsory membership usually is required only of workers who are employed after the effective date of the plan.

computation base years: A basis used in calculating one's average monthly age and/or average indexed monthly earnings for purposes of determining Social Security benefits. (*See also: average monthly wage.*)

concealment: In insurance, failure of the insured to disclose a material fact to the insurance company at the time application is made. The telling of only part of the truth or hiding the truth altogether.

condition: A provision in a contract that has the effect of modifying, suspending or revoking the principal obligation if a future, uncertain event happens or fails to happen.

conditional assignment: An assignment made for the purpose of securing a debt and canceled on payment of the obligation. (*See also: assignment.*)

conditional binding receipt: (*See: binding receipt.*)

conditional coverage: Insurance coverage applied for and paid for at the same time, but not yet issued.

conditionally renewable contract: A contract of health insurance that provides that the insured may renew the contract from period to period or continue the contract to a stated date or an advanced age, subject to the right of the insurance company to decline renewal, but only under conditions specified in the contract.

conditional premium receipt: In life insurance, receipt given to the applicant if all or part of the premium is paid at the time of application. This receipt does not provide absolute interim insurance until the company acts on the application, but stipulates that the company will assume the risk of the death or a change in the health of the insured after the date of the application if it later approves the application or, more frequently, if the insured meets with the company's rules of insurability for the plan applied for as of the date of the application. (*See also: interim term insurance.*)

conditional receipts: In insurance, receipts given to applicants when they pay a premium at the time they make application. Such receipts bind the insurance company if the risk is approved as applied for, subject to any conditions stated on the receipt.

conditional transfer: A transfer of control that will take place only if certain conditions are satisfied.

conditional vesting: That form of vesting in a contributory pension plan under which entitlement to a vested benefit is conditional upon the non-withdrawal of the participant's contributions.

condition concurrent: A contract provision requiring that two events must occur simultaneously, such as delivery of goods and their payment. A tender of performance by either party and rejection by the other party creates liability on the part of the one rejecting.

condition precedent: A legal stipulation in some contracts that one event must precede the other for the second to take place. For example, in an insurance policy, the insurer is not liable unless and until the insured pays a premium. At law, it is a provision in a contract stipulating that rights and duties shall arise only after the happening of an event. The happening of the event is the condition precedent.

conditions: Limiting and defining provisions within an insurance policy that along with the insuring agreement and exclusions, complete the contract.

condition subsequent: A contract provision stating that upon the occurrence of an event, one of the parties is, for example, released from previous duties and rights. The occurrence of the event is the condition subsequent.

confidential risk report: A report on the suitability of an insurance risk based on an investigation of physical and moral hazards.

confinement clause: A clause in some health insurance policies that specifies that disability income benefits are payable as long as the insured is confined at home, in a hospital, or in a sanitarium.

confining sickness: An illness that confines the insured to his or her home, a hospital or sanitarium.

conformity with state statutes provision: A provision that may be included in health insurance policies stating that regardless of whether or not a policy conforms to the state law at the issue date, the policy will be interpreted as though it does conform to the laws.

consent: To give approval. In life and health insurance, a policy may not be taken out on a person without that person's approval. Consent is given when the insured signs the application.

conservation: In insurance, efforts expended by agents and companies to keep insurance in force. Conservation consists not only of the prevention of lapses, but also of the reinstatement of business that already has lapsed. (*See also: persistency.*)

conservator: A caretaker appointed by a court to manage the affairs of an incompetent or to liquidate a defunct business.

consideration: One of the elements of a binding contract: the exchange of values by the parties to the contract. Such values may be money, promises, property, etc. In insurance, the policyowner's consideration is the first premium payment and the application; the insurance company's consideration is the contract itself.

consideration clause: That part of an insurance contract that sets forth the amount of initial and renewal premiums and the frequency of future payments.

consortium: The joining of several parties to one action; an international business or banking agreement or combination; the legal right of one spouse to the company, affection and service of the other.

conspiracy: A corrupt or unlawful combination or agreement between two or more persons to do by concerted action an unlawful act or do a lawful act by unlawful means.

consultant: In insurance, an independent adviser specializing in pension and profit-sharing plans. Commonly, a licensed agent.

Consumer Credit Insurance Association: An organization of insurance companies that specializes in the writing of credit life and credit disability insurance. Formed in 1951, it acts as a trade association of insurance companies engaged in the business of underwriting creditors' life insurance, promoting high ethical standards for the consumer credit insurance business, and disseminating insurance information.

contemplation of death: A phrase used to describe the apprehension or expectation of approaching and impending death that arises from some presently existing sickness or physical condition or from some impending danger. As applied to transfers of property, the phrase means that thought of death is the impelling cause of transfer, and the motive that induces transfer is a thought that leads to testamentary disposition.

contemplation of death, gift in: Prior to the 1976 Tax Reform Act, the presumed purpose of a free transfer of property made within three years of the donor's death was the avoidance of estate tax on the property involved in the gift transfer. The value of the gift, therefore, was included in the donor's estate for tax purposes, as the Internal Revenue Service presumed that the gift was made in contemplation of death. This presumption and term were eliminated by the 1976 Act. Post–1981 gifts (in excess of $10,000 per year per donee) made within three years prior to death, plus any gift taxes paid on such gifts, are with certain exceptions generally not included in the gross estate. Effective for the estates of decedents dying after 1981 (except for gifts of life insurance) as provided by the Economic Recovery Tax Act of 1981. (*See also: gross-up rule.*)

contestable: The right reserved by an insurance company to refuse or contest payment of a claim, usually for reasons of fraud or a material misrepresentation in the application. (*See also: contestable clause* and *incontestable clause.*)

contestable clause: That section of an insurance contract that states conditions under which the policy may be contested or voided. (*See: incontestable clause.*)

contestable period: The period of time during which an insurer may contest a claim on a policy because of misleading or incomplete information furnished with the application. The maximum contestable period allowed by law is two years. (*See: incontestable clause.*)

contingency reserve: A portion of surplus that most life insurance companies set aside to cover possible investment or mortality losses and operating contingencies that may arise, and thereby provide a sound margin of safety. Such funds are listed in the financial statement as contingency reserves.

contingency reserve, group life insurance: (*See: group life insurance, contingency reserve.*)

contingency surplus: (*See: contingency reserve.*)

contingent: Depending upon the happening of some future event.

contingent annuitant: (*See: annuity, joint and survivor.*)

contingent annuity: An annuity presently established and funded, but with payments to commence upon the occurrence of an uncertain event, such as the death of a named person other than the annuitant. (*See also: annuity, joint and survivor.*)

contingent beneficiary: In life and health insurance, an alternate beneficiary designated to receive payment, usually in the event that the original beneficiary pre-deceases the insured. When policy proceeds are held under a deferred settlement agreement, the person designated to receive payment of the remainder in the event that the beneficiary dies before the policy proceeds have been paid out is also sometimes called a contingent beneficiary.

contingent business insurance: Coverage of the insurable interest of an individual in the continued operation of another business, such as a supplier or a major customer.

contingent commission: *(See: commission, contingent.)*

contingent fund: A reserve to cover possible liabilities resulting from a chance happening.

contingent liability: A liability that has not yet materialized at the time of a financial statement, but that might occur at a future date.

contingent life insurance trust: A trust designed to solve the legal and financial problems confronting a minor or incompetent child if both parents die. Such a trust becomes effective only in the event of the death of the primary beneficiary (wife or husband) of a life insurance policy (or policies) with a third party named trustee.

contingent payee: *(See: contingent beneficiary.)*

contingent trust: An express trust whose operation is dependent upon a future event.

contingent vesting: In reference to pension benefits, that form of vesting under which entitlement to a vested benefit depends upon the circumstances surrounding the employee's termination of service or his or her conduct at the time of and after leaving the company.

continued term insurance: *(See: extended term insurance.)*

continuing care retirement community (CCRC): A community of independent living units with a nursing facility that offers lifetime nursing care and service. There is usually a large, onetime entrance fee followed by monthly charges.

continuing education: In many states, the term describing mandatory, ongoing educational requirements to maintain high standards of insurance sales professionals.

continuous disability: One that persists. Most health insurance contracts require that the insured's disability be continuous in order for him or her to continue receiving benefits. However, a trial effort to return to work, or work done as medical therapy, usually is not construed as breaking the continuity of disability.

contract: In insurance, the policy is a legal contract. The chief requirements for the formation of a valid contract are (1) parties having legal capacity to enter into a contract; (2) mutual assent of the parties to a promise or set of promises, generally consisting of an offer made by one party and an acceptance thereof by the other; (3) a valuable consideration; (4) the absence of any statute or other rule making the contract void; and (5) the absence of fraud or misrepresentation by either party. A life or health insurance policy meeting these requirements qualifies as a contract. (*See also: contract of insurance.*)

contract, group: (*See: group contract.*)

contract of adhesion: (*See: adhesion.*)

contract of agency: (*See: agency agreement or contract.*)

contract of decedent: An agreement entered into before the death of a deceased person.

contract of insurance: A legal and binding contract whereby an insurer agrees to pay an insured for losses, provide other benefits, or render service to, or on behalf of, an insured. The contract of insurance is often called an insurance policy, but the policy is merely the evidence of the agreement. In life and health insurance, the contract of insurance consists of the policy, the application, and any attached supplements, riders, or endorsements.

contract of personal representative: A contract entered into by an executor, administrator or trustee in conjunction with his or her fiduciary role.

contract rates: Life insurance settlement option rates stipulated in the contract itself. Current rates are those that reflect the price of money at the time a settlement option is made by a beneficiary. Contract rates govern if the settlement agreement is one set forth in the contract. Current rates are usually applied if the settlement arrangement differs from those described in the contract.

contra preferendum: A legal concept that any ambiguity in a contract must be interpreted against the person who drew the contract, since he or she had the opportunity to make it clear. Since insurance contracts are written by the insurance company, any ambiguity would be interpreted in favor of the insured.

contribution: An insurance company's obligation to pay all or part of a loss. The amount payable by an insurer under an insurance contract that is one of two or more contracts covering the same loss. (*See also: contributions.*)

contribution carryover: That amount of employer contribution that exceeds 15 percent of the participants' payroll under a profit-sharing plan and is currently nondeductible from taxable income. If the contribution formula requires the employer to contribute more than 15 percent of payroll in a particular year, the employer's deduction is still limited to 15 percent. Nevertheless, the excess contribution may be carried forward and deducted in succeeding years, to the extent the total deduction in a given year does not exceed 25 percent—15 percent for current contributions plus 10 percent carryover. (*See also: credit carryover.*)

contribution formula: As used in a qualified profit-sharing trust or money-purchase pension plan, that formula that determines what amounts or percentage of earnings the employer will contribute to the trust.

contribution limits: The maximum amount that may be placed into a retirement income plan. This amount is usually a percentage of annual income up to a ceiling cut-off level.

contribution plan: In insurance, a system of dividend calculation in which the dividend allotted to each policy is in direct proportion to its contribution to the total amount of surplus to be distributed.

contributions: In pension and other social insurance plans, payments made by covered persons, employers, or both, to meet all or a portion of the costs of the plan.

contributory: A pension or employer-sponsored insurance plan in which part of the contributions or premiums is paid by the employee and part is paid by the employer or union.

contributory group insurance: Group insurance in which premiums are paid jointly by employer and employees.

contributory plan: Any employee group insurance or retirement plan under which the employer and employees share the cost for the coverage. Employee contributions are made through periodic payroll deductions. (*For comparison, see: noncontributory plan.*)

contributory retirement plan: One in which the participant pays part of the cost of purchasing the annuity or building up the fund from which benefits are paid.

control: (*See: control of a line.*)

controlled business: An insurance account that an agent or broker can control by virtue of his or her influence with the buyer, as contrasted with controlling by actual agreement. An agent's own family members are examples of controlled business. Many states limit the controlled business an agent/broker may have to a certain percent (usually 25 percent) of total volume.

controlled businesses: For purposes of a Keogh plan, all of the unincorporated businesses (if more than one) of which the self-employed person is the sole proprietor. All must be treated as one business as far as Keogh plans are concerned. The term may also refer to corporations for purposes of a qualified pension plan.

controlling interest: Any business ownership interest in excess of 50 percent. From a practical standpoint, especially when ownership interests are in a number of people, an interest of less than 50 percent may be controlling.

control of a line: In insurance, the term referring to a situation where the policyowner gives the agent or broker the authority to place the insurance where the agent or broker sees fit.

control provision: A provision in some insurance policies, usually juvenile, that states that control is to be exercised by a person other than the insured for a limited or indefinite period.

convention: In insurance, the general term used to refer to the annual financial statement (convention form) and to the examination of insurance companies by insurance commissioners. The word convention derives from the fact that the National Association of Insurance Commissioners was originally named the National Convention of Insurance Commissioners. Also refers to a large gathering of sales representatives, who have qualified to attend by meeting certain performance prerequisites.

conventional method: In life insurance, a method of accounting for policy cash values, policy loans and premiums. The conventional method considers insurance strictly from the standpoint of its actual yearly cash value and expense elements.

conventional programming: (*See: programming* and *capital utilization method.*)

convention blank: The uniform annual financial statement submitted to the National Association of Insurance Commissioners by all state insurance departments in the United States.

convention form: (*See: convention blank* and *convention reports.*)

convention reports: Detailed insurance company statements filed with the state insurance departments. (*See also: convention blank.*)

convention values: (*See: commissioners values.*)

conversion: In life insurance, the exchange of an insurance policy of one kind for a policy of a different kind. Specifically, the exchange in accordance with the terms of a specific policy. Also, under a group policy, the right of the insured individual to apply for an individual policy without evidence of insurability within a stipulated period of time before the termination of group insurance coverage.

conversion, attained age: The conversion of a life insurance policy whereby the premiums are based on the insured's age attained at time of conversion.

conversion fund (supplemental)::   A fund used with ordinary life or limited payment life policies that enhances the cash value at retirement to provide desired monthly retirement income.

conversion, original age: The conversion of a life insurance policy whereby the premiums are based on the insured's original age at issue, with the insured required to pay the difference in premiums, plus interest, for the time the policy has been in force.

conversion privilege: In group insurance, a provision that gives the employee the right to convert group life coverage to an individual insurance policy, such as whole life or endowment. Rates are based upon attained age without evidence of insurability. Also, universal life and some variable products contain a provision that allows the policyowner to convert or exchange the policy for a traditional plan of coverage within a specified time after issue.

convertible: In life insurance, a provision in some policies giving the insured the right to exchange the policy for another without evidence of insurability.

convertible insurance: Insurance that may be converted to insurance of another form. Typically it is a term policy that is convertible into a permanent form, or group health/life coverage convertible to individual coverage.

convertible term insurance: In life insurance, a term contract that may be converted to a permanent form of insurance without medical examination, if conversion is made within a limited period as specified in the contracts. The premium is based on the attained age of the insured at the time of conversion.

cooperative insurance: A term used to describe insurance plans covering mutual associations, such as fraternal, employee, industrial, or trade union groups.

coordination of benefits (COB):   (*See: nonduplication of payments (or benefits).*)

corporate health plans: Employer-provided group health plans, operated for employees as benefits and/or incentives.

corporation: An association of stockholders created as an entity under law and regarded as an artificial person by courts, offering limited liability to stockholders, continuity in existence, and easy transferability of ownership interests.

corridor: With universal life and variable universal life policies, the minimum amount of pure insurance protection permitted by law in relation to cash value. If a minimum corridor ratio is not maintained, the policy will be treated as an investment for income taxation purposes.

corridor deductible: The name for the deductible that lies between the benefits paid by the basic plan and the beginning of the major medical benefits when a major medical plan is superimposed over a basic health plan.

corridor ratio: The legal ratio between death benefit and cash value within a life insurance policy. This ratio must be maintained if the policy is to retain its life insurance status under current law. In variable and universal life products, in which the cash value functions independently of the death benefit, the death benefit will automatically increase when the cash value reaches a certain level.

co-settlor: One of two individuals who create a trust.

cost: Amount paid or charged.

cost, current service: (*See: current service cost.*)

cost, gross: (*See: gross cost.*)

cost of insurance: The cost or value of the actual net insurance protection in any year (face amount less reserve), according to the yearly renewable term rate used by a company on government published term rates.

cost of insurance element: In an IRA, that part of a life insurance product used as an investment vehicle for a plan that provides a pure insurance benefit and is not tax deductible.

cost of living adjustment (COLA):   A rider available with some policies that provides for an automatic increase in benefits, offsetting the effects of inflation.

counsel: Legal advice; also, a lawyer or lawyers engaged to give such advice or to conduct a case in court.

counter agent: In insurance, an underwriting employee who accepts and acts upon applications submitted by buyers and brokers *over the counter* in an agency of an insurance company.

countersignature: Signature of licensed insurance agent or representative on a policy to validate the contract.

countersignature law: Statute regulating the countersigning of insurance policies in a particular state. A law requiring that all insurance contracts covering property or persons in a state be countersigned by an insurance company representative located in that state; usually a licensed resident insurance agent.

coupon policy: (*See: guaranteed dividend policy.*)

cover: The act of offering insurance coverage; to include within the coverage of an insurance contract.

coverage: The guarantee against specific losses provided under the terms of an insurance policy. Frequently used interchangeably with the word protection. The amount and extent of the insurance provided under an insurance contract. Often used to mean insurance or insurance contract. Used synonymously with the words insurance or protection.

coverage, conditional: (*See: conditional coverage.*)

covered expenses: In an insurance contract, those costs for which benefits are payable or which may be applied against a deductible amount. For example, under a medical expense contract, those expenses, such as hospital, medical and miscellaneous health care, incurred by the insured and for which he or she is entitled to receive benefits.

cover note: Written statement by an insurance agent informing the insured that coverage is in effect; used in lieu of a binder, but differing in that the binder is prepared by the insurance company, while the cover note is prepared by the broker or agent.

credit beneficiary: *(See: beneficiary.)*

credit carryover: In a profit-sharing plan, that percentage of deductible contributions that is not used and that can be applied in subsequent years. Each year the employer is allowed to contribute 15 percent of payroll toward his or her profit-sharing plan and deduct it from taxable income. If his or her contribution is less than 15 percent in a particular year, the participant can contribute the unused percentage in succeeding years (in addition to the annually allowable 15 percent) and also deduct it from taxable income. However, deductible contributions are limited to a total amount not greater than 25 percent of the participants' payroll: 15 percent for the current year's contributions plus 10 percent due to credit carryover.

credit disability insurance: *(See: credit life insurance.)*

credited service: Under a pension plan, a period of time before or after the effective date of the plan that is recognized as service for one or more plan purposes, such as determination of benefit amounts, entitlement to benefits and vesting.

credit life insurance: A policy issued on the life of a borrower to cover the repayment of a loan in the event the borrower dies before the loan has been repaid. With the creditor as beneficiary, usually written using decreasing term on a relatively small, decreasing balance installment loan. The loan may reflect direct borrowing or a balance due for merchandise purchased on the installment plan. In the event of the borrower's death, the balance due is canceled. Similar to mortgage insurance, except that generally: (1) amounts are smaller; (2) periods covered are shorter; (3) creditor, instead of a member of the borrower's family, is named beneficiary; and (4) written nonmedically from ages 18 to 65. Sometimes written on a group basis, sometimes on an individual basis.

credit life insurance, group: *(See: group credit life insurance.)*

creditor clause: In life insurance, a provision that may be included in a policy and that is intended to prevent creditors from seizing the proceeds. (*See also: spendthrift clause.*)

creditors: Third parties to whom an individual is indebted.

credit report: (*See: commercial inspection report.*)

crisscross arrangement: (*See: cross purchase.*)

critical premium: The first premium an insured pays after the policy is in force, the initial premium having been collected by the agent at the time of policy application or delivery. It is considered critical in terms of high lapse potential, with the greatest number of policy lapses occurring at this time.

critical premium contact: A follow-up practice of many agents who, as the critical premium due date draws near, contact policyowners to remind and reassure them of the benefits provided by the policy and to encourage them not to let the policy lapse.

cross purchase: An arrangement of buy-sell agreements made by business owners, that provides that in the event of one owner's death, the surviving shareholders or partners are bound to purchase, and the estate of the deceased to sell the deceased's interest in the business. A cross-purchase agreement is often funded with life insurance policies owned by each principal on the lives of all other principals.

crude death rate: The ratio of total deaths to total population during a given period of time, such as a year.

crude mortality rate: (*See: crude death rate.*)

current assets: Those assets that are expected to return to cash within one year after completing a short operating cycle of cash—inventory—accounts receivable—cash.

current compensation: That compensation that provides an employee with an immediate benefit, the most obvious example of which is his or her current base pay.

current debt: (*See: current liabilities.*)

current disbursement: In retirement planning, the most expensive means of funding a pension plan. Sometimes referred to as *pay as you go*. Distribution and funding of pension benefits when they come due.

current disbursement method: A retirement plan in which the employer pays each retired employee's monthly pension as each payment becomes due. Pension funds do not accumulate either through a contract or in an irrevocable trust.

current future service benefit: In retirement plans, the amount of pension benefits payable for each period (usually one year) of extra participation beyond the minimum requirement.

current interest rate: General term used to describe the interest rate of earnings credited to variable and universal life products (versus the fixed rate of traditional life insurance policies).

current liabilities: Short-term debts and obligations that must be paid in full within one year.

currently insured: Under Social Security, a status of limited eligibility that provides only death benefits to widows or widowers and children; does not provide old-age or disability benefits. To qualify as currently insured, a worker must have at least six quarters of coverage in the 13-quarter period ending with the quarter in which he or she dies or becomes eligible for old-age or disability benefits.

current rates: *(See: contract rates.)*

current service: Participation in a pension plan after its adoption. Current service benefit or credit is the amount of pension payable for each year of surplus participation, and current service cost is the estimated cost of providing pensions based on such participation. *(See also: past service.)*

current service benefit: In a pension plan, the portion of a participant's retirement benefit relating to his or her credited service in a given period (usually a year).

current service cost: In a pension plan, the cost to make provision for annuity credits earned by employees in the current year.

current value: The fair market value of a security or other property at the present time.

curtesy: The common-law right that a husband has to a life interest in all his deceased wife's realty, provided a child was born to them.

custodial care: In a medical context, the care necessary to meet personal needs, such as walking, bathing, dressing and eating.

Medical training is not required, but this care must be provided on a doctor's order.

customary and reasonable charges: In health insurance, the basic concept used in determining the benefit package in a major medical plan: to pay all reasonable and necessary medical costs, but not to pay excessive or unnecessary costs. Insurance companies and government providers may refuse to cover excessive expenses if they determine that charges made were not within customary and reasonable limits. (*See also: inside limits.*)

cut-off provision: In health insurance, a provision that regulates the period during which benefits are payable under major medical and comprehensive medical expense insurance.

cut rate: An insurance premium charge that is below a scheduled rate.

cy pres doctrine: A legal concept whereby, when a person expresses something in a document (e.g., a will) and for some reason the precise intention expressed therein cannot be carried out, a court interprets the document *cy pres* and orders the matter to be carried out as nearly as possible to the original intentions.

D

daily hospital benefit: In medical expense health policies, benefit coverage for hospital charges such as room, board, nurses and other routine services provided on a per diem (daily) basis. Sometimes referred to as DBR (daily board and room).

data interview: In insurance selling, a meeting during which the agent and prospect learn more about each other, and the prospect learns more about his or her own insurance needs. It is a critical step in the whole process of recognizing and solving problems associated with estate accumulation and distribution. (*See also: fact-finding interview.*)

date of exhaust, exact: (*See: exact date of exhaust.*)

date of expiration: (*See: expiration date.*)

date of issue: The date the insurance application is approved and the policy is issued by the insurance company. This is not necessarily the same as the date of the policy or the date the insurance becomes effective. However, life insurance policies frequently determine suicide and incontestability clauses based on the date of issue.

date of last payment: For home service insurance policies, the premium due date of the last period, week or month for which a premium was paid; this is not necessarily the date on which the last premium payment was made.

date of maturity: The stipulated date upon which a debt must be paid. The term is usually applied to those debts evidenced by a written agreement, such as a note, bond, etc. Also, the date upon which a life insurance policy endows if the insured is still living.

date of policy: The date appearing on the front page of an insurance policy indicating when the policy went into effect.

days of grace: (*See: grace period.*)

death benefit: Policy proceeds to be paid upon the death of the insured. In life and AD&D health policies, the face amount to be paid to a beneficiary upon proof of death of the insured. The sum payable as the result of the death of the insured. In a pension plan, the benefit payable to the beneficiary on the death of a participating employee. (*See also: principal sum.*)

death benefit for parents: Under Social Security, a monthly death benefit beginning at age 62, payable to each natural or adoptive parent or stepparent of a deceased, fully insured individual, if the parent or stepparent was dependent upon the insured for at least one half of his or her support and has not remarried since the individual's death (unless to a person also eligible for certain Social Security benefits).

death claim: In life insurance, certain forms giving due proof of the death and establishing the claimant's right to such proceeds that the person entitled to the proceeds must complete when an insured dies. When filed with the company, the company is said to have a death claim.

death, contemplation of: (*See: contemplation of death.*)

death duty: (*See: state death taxes.*)

death fund: Prior to the development of life insurance, the sum collected by members of a group in anticipation of the deaths of members.

death, premature: (*See: premature death.*)

death rate: For insurance purposes, the proportion of persons in each age group who die within a year, usually expressed as so many deaths per thousand.

death rate, crude: (*See: crude death rate.*)

deaths, discounts for: A reduction in the anticipated cost of providing benefits that results from assuming that a certain number of participants in a group pension plan will die before retirement. A recognized mortality table is used as the basis for these assumptions. The greater the number of deaths, the greater the discount for death for survivors.

death taxes: (*See: state death taxes, estate tax* and *inheritance tax.*)

death test: In life insurance, a concept that may be used in determining the appropriateness of an insurance plan. If a plan meets the death test, it will create an estate of so many dollars (the amount dependent on each prospect's needs) immediately upon death. As compared to the living test that works with the death test to provide an ideal plan. (*See also: living test.*)

debit: A combination insurance agent's group of policyowners from whom premiums are regularly collected. A debit book is the agent's list of active policyowners. The term also applies to the territory in which an agent collects premiums.

debit agent: In insurance, an agent who collects premiums for and sells industrial insurance. The terms *debit, industrial* and *combination* are generally used interchangeably with respect to types of insurance, insurance agents, insurance marketing methods, etc. Also known as home service agent.

decedent: A deceased person.

declaration: In insurance, a statement made by the applicant at the time of policy application, usually relative to underwriting information that the insurer deems vital, and to which the applicant is probably the one best able to supply accurate information. In life and health insurance policies, the declaration is copied into the policy. Also, that part of an insurance policy that contains information regarding the insurance risk, on the basis of which the policy is issued.

declare a dividend: To announce or approve a cash payment (dividend) to a corporation's shareowners out of the company's earnings or surplus.

declared interest rate: In a universal life policy (or in the general account of a variable universal life or interest sensitive whole life policy) cash values earn a minimum interest rate. However, they will actually be credited with a current rate of return that may be substantially higher. This rate is declared by the insurance company and may be periodically changed.

declination: Rejection of an application for insurance by the insurer.

decline: To refuse or reject an applicant for insurance.

decreasing term insurance: Term life insurance whereby the face value slowly decreases over time in scheduled steps from the date the policy goes into force until the date the policy expires, while the premium remains level. The intervals between decreases are usually monthly or annually.

deductible: In many health insurance policies, an amount of expense or loss to be paid by the insured before an insurance policy starts paying benefits. The insurance company pays benefits only for losses in excess of the stated amount.

deductible clause: An insurance policy provision that specifies an amount to be deducted from any loss, leaving the company liable only for the excess of that stated amount.

deductible, corridor: (*See: corridor deductible.*)

deductible coverage: An insurance policy provision stipulating that only the loss in excess of a minimum figure is covered.

deductible coverage clause: A provision in an insurance policy that states that, in return for a reduced rate, the insured will assume losses below a specified amount. In a health insurance policy, for example, that portion of covered hospital and medical charges that an insured person must pay before the policy's benefits begin.

deductible period: (*See: recurrent disability provision.*)

deductions: Amounts or items subtracted as allowable expenses from gross income for income tax purposes or from gross estate for death tax purposes.

defamation: The act of harming someone's character, fame, or reputation by false and malicious words, including libel and slander. Many state insurance laws provide penalties for verbal or printed circulation of derogatory information calculated to injure the business or reputation of any insurance company or agent, or for aiding in such activities.

default: In insurance, the policyowner's failure to make a premium payment by a policy's final due date or by the end of its grace period.

defeasance: A clause included in some insurance policies that provides that performance of certain specified acts will nullify the contract agreement.

deferment clause: (*See: delay clause.*)

deferred annuity: A life annuity contract in which the first payment is not paid to the annuitant until after a specified number of years or until the annuitant attains a specified age. Deferred annuities may be purchased either on the single premium or annual premium basis. Annual premium deferred annuities are usually known as retirement annuities. (*See also: retirement annuity.*)

deferred compensation: The deferral of an employee's compensation to some future age or date. The employee accepts a promise to receive payment at a later date (such as at retirement or in the form of a death benefit paid to a beneficiary) for work performed currently. A plan of deferred compensation is frequently used to provide fringe benefits to selected personnel. When arranged in accordance with IRS requirements, it benefits the key employee because the money is not taxed until the later date, usually upon retirement, when income is reduced and the deferred funds will then be taxed at a lower rate.

deferred payments: Payments of compensation or benefits to be made at some future date.

deferred premium file: A file maintained by an insurance company office and used to record and report when premium payments are due and made.

deferred premiums: In life insurance, the unpaid premiums (not yet due) as of December 31 on an individual policy where premiums are payable other than on an annual basis.

deferred vesting: In a pension or profit-sharing plan, a form of vesting in which rights to benefits are acquired by a participant upon the fulfillment of specified requirements (usually in terms of attained age, years of service and/or plan membership).

deferred wage concept: The idea that a pension is simply income held for future payment in lieu of cash increases in wages. (*See also: deferred compensation.*)

deficiency reserves: Additional funds required by state laws to be held by insurance companies when the gross premiums are less than the net premiums.

defined benefit plan: A type of pension plan under which benefits are determined by a specific benefit formula. The required annual deposits depend on the benefits to be provided and the number of years in the accumulation period. (*See also: fixed benefit retirement plan.*)

defined contribution plan: A tax-qualified retirement plan in which annual contributions are determined by a contribution formula set forth in the plan. The benefits paid to a participant vary with the amount of contributions made on his or her behalf and with the length of service under the plan.

definite benefit: In employee retirement plans, pension benefits equivalent to a definite percentage of pay, multiplied by length of service or by years of participation in a plan.

definite benefit plan: A pension plan that provides a definite schedule of benefits and undertakes to meet whatever costs prove to be necessary. (Contrasted to a money-purchase plan that provides a definite schedule of contributions, but promises to pay at the time of retirement only whatever benefits the accumulated funds have provided.) The definite benefit is usually a specified percentage of pay for each year of service or participation, but may also be a single flat sum or a flat sum per year of service. Sometimes called fixed benefit. (*For contrast, see: money purchase plan.*)

degree of risk: In insurance, the probable deviation of actual experience from expected experience.

delay clause: A provision in an insurance policy that permits the insurance company to delay, for a period of no longer than six months, the granting of any loan against the cash value of the policy, except for purposes of paying premiums. This provision is rarely invoked.

delayed payment clause: In insurance, a provision that permits the insurer to withhold payment of proceeds to the beneficiary for a specified period after the death of the insured. Should the beneficiary die within this period, the proceeds are paid to the contingent beneficiaries, if any, or to the estate of the insured.

delivered business: Insurance policies that have been issued and delivered to the policyowner, but for which the initial premium has not yet been paid. In life insurance, delivery generally may be made only if the first premium is or has been paid at the time of delivery.

delivery of policy: The presentation of an insurance policy to the insured. Actually, delivery is determined by the intent of the parties and does not necessarily require that the policy physically change hands. A conditional receipt or binding receipt (or, at times, verbal acknowledgement) may constitute delivery.

delivery receipt: In insurance, a dated receipt signed by the policyowner, stating that he or she has received the policy.

demise: To die; death; to convey an estate to another by will or lease; to transfer by descent or bequest.

demography: The study of populations from the standpoint of their vital statistics.

demonstrative legacy: A gift provided for in a decedent's will by a particular fund or from specific property. It differs from a specific legacy in that, if the specified funds do not exist or are not sufficient to pay the legacy, the demonstrative legacy does not abate, but may be provided, nevertheless, from general funds.

dental expense insurance: A form of medical expense health insurance covering the cost of treatment and care of dental disease and injury to the insured's teeth. This coverage is more commonly included in group health insurance policies than in individual health policies.

dependency period: For life insurance purposes, the years when children are dependent upon parents. This usually is considered to be until the youngest is 18 years old, because that is the period during which Social Security benefits are payable to eligible spouses caring for eligible children of deceased, disabled or retired workers.

dependency period income: One of the basic uses for life insurance. Income for the family during the years until the youngest child reaches maturity (usually age 18).

dependent: For legal and tax purposes, the lawful spouse and each unmarried child who is not employed on a regular full-time basis and who is dependent upon the declaring individual for support and maintenance. The term includes stepchildren, adopted children and foster children.

deposit: The contributions or payments made to a pension fund by the employer and/or employee.

deposit administration: A method of pension funding in which contributions are placed with an insurance company and used to purchase annuities when employees retire; in contrast to conventional group annuities, under which the funds are immediately used to purchase units of deferred annuities for all participants. As in the trusteed plan, the insurance company acts as the trustee until annuities are actually purchased. Also known as group deposit administration annuity.

deposit administration group annuity: A group contract providing a deposit fund prior to retirement of participants, with annuities bought for them from the fund at their retirement.

deposit administration plan: A retirement plan in which benefits are funded by payments to a deposit account held by an insurer, who credits interest and withdraws the amounts required for the purchase—upon retirement or at other specified times—of stipulated annuities for individual employees. Funds in the deposit account are not allocated to specific benefit credits or to individual employees.

deposit premium: A premium deposit required by an insurance company on those forms of insurance subject to premium adjustment. Also called provisional premium. (*See also: advance premium.*)

deposits, dividend: (*See: dividend deposits.*)

deposit term life insurance: A kind of term insurance, normally sold for ten-year terms, with the first-year premium being more than twice the amount of the annual premiums to be paid for the remaining years. This higher first-year premium is called a deposit. If the insured dies, double the deposit is added to the death benefit; if the insured lives, double the deposit is returned at the end of the term. The insured forfeits the deposit and receives no refund if the policy lapses.

descendant: One who descends from another; one's child, offspring.

descent: With respect to estates, succession to ownership by inheritance; the passage of estate, upon the death of the owner, to heirs by law.

determination letter: In employee retirement planning, an official ruling issued by the Internal Revenue Service, advising as to the deductibility of employer contributions under a pension or profit-sharing plan, stating whether or not the proposed plan qualifies under the provisions of Section 401(a) of the Internal Revenue Code. Although the law does not require or provide for advance approval by the IRS in order to obtain tax treatment accorded qualified deferred compensation plans, most employers seek such approval, considering the substantial sums involved.

devise: A disposition of real property, distributed according to the terms of a last will and testament. It is distinguished from a bequest or legacy, which is a gift of personal property by a will.

diagnostic coverage: Medical insurance that pays expenses up to a stated amount for such diagnostic services as x-ray examination or other laboratory tests.

diagnostician: A physician who determines the nature of an ailment.

difference in conditions: In insurance, a rider that expands coverage written on a named period basis, whereby all risks subject to exclusion are incorporated into the coverage.

direct approach: (*See: cold canvassing.*)

direct cause: The active, efficient cause that sets events in motion and that is sufficient, in itself, to bring about a result.

direct mail: In insurance, a prospecting method designed to assist the agent in securing or qualifying prospects, whereby substantial quantities of standardized letters are sent out by the agency, the agent or the insurance company.

directory trust: A trust that is not completely and finally established, but only defined in terms of its general purpose and to be carried out in detail according to later specific directions.

direct placement: The direct selling of a security to a financial institution, such as an insurance company, by the issuer of the security.

direct selling system: A marketing method whereby the insurance company deals directly with the policyowners and utilizes salaried employees, rather than commissioned agents.

direct trust: (*See: express trust.*)

direct writer: An insurance company that sells its policies through salaried employees or agents who represent it exclusively, rather than through independent agents or insurance brokers. Also, the insurer that contracts with the insured, as distinguished from the reinsurer.

disability: A physical or mental impairment caused by accident or illness that partially or totally limits one's ability to perform duties of, say, his or her own occupation or any occupation for which the individual is reasonably suited by education, training, or experience. In insurance policies or government benefit programs, definitions of disability may vary.

disability benefit: Provision in a life insurance policy that states that, in the event of an insured's total disability, the insurance company will waive payment of premiums falling due during the disability period and, in some cases, will also pay an income during disability. Also, the benefits payable under a disability income policy.

disability benefits insurance: Insurance providing benefits to employees for accident or sickness that is not covered by workers' compensation laws.

disability benefits law: A disability benefits system, established by statute, under which employees, temporarily out of work because of nonoccupational disability caused by either illness or injury, receive certain benefits, provided they meet minimum specified requirements.

disability buy-out insurance: A type of disability insurance coverage, issued in connection with a buy-sell agreement that, in the event of a business partner's (or stockholder's) total disability, pays a stated benefit for the purpose of buying out the business interest of the disabled associate.

disability, continuous: (*See: continuous disability.*)

disability freeze: Under Social Security, a provision that preserves the insured status and benefit level of those who become disabled. Thus, in any later calculation of benefits, the disability period is excluded in determining the average monthly wage or average indexed monthly earnings, as appropriate, on computing the worker's Primary Insurance Amount.

disability income: A disability benefit provided by a specific health insurance contract that pays a regular monthly income if the insured is disabled by sickness or accident. Also, under certain life insurance contracts, a limited disability income may be provided under a rider in the event of total and permanent disability of the insured. (*See also: disability income benefit for worker* and *disability income benefits for worker's dependents.*)

disability income benefit for worker: Under Social Security, a monthly benefit, equal to the worker's Primary Insurance Amount, paid to a disabled worker who meets stipulated requirements.

disability income benefits for worker's dependents: Under Social Security, a monthly benefit paid to dependents of persons drawing disability benefits. Eligible dependents, and their benefit amounts, are the same as though the worker had retired at the time of disability.

disability income checkup: In insurance, an analysis of the prospect's disability income situation. It is designed to help the prospect determine how much of a reduced income would be required in the event of disability, how much of that income would be provided under the prospect's present plans, and how to supplement and increase the coverage, if necessary.

disability income insurance: A form of health insurance that provides periodic payments under certain conditions to replace income lost when the insured is unable to work as a result of an accident or illness. This is a stated amount (valued) contract.

disability insurance, group: (*See: group disability insurance.*)

disability insurance, mortgage: (*See: mortgage disability insurance.*)

Disability Insurance Training Council: An organization established by the International Accident and Health Association for the promotion of health insurance education on an institutional level, primarily through adult or continuing education divisions of colleges and universities.

disability, partial: As it relates to disability insurance coverage, a disability that prevents the insured from undertaking a part of the duties of his or her occupation. The exact degree of such inability that must exist in order to constitute partial disability depends upon the terms of the individual policy.

disability, pension: A pension payable in the event that an employee becomes totally and permanently disabled before normal retirement age.

disability, permanent-total: Disability equivalent to a complete and permanent loss of earning power. Different health insurance policies define permanent-total disability in various ways and often specify that certain injuries (such as total loss of sight, loss of both hands or both legs) constitute permanent and total disability, regardless of the injured's ability to undertake gainful employment.

disability premium waiver insurance: A provision (sometimes included automatically, sometimes optional and requiring an additional premium) in a life insurance contract or rider that provides that no further premiums will be due during a period of disability, providing the disability (as defined in the contract) extends beyond the stated period (usually six months).

disability provision: A provision in an insurance policy that explains the term and benefits provided in the event the insured becomes disabled and defines what is meant by disability.

disability retirement benefits: Pension benefits paid because of retirement due to disability.

disability, temporary-partial: A disability causing a partial loss of earning power, but from which full recovery can be expected.

disability, temporary-total: A disability that prohibits the insured from performing any of his or her duties, but from which complete or partial recovery can be expected.

disability, total: There are various definitions of total disability in health insurance. The two most common state that the totally disabled individual is incapable of: (1) performing any of the duties of his or her occupation commensurate with education and training; or (2) performing any income-earning job, without regard to education and training. The actual definition will depend upon the wording in the policy. (*See also: partial disability.*)

disbursement method, current: (*See: current disbursement method.*)

disclaimer: In the legal sense, a repudiation, or refusal to accept an interest, right, property, estate, claim or power offered to or vested in or alleged to be a person's inheritance.

discount: The difference between an amount due at a future date and its present value at a specified rate of interest. In estimating pension costs, to discount for mortality or turnover is to deduct or make allowance for those employees who will die or terminate employment before retirement. Also, based on an assumed rate of interest, a benefit due in the future can be purchased with discounted dollars today.

discounted premiums: In insurance, premiums paid in advance by means of lump-sum payment. Such payments are less than the sum of shorter, modal premiums. In general, the less frequent the premium made (such as annually v. monthly) the greater the discount.

discount for turnover: (*See: turnover, discount for.*)

discounting for mortality: (*See: advance discounting for mortality.*)

Discretionary Rule: Under a pension plan, the legal power of the Commissioner of Internal Revenue to approve any classification of employees that does not discriminate in favor of officers, stockholders, supervisors, or highly paid employees.

discrimination: For insurance purposes, treating certain groups of people unfairly in the sale and/or pricing of policies. It also refers to the favoring of certain agents or agencies by handling of like risks in different ways. Actually, the nature of underwriting is based upon discrimination of the good risk from the poor risk. What is prohibited is treating any of a given class of risk differently from other like risks. In pensions, discrimination is the favoring of officers, shareowners, supervisory or highly compensated employees over others.

dismemberment: (*See: accidental dismemberment, double dismemberment* and *single dismemberment.*)

dismemberment insurance: A form of health insurance that provides payment in event of accidental loss of one or more bodily members or the sight of one or both eyes. Dismemberment insurance frequently is combined with accidental death insurance in a form called accidental death and dismemberment insurance.

distribution plan: (*See: settlement options.*)

distributive share: That portion of a partnership's net profits (or losses) to which each member of a partnership is entitled and that must be included in that member's taxable income. It is immaterial whether the distributive share is actually distributed or kept in the business.

diversification: In insurance, the spreading of the risk, accomplished by several different techniques, such as geographically, by type of risk, by type of coverage, or by insuring more risks that are separate exposures. Also applies to spreading investment risks, such as the diversification of cash value among different investment accounts in a variable or variable universal life policy.).

dividend: In participating life insurance contracts, the refund of that part of the premium paid that still remains after the company has set aside the necessary reserve and has made deductions for claims and expenses. The dividend may also include a share in the company's investment, mortality, and operating profits. Sometimes called return of premium overcharge.

dividend accumulation: *(See: accumulated dividends and accumulation.)*

dividend additions: In life insurance, paid-up additional insurance purchased with dividends on existing policies. Participating policies provide that their dividends may be used as single premiums at the insured's attained age to purchase paid-up insurance as additions to the amount of insurance specified on the face of the contract. *(See: paid-up additions.)*

dividend class: The method used by participating companies to pay dividends to policyowners, whereby the total population of policyowners is grouped into categories in which members bought the same policy at the same age and are currently the same age. This method allows precise determination of how much premium should be returned to each class as a dividend.

dividend deposits: In participating life insurance, cash dividends and interest arising from the policy, but left on deposit with the company under the terms of the dividend option.

dividend, extra: A dividend that is paid in addition to any regular, periodic dividends. *(See also: dividend.)*

dividend options: In life insurance, the different ways in which the insured under a participating policy, may elect to receive surplus earnings: in cash; as a reduction of premium; as additional paid-up insurance; left on deposit at interest; or as additional term insurance.

dividend, postmortem: (*See: postmortem dividend.*)

divisible surplus: In participating life insurance policies, the amount of surplus earnings available for distribution among the policyowners in the form of dividends.

domestic company: A company is a domestic company in the state or province in which it is incorporated or chartered.

domestic society: A fraternal benefit insurance society headquartered within the state in which it is chartered.

domicile: An individual's fixed, permanent home. In law, a person can have only one domicile, although he or she can have many residences.

domiciled company: An insurance company with its head office in the same state as is the person referring to it.

dominant problem: The major shortcoming in an insurance prospect's current estate situation that must be solved in order for the prospect to realize his or her financial and family objectives.

donee: One who receives a gift.

donee beneficiary: (*See: beneficiary.*)

donor: One who makes a gift.

double dismemberment: Loss of any two limbs, the sight of both eyes, or the loss of one limb and sight of one eye.

double indemnity: A provision in a life insurance policy, subject to specified conditions and exclusions, under which double the face amount of the policy is payable if the insured dies as a result of an accident. Generally, the insured's death must occur prior to a specified age and result from accidental bodily injury caused solely through external, violent and accidental means, independently and exclusively of all other causes, and within 60 or 90 days after such injury. (*See also: accidental death benefit.*)

doubling up: In business insurance, a technique used in some buy-sell agreements that increases the coverage on insurable shareholders to offset the lack of coverage on those who are uninsurable.

dower: Historically, the right a widow has to the property of her deceased husband; a right which, at common law, comprises a life interest in one-third of such property.

draft: A negotiable instrument, often used by insurance companies to pay claims, whereby instead of ordering a bank (as in a check) to pay, the payer (the insurance company) orders itself to pay.

dread disease insurance: Health insurance coverage providing unallocated, blanket reimbursement of expenses incurred for the treatment of specified diseases, up to a specified maximum amount.

drop at (date):   In insurance, an order for nonrenewal of a policy as of a certain date.

drop-ins (dump-ins):   Refers to lump sum or large single premium payments. (*See also: additional premium.*)

dry trust: A trust that vests the legal title in the trustee and does not require the performance of any active duty on his or her part to carry out the trust.

dual line stock company: An insurance company that issues both participating and nonparticipating life insurance policies.

duplicate coverage: In health insurance, a term usually applied to coverage other than loss of time, under which an individual is insured by two or more policies providing the same type or overlapping benefits and often resulting in overinsurance.

duration of risk: In insurance, the period of time for which a risk is to run.

duress: The compulsion under which a person acts through fear of personal suffering. A contract obtained by means of duress is voidable.

E

earned income: Gross salary, wages, commissions and fees, derived from active employment. Contrast to unearned income that includes income from investments, rents, annuities, and insurance policies. (*See also: compensation.*)

earned premium: The amount of premium that would compensate the insurance company for its loss experience, expenses and profit year to date.

earnings: Money derived from personal services, that is, salary, wages, and commissions.

earnings limitation: The limitation on the amount of income a person who is receiving Social Security benefits can earn before those benefits are reduced. Both the earnings limitation amount and the benefit reduction are subject to escalation.

earnings, gross: (*See: gross earnings.*)

economic benefit: In a split-dollar or other employer-provided insurance plan, that amount that the insured employee or party must report currently as income. The economic taxable benefit equals the value of the insurance protection payable to the insured's beneficiary under the basic plan, plus the dollar value of any dividends used for the insured's benefit, less the insured's share of the gross premium. In a Section 79 plan, the value of the insurance received by an employee above the $50,000 allowed income tax-free under the Internal Revenue Code.

economic life value: The dollar value of an individual's earning ability. This involves either a direct or indirect income or cost value to families (such as the death of a husband or wife), businesses or organizations. (*See also: human life value.*)

educational endowment: An endowment policy designed to provide children with money for education. The policy may be either on the parent or the child. Normally, an educational endowment matures when the child reaches college-age.

education insurance: Life insurance purchased to ensure that a child has the funds necessary to pay for his or her college education. For instance, a cash value policy may be taken out on the life of a parent. If the parent lives, the cash value is available as a college fund; if the parent dies, the proceeds are then available.

effective control: In a closely-held corporation, ownership of more than 50 percent of the voting stock or more than 50 percent of the total value of all classes of stock. In publicly-held businesses, effective control can generally be achieved with less than 50 percent ownership of stock.

effective date: The date on which a retirement plan or an insurance policy goes into effect and coverage begins.

Eianoi: Ancient Greek society that was influential in developing the idea of life insurance.

elapsed years: When calculating one's average monthly wage or average indexed monthly earnings for purposes of Social Security benefits, generally, the number of years obtained by subtracting 1951 (or if later, the year in which the worker attains age 22) from the year the worker dies, becomes disabled, or attains age 62.

elective benefits: (*See: elective indemnities.*)

elective indemnities: Under disability plans, a lump sum that the insured may elect to receive, in accordance with the policy schedule, in lieu of any regular income payments provided, if he or she suffers an accidental injury resulting in a sprain, dislocation, fracture, or amputation of fingers or toes.

eligibility period: The period of time during which potential members of a group life or health insurance plan may enroll without providing evidence of insurability. Also, the period of time under a major medical policy during which reimbursable expenses may be accrued.

eligibility requirements: In pension plans, rules to determine which employees may enter into the plan. (*See also: eligible employees.*)

eligible employees: Within a given group or company, employees who may participate in a company benefit plan, such as a pension plan, profit-sharing plan, etc. For purposes of Section 403(b) of the Internal Revenue Code, common-law employees of Section 501(c)(3) employers who may participate in a tax-deferred annuity.

eligible expense: In health insurance, expenses covered under the terms of the policy, as under the broad terms of major medical or comprehensive medical expense insurance.

elimination period: (*See: waiting period.*)

emergency accident benefit: In health insurance, a hospital benefit payable for out-patient emergency treatment of an injury.

emergency expense benefits: (*See: funeral or emergency expense benefits.*)

emergency fund: One of the basic uses for life insurance proceeds. A reserve death benefit fund provided by the insured to protect his or her family against sudden large, unbudgetable expenses, such as accidents, operations, etc. The increasing loan value of a life insurance policy also constitutes, and is often referred to as, an emergency fund for the insured while he or she is living.

employee: For purposes of retirement plans, an individual who works for a person or organization having the right to direct and control that individual in the way he or she works, both as to the final results and as to details of when, where and how the work is to be done. Hence, for purposes of a pension or profit-sharing plan, an independent contractor cannot be considered an employee. An employee, however, may also be a self-employed person, an owner-employee, a junior partner or a common-law employee. (*See also: self-employed individual, owner-employee, junior partner* and *common-law employee.*)

employee benefit programs: Programs through which benefits are offered to employees by an employer, covering such contingencies as medical expenses, disability, retirement, and death, usually paid for wholly or in part by the employer. Sometimes called fringe benefits because they are usually separate from wages and salaries.

employee, common-law: (*See: common-law employee.*)

employee contribution: Deduction from an employee's pay, applied toward the cost of a retirement or other benefit plan.

employee organization: Any organization, such as a labor union, that exists for the purpose of dealing with an employer on matters of employment, such as benefit plans, conditions, etc.

employee pension benefit plan: Any plan, fund or program established and maintained by an employer or an employee organization that provides retirement benefits to employees or provides deferred income until employment is terminated.

Employee Retirement Income Security Act: Known as ERISA, a federal law, passed in 1974, establishing government requirements for private pension and profit-sharing plans, including vesting requirements, funding mechanisms and general plan descriptions. The law also specifically increased the tax deduction limits available to self-employed individuals utilizing Keogh plans, raising the dollar limit from $2,500 to $7,500 and the percentage limit from 10 percent to 15 percent. The Economic Recovery Tax Act increased these deductible limits in 1981; the Tax Reform Acts of 1984 and 1986 raised the limits even further. Currently, the maximum deductible amount is the lesser of 25 percent of compensation or $30,000.

employee stock ownership plan: A qualified retirement plan that receives favorable tax treatment under the Internal Revenue Code. The plan trustee must invest contributions primarily in securities of the employer. However, a qualified ESOP can provide an incidental death benefit funded by life insurance.

employee stock ownership trust: A trust formed to borrow money on behalf of the parent company, with repayments made to the trust in the form of annual contributions to an ESOP.

employees' trust: A medium through which a pension plan is financed and given effect.

employee welfare benefit plan: Any plan or program that is established or maintained by an employer or an employee organization for the purpose of providing its participants or their beneficiaries with medical, surgical or hospital care, or benefits in the event of sickness, accident, disability, death or unemployment, or vacation benefits or training programs or similarly related programs (other than pension or retirement programs).

employer: In an employee benefit plan, any person acting directly as an employer or indirectly in the interest of an employer. This includes a group or association of employers acting for their respective employer members.

employer's liability insurance: Insurance coverage against the common-law liability of an employer for injuries to employees, as distinguished from the liability imposed by a workers' compensation law.

employment benefit plan: Any employee life, health, retirement or other benefit plan (such as parental leave or day care facilities) provided totally or partly by an employer.

endless chain prospecting: In insurance, a method of referred lead prospecting whereby satisfied policyowners are asked to recommend an agent to friends and associates.

endorsement: A written modification to an insurance policy, usually written on the printed policy page. An endorsement may also be in the form of a rider. No endorsement is valid unless signed by an executive officer of the company and attached to and made a part of the policy. (*See also: rider.*)

endow: A life insurance policy is said to endow when its cash value equals the face amount. The policyowner then receives, in cash, the face amount. Also, to give or bestow, as money to a favorite school or charity.

endow at age 100:   A characteristic of the whole life policy in that the policy is so designed that the cash value will equal the face amount of the policy at the insured's age 100.

endowment: In life insurance, a contract that provides for the payment of the face amount at the end of a fixed period, or at a specified age of the insured, or at the death of the insured before the end of the stated period.

endowment amount: (*See: face amount.*)

endowment at age ( ):   The name and description of an endowment policy, indicating the time when the endowment matures (i.e., an endowment at age 65 endows when the policyowner is 65 years old).

endowment insurance policy: (*See: endowment policy.*)

endowment policy: A life insurance policy in which the cash value and face value are equal to each other at the policy's maturity date; a policy under which the face amount is payable on a specified future date (maturity date) if the insured is then living, or at the insured's death if that should occur sooner. Essentially, it is an insured endowment.

enemy alien: An individual or company whose nation is at war with another nation. Insurance contracts between enemy aliens are held to be against public policy and are void.

enrollment card: In a group life insurance plan, an information and registration certificate filled out by each employee.

entail: An estate limited in succession to issue or to certain classes of issue, rather than descending to all heirs.

entire contract clause: An insurance policy provision stating that the application and policy contain all provisions and constitute the entire contract. No promises or special agreements of the agent can be part of the insurance company's obligation unless they are set out as a part of the contract and signed by the proper officers.

entirety, estate by: Joint ownership by both husband and wife, with the right of survivorship. In most states this has been abolished and replaced by joint tenancy, having the same result.

entity plan: A buy-sell business continuation agreement in which the business entity assumes the obligation of purchasing a deceased owner's interest in the business, thereby proportionately increasing the interests of surviving owners.

entry age normal: Under an employee retirement plan, the age at which an individual would first have been eligible for participation in the plan had it been in effect at that time.

entry age normal funding: A pension funding method involving the projected cost concept of pension planning.

equitable asset: An asset held by the executor of an estate that is not subject to debts. Only a decree by an equity court can make an equitable asset available for satisfaction of certain obligations.

equity: Money value of property or an interest in property after all claims have been deducted. In connection with cash values and policy loan indebtedness, the policyowner's equity is the portion of cash value remaining to the policyowner after deduction of all indebtedness on account of loans or liens secured by the policy. As a principle of insurance, fair and impartial treatment; the principle that insurance premiums shall be set according to the degree of risk assumed and the benefits granted. In insurance law, equity is the name given to the rules and decisions that originated with the former equity courts, as distinguished from those that were handed down by law courts dealing with the common law and statute law. The importance of equity in cases concerning insurance lies in the fact that equitable remedies may be available when the legal remedy may not be adequate for the injured party. Also used to indicate a risk or ownership right in property or a business, etc., as shares of stock.

equity annuity: *(See: variable annuity.)*

equity, estimated total: *(See: adjusted net worth.)*

equity linked: An insurance concept under which the amount of insurance varies according to market value of equity investment. *(See also: variable life insurance.)*

equity rate: The insurance rate applied to a very large risk that has had an outstandingly good or bad record of claims; the ordinary rate would not truly represent the risk.

equity value holding: An investment that has a market value and/ or a rate of return that may fluctuate from time to time and therefore is subject to degree of investment risk. Typical examples are stocks, most bonds, and mutual funds.

ERISA: The Employee Retirement Income Security Act of 1974. Provided broad pension changes in employee benefit laws, including Keogh, IRA, Section 403(b), pension, profit-sharing and other employee benefit plans. *(See also: Employee Retirement Income Security Act.)*

estate builder policy: A popular life insurance policy sold to parents on the lives of their children. When the insured child attains a specified age, commonly age 21, the face amount is automatically increased by up to five times the original amount without additional premium cost or medical examination. Often called a jumping juvenile policy.

estate planning: The total process of planning an estate, including: (a) estate creation and conservation during the owner's life; (b) the minimization of estate shrinkage at death; (c) the creation of adequate liquidity for estate settlement costs; and (d) a plan for proper estate distribution to the owner's heirs.

estate protection: A general term describing any plan or set of plans designed to carry out a person's wishes regarding his or her estate. Estate protection differs from estate planning in that the focus of estate protection is to keep the accumulated estate as intact as possible including provision for the replacement of necessary shrinkage with adequate life insurance.

estate settlement: The procedure of distributing the estate of a decedent, first paying all existing debts and transferring the remainder to heirs. If the deceased had a will and named an executor, the executor pays all debts and distributes the proceeds of the estate. If the will does not name an executor, the court will appoint an administrator to handle the executor's role.

estate shrinkage: The amount by which the value of an estate can be reduced during the transfer to the estate owner's heirs at his or her death. Between the date of the decedent's death and the time of ultimate distribution to his or her beneficiaries, there can be substantial depletion of estate assets. This loss falls on the decedent's family or other beneficiaries.

estate tax: A tax levied upon the right to transfer property at death, imposed upon and measured by the estate that the deceased leaves. (*See also: federal estate tax.*)

estate transfer: The process of distributing or dispersing assets of an estate, either during an individual's lifetime or after death.

estimated premium: In insurance, a temporary premium charged, based on projected loss experience. The amount is eventually adjusted to reflect the actual loss experience.

estimated total equity: (*See: adjusted net worth.*)

evidence of insurability: A statement or proof of a person's physical condition, occupation, etc., affecting the acceptance of the applicant for insurance.

exact date of exhaust: In life insurance, the future date on which the cash value of a policy will be equal to or exceeded by the total indebtedness (loan plus accrued interest) unless a premium, loan or interest payment is made prior to that date.

exact interest: Interest computed on the basis of 365 days of the year.

examination: The medical examination of an applicant for life or health insurance. Also, a periodic audit of an insurance company's books by regulatory authorities.

examination under oath: A clause in some insurance policies that permits the insurance company to obtain statements on claims and related facts from an insured under oath. Perjury charges may result from false claims.

examined business: In life and health insurance, the situation in which an applicant has been examined and has signed the application, but has paid no premium.

examiner: In life and health insurance, medical personnel authorized by the medical director of an insurance company to make medical examinations. Also, persons assigned by the insurance commissioner to audit the affairs of an insurance company.

excepted period: *(See: waiting period.)*

exception of proceeds provision: *(See: spendthrift provision.)*

exceptions and reductions provision: An insurance policy provision that limits the insurance company's liability by excluding coverage for certain losses, such as suicide, or reducing benefits for other losses, such as mental illness.

excess arrears: In insurance, more than permitted arrears beyond the grace period. Should an insured's premiums fall too far into arrears, the policy will lapse.

excess compensation: In reference to an integrated employment retirement plan, that portion of compensation, in excess of a certain amount, upon which retirement benefits can be calculated.

excess contribution: In qualified retirement plans, that a contribution to an IRA that exceeds the deductible limits or that is made by or for the benefit of an ineligible IRA participant, subject to a penalty tax. Under a qualified Keogh plan, contributions made by an employer in excess of the contribution formula limit in the plan for self-employed individuals and/or common-law employees. Subject to an annual excise tax against the employer.

excess cover for catastrophe: A type of reinsurance that takes effect in the event of loss above a stated amount.

excess initial expenses: In life insurance, a company's first-year expenses that exceed first-year expense loading. These are generally a result of higher first-year commission rates and the expense of selection and issue.

excess insurance: Health coverage against loss in excess of a stated amount or in excess of coverage provided under another insurance contract.

excess interest: In life insurance, the difference between the rate of interest the company guarantees to pay on proceeds left under settlement options and the higher interest usually allowed on such funds by the company. Also, the difference between the guaranteed rated return on cash value and the higher, current rate in universal life and other interest-sensitive policies.

excess limit: A maximum limit set by the insurance company's underwriters showing the highest amount of insurance that will be offered in a given situation, which limit is in excess of the basic limit.

excess line broker: In insurance, a person licensed to place coverage not available in his or her state (or not available in sufficient amount) through insurers not licensed to do business in the state where the broker operates. Sometimes called surplus line broker.

excess of loss reinsurance: An amount of reinsurance indemnifying the ceding company for the excess of a stipulated sum in event of loss.

excess plan: With respect to employee retirement plans, a plan that provides benefits only with respect to earnings in excess of the maximum Social Security earnings base for old-age benefits.

excluded period: (*See: probationary period.*)

exclusion: A provision in an insurance policy excluding certain risks or otherwise limiting the scope of coverage. Certain causes and conditions, listed in the policy that are not covered.

exclusion allowance: Under tax-deferred annuity plans, the amount of nontaxable contributions an individual may put in a retirement account. Contributions may exceed the limit, but only the portion within the exclusion allowance is excludable from taxable income.

exclusion clause: In insurance, a policy provision that excludes certain risks from coverage, such as aviation, war, or preexisting conditions.

exclusion ratio: With respect to annuity income taxation, a fraction used to determine the amount of annual annuity income exempt from federal income tax. The fraction is found by dividing total contributions or investment in the annuity contract by the expected return.

exclusions: Specified hazards, listed in an insurance policy, for which benefits will not be paid.

exclusive agency system: An insurance marketing approach whereby agents sell and service insurance under contracts that limit representation to one or more insurers under common management and that reserve to the insurer the ownership, use, and control of policy records and the expiration data. (*See: agency system.*)

exclusive agent: In insurance, an agent granted the sole rights to sell a company's products within a given market or territory.

executed contract: A legal agreement that has been carried out by two or more parties.

executed trust: A trust in which the estates and interest in the subject matter of the trust are completely limited and defined by the instrument creating the trust and require no further instruments to complete them.

executor: The person or entity appointed by the court to carry out the provisions of a will. The court will appoint the person named in the will as executor, provided that person consents and qualifies. (*See also: administrator.*)

executory: A legal characteristic of some types of contracts, such as insurance, whereby the completion of the agreement will occur in the future as opposed to the present time.

executory trust: One that requires the execution of some further instrument, or the doing of some further act, on the part of the creator of the trust or of the trustee, toward its complete creation or full effect.

exemption of proceeds provision: (*See: spendthrift provision.*)

exempt pension trust: A tax-exempt trust; part of a pension plan established by an employer for employees. To be exempt, the plan must be approved by the Commissioner of Internal Revenue.

ex gratia payment: Settlement of a claim by an insurer, even though the company does not feel it is legally obligated to pay. Settlement is made in order to prevent an even larger expense to the company as a result of having to defined itself in court, or for goodwill purposes.

exhaust loan: In life insurance, a policy loan resulting in termination of the policy.

exhibit: In insurance, one of the sections of the convention form annual statement, such as gain and loss exhibit, policy exhibit, etc.

expectancy policy: A special type of health policy, providing term insurance coverage during pregnancy.

expectation of life: In insurance, the mean number of years, based on mortality table figures that a large group of persons of a given age will live. (*See also: life expectancy.*)

expected morbidity: The expected incidence of sickness or injury within a given age group during a given period of time.

expected mortality: The number of deaths that should occur among a group of persons during a given period, based on the mortality table being used.

expenditure, capital: The amount of money paid for a fixed asset.

expense: The overhead cost involved in running the business, aside from losses of claims. To an insurer, the cost of putting business on the books. (*See also: expense loading.*)

expense allowance: In insurance, compensation or reimbursement in excess of prescribed commissions. Money paid by an insurer to an agent or agency head for incurred expenses.

expense charge: In variable and universal life policies, all costs are individually deducted and accounted for within the policies. These expense charges are fixed amounts or percentages deducted from gross premiums paid and cash value, as specified in the policy.

expense constant: In insurance, a flat charge added in the computation of the premium where the pure premium is so low that the cost of issuing and servicing the policy cannot be recovered. (*See also: loss constant.*)

expense factor: (*See: loading.*)

expense loading: In insurance, the amount added to the premium during the rate-making process to cover the expenses of maintaining the business, commissions, administration and overhead.

expense of management: (*See: loading.*)

expense ratio: In insurance, that part or percentage of the premium devoted to paying the acquisition and service costs of insurance written.

expense reimbursement allowance: In life insurance, compensation paid to agents or agency heads by the insurer that is in excess of prescribed commissions, in order to assist them in absorbing the overhead expense of agency operation.

expense reserve: A fund set aside to pay future expenses.

expenses incurred: In insurance, expenses paid and expenses to be paid.

expenses paid: Money disbursed by the insurance company for conducting business other than for the purpose of paying claims.

experience: The loss record of an insured or of a type of insurance written. This record is used in adjusting premium rates and predicting future losses. Also, a statistical compilation relating premiums to losses. (*See also: calendar year experience* and *policy year experience.*)

experience and service table: Used in establishing pension funding rates, a table that indicates the percentage of employees at each eligible age who are expected to terminate their service before attainment of the next higher age. The withdrawal rates in the table are applied in the manner of mortality rates to a hypothetical group of employees coming into a pension plan at the youngest permissible age, in order to indicate the probability that any participant at any given age will remain with the employer until retirement or until he or she has satisfied the requirements for vesting.

experience, calendar year: (*See: calendar year experience.*)

experienced mortality or morbidity: The actual mortality or morbidity experience of an indicated group of insureds, as compared to the expected mortality or morbidity. (*See also: expected mortality* and *expected morbidity.*)

experience modification: The adjustment of premiums as a result of the application of experience rating; usually expressed as a percentage. (*See also: experience rating.*)

experience, policy year: In insurance, experience measured during 12-month periods beginning with a policy's date of issue.

experience rating: In group health insurance, a review of the previous year's group claims experience (or loss) used to establish premiums for the next period.

experience refund: In life reinsurance, a predetermined percentage of the net reinsurance profit that the reinsurer returns to the ceding company as a form of profit sharing at year-end.

expiration: The date on an insurance policy indicating termination of coverage.

expiration card: In insurance, a record or file, generally kept in tickler form by the agent, of the dates on which policies terminate coverage.

expiration date: The date on an insurance policy that indicates when coverage ends.

expiration file: A record often kept by insurance agents, indicating the expiration dates of the policies they have written or are servicing.

expiration notice: Written notification to an insured showing the termination date of an insurance contract.

expiry: Termination of a term insurance policy at the end of its period of coverage.

exposure: In insurance, the possibility of loss. In mortality or morbidity studies, the total number included in the study.

express covenants: Those parts of a contract created by specific words of the parties and that state their intention.

expressed authority: The specific authority given in writing to the agent in the agency agreement. (*For contrast, see also: apparent authority.*)

express trust: A trust created or declared in express terms, usually in writing, as distinguished from one inferred by law from the conduct or dealings of the parties, as with a constructive trust.

extended coverage: An additional agreement or rider broadening an insurance contract. A provision in certain health policies (usually group) to allow the insured to receive benefits for specific losses sustained after termination of coverage, such as maternity expense benefits incurred in a pregnancy in progress at the time of termination.

extended term option: In life insurance, the nonforfeiture option that provides that the net cash surrender value of a policy may be used as a net single premium at the attained age of the insured to purchase term insurance at the face amount of the original policy for as long a period as possible.

extra dividend: A dividend that is paid in addition to regular, periodic dividends.

extra percentage tables: Mortality or morbidity tables indicating the percentage amount increase of premium for certain impaired health conditions. A form of substandard rating.

extra premium: In insurance, the amount charged in addition to the regular rate to cover an extra hazard, special or substandard risk.

extra premium removal: The removal of the extra premium when the cause for it ceases to exist. (*See also: extra premium.*)

extra protection benefit: An insurance policy provision that provides an extra amount of insurance payable if death occurs during the term of the provision.

F

face: In insurance, the first or front page of a policy. (*See also: face amount* and *face of policy.*)

face amount: In life insurance, the amount payable in the event of death, as stated on the front page of the policy. Since the amount of insurance protection provided under a given policy is usually stated on the face or first page of the contract, the term is commonly used when referring to the principal sum involved in the contract. The actual amount payable by the company may be decreased by loans or increased by additional benefits payable under specified conditions, or as stated in a rider.

face amount certificates: An investment contract or other security that represents an obligation on the part of its issuer to pay a stated or determinable amount at a fixed or determinable date or dates more than 24 months after its date of issue in consideration of the payment of a single lump-sum contribution or of periodic contributions. If used as an investment vehicle for a 403(b) plan, it is called an annuity contract.

face of policy: The front or first page of an insurance policy. It usually includes the name of the insurance company, the amount payable in the event of death or at policy maturity, as well as certain insuring clauses or riders.

face value: (*See: face amount.*)

facility of payment: A provision found in home service policies that allows the insurance company to pay proceeds to someone other than the beneficiary if there is no beneficiary named or if the beneficiary cannot be located.

fact-finding interview: In insurance, an interview that is intended to gain the prospect's full cooperation, obtain essential personal and financial information and determine his or her needs and objectives. (*See also: data interview.*)

Fair Credit Reporting Act: Federal law that requires written notification to an individual whose credit is to be investigated by an inspection company, sets guidelines to be followed by the inspection company and grants the individual access to the information reported.

fair market value: A legal term variously interpreted by the courts, but generally meaning the price at which a willing buyer will buy and a willing seller will sell an asset.

fair value: Value that is reasonable and consistent with all of the known facts.

family dependency period: In insurance, a term referring to the years when the spouse of a deceased wage earner is caring for dependent children, generally considered to continue until the youngest child is 18 years old.

family expense policy: A health insurance policy that covers the medical expenses of the policyowner and his or her immediate dependents (usually spouse and children).

family income: The total income earned by a family unit and used for family maintenance. Such income might be earned by more than one family member, such as in a situation where both spouses are employed. (*See also: family income policy* and *family income rider.*)

family income policy: A life insurance policy that combines whole life and decreasing term to provide income protection against the premature death of the family breadwinner. If the insured dies within a specified period, the family will receive a stated amount of income from date of death until the end of the period. The face amount of the policy is then paid to the family. (*For comparison, see: family maintenance policy.*)

family income rider: Similar to the family income policy except that the decreasing term coverage is written as a rider to a whole life policy rather than as combination of both coverages.

family life insurance: (*See: family policy.*)

family maintenance policy: A life insurance policy combining level term and whole life to provide income protection against the premature death of the family breadwinner. If the insured dies within a specified period (say, 20 years) the family will receive a stated monthly amount from the date of death to 20 years in the future. The face amount of the policy is then paid to the family. (*For comparison, see: family income policy.*)

family policy: A policy that combines whole life and convertible term to provide insurance on each family member in units of coverage. Each unit generally consists of $5,000 of whole life on the wage earner, $1,250 of convertible term on the spouse and $1,000 of convertible term on each child.

family protection contract: (*See: family maintenance policy.*)

family rider: An optional policy supplement attached to the insurance policy issued to the head of a family and insuring other members of the family, generally the spouse and children.

family situation: For life and health insurance purposes, any group having at least two people, including at least one income provider upon whose earnings the family depends for its financial support. Generally, the family must also include one or more dependent children.

family split-dollar life insurance plan: An insurance plan whereby two family members (usually a parent and a married child) share the premium payments for insurance on one of their lives (usually the child's). Generally, the child applies for insurance and makes a collateral assignment to the parent, paying as much as his or her budget permits. The parent then pays the balance of the premium, for which the child gives the parent a cumulative note replacing any prior note and documenting the child's total indebtedness to the parent with respect to the policy. At termination of the plan for any reason, the parent collects the debt from the policy cash value or death proceeds, and the balance belongs to the child or child's survivors.

family term insurance: Decreasing term insurance designed for the decreasing responsibilities of a family head; usually sold in $10 monthly income units. Designed to provide income to the family from the time the family head dies until the end of a selected term period. (*See also: family income policy* and *family maintenance policy.*)

Fannie Mae: A nickname for the Federal National Mortgage Association.

Federal Deposit Insurance Corporation: An agency of the federal government that insures bank deposits up to a stated maximum.

federal estate tax: A federal tax levied upon the property of an individual at death. Ownership of a life insurance policy constitutes property and is therefore subject to federal tax. The value of life insurance policies owned by the deceased on the lives of others is also taxable.

federal gift tax: A federal tax on lifetime gifts of property in excess of certain exemptions. Under current tax laws, there is an annual $10,000 exemption for each donee where the gifts are gifts of present interest. Life insurance is property for purposes of this tax and is considered in terms of its living value (cash value and/or gift premiums).

Federal Housing Administration: A federal agency that provides insurance protection to lenders against default on home loans made on mortgages issued under its supervision. FHA loans are mortgage loans guaranteed by the Federal Housing Administration.

federal income tax: A federal tax on individual or business incomes.

Federal Insurance Contributions Act (FICA):   A federal law imposing a payroll tax to assist in funding Social Security benefits.

Federal National Mortgage Association: A subsidiary of the Housing and Home Finance Agency, that assists those unable to obtain adequate housing under established home financing programs by purchasing eligible mortgages and selling them to institutional and other investors.

Federal Savings and Loan Insurance Corporation: A federal organization that insures savings deposits in savings and loan and similar institutions, up to a maximum amount per account.

Federal Security Agency: The federal agency that is responsible for administering the Social Security Act and the Federal Unemployment Insurance Act.

federal unemployment insurance tax: A joint state and federal tax designed to provide unemployment compensation benefits for eligible individuals.

Federal Welfare and Pension Plans Disclosure Act: A pre-ERISA (1974) federal law governing reports on financial status of pension plans. For plans covering more than 25 persons, a description of the plan must be filed with the U.S. Department of Labor. If the plan covers more than 100 persons, an annual financial report is required.

fee: Depending on the context, either a remuneration for services or an inheritable estate in land.

fee simple: An estate inheritance without restrictions, by which an owner is entitled to the entire property without limitations or conditions, as are his or her heirs.

fee simple, absolute: (*See: fee simple.*)

fee simple, limited: An estate less than fee simple, under which the owner has rights only so long as certain conditions prevail, otherwise, the estate is terminated. Important in cases of insurable interest.

fee tail: An estate limited to a particular class of heirs of the person to whom the property or estate is granted.

Fellow of the Institute of Actuaries: A designation for an individual who has been examined by and becomes a member of the Institute of Actuaries.

Fellow of the Life Office Management Institute: A designation attained through successfully participating in an educational program conducted by LOMA.

Fellow of the Society of Actuaries (FSA): A designation given to members of the Society of Actuaries, earned by the completion of ten examinations in mathematics, statistics, insurance, actuarial science, accounting, finance and employee benefits. The examinations and course materials are prepared by the Society of Actuaries. (*See also: Society of Actuaries.*)

fiduciary: One who occupies a position of special trust and confidence, as in handling or supervising the affairs or funds of another. Trustees, executors, administrators, corporate directors, etc., are fiduciaries. The mere fact that somebody is trusted by somebody else, however, does not establish a fiduciary relation. The relation must be one fitting a recognized legal category. A fiduciary under ERISA, for instance, must meet certain statutory tests and is prohibited from engaging in defined acts.

fiduciary bond: A bond that guarantees the faithful performance of a fiduciary.

fiduciary loan: An unsecured loan.

field: For insurance purposes, a type or line of coverage. An area or territory covered by an agent, agency or insurance company.

field force: The agents and company supervisory personnel who operate in the branch offices and general agencies of an insurance company. These people, selling and servicing the company's insureds, are said to be working "in the field."

field representative: (*See: agent.*)

field underwriter: (*See: agent.*)

field work: The sales and service work (calls, interviews, prospecting, etc.) done by an insurance agent, usually outside of the office, as compared to office work or paperwork.

fifth dividend option: In life insurance, an arrangement under which one-year term additions are purchased each year out of current dividends, or any dividend accumulations, in an effort to maintain level protection for a period at least up to the insured's retirement age. Often used with a split-dollar plan.

final average formula: In an employee retirement plan, a method of determining pension benefits based on the participant's average compensation during a specified period, such as five or ten years immediately preceding retirement.

final earnings basis: In an employee retirement plan, a pension benefit formula that bases benefits on earnings immediately prior to retirement, usually the last full year, in contrast to the more customary method of basing benefits on average or career earnings. Some plans base benefits on final average earnings that are average earnings during a specified period, such as five years prior to retirement.

final expense fund: (*See: clean-up fund.*)

final expenses: Costs incurred during a last illness, funeral and burial costs, debts, probate expenses, death taxes and any other taxes or obligations that must be paid in order to settle the estate of a decedent.

final pay plan: In reference to pension plans, one in which benefits are based upon the participant's pay immediately preceding retirement or averaged over the last five or ten years preceding retirement. (*See also: final earnings basis* and *final average formula.*)

financed insurance: In life insurance, the payment of insurance premiums, in whole or in part, with funds obtained by systematic borrowing, usually from the cash value of the contract.

financed premium: In insurance, premiums paid with funds borrowed outside the contract itself.

finance plan: A contractual agreement between an insurance company and a new agent by which the company agrees to supplement commission income, and the agent agrees to meet certain standards of sales activity, production results and training during a defined period of months.

financial planning: The comprehensive analysis of an individual's or business' current financial condition, including sources of present income, net worth and expenditures; projection of finances into the future; budget guidelines; and use of financial investments, such as stocks, bonds and insurance, retirement plans, etc., to achieve financial objectives and the eventual transfer of assets to designated heirs.

financial statement: A statement of the financial condition or performance of a company; a condensed form of the annual statement.

financing method: In an employee retirement plan, the method used to fund and handle the finances of a pension plan, using group annuities, deposit administration, individual policies, or a trusteed plan.

finder's fee: A sum paid to an individual for finding or establishing the contact that makes a financial transaction possible. For example, a large borrower may pay a finder's fee to an individual who knows of an insurance company that is willing to and does lend funds to the borrower.

fine print: Small type in an insurance policy contract, supposedly containing the exclusions, reductions, exemptions, and limitations of the coverage. (Most state laws include specification of the minimum type size that can be used in a policy and also usually provide that exclusions, etc., cannot be printed in type smaller than the type stating the benefits; therefore, the popular concept of fine print no longer has validity.)

first-dollar coverage: A term generally applied to medical expense policies that pay covered expenses from the first dollar up to specified limits, without the use of deductibles or waiting periods. The term often is used to describe basic hospital expense insurance that has benefits payable starting with the first dollar of medical expense and from the time the first such expense is incurred.

first party insurance: Insurance that applies to the insured's own property or person.

first policy year: The year during which a policy was first issued. (*See also: first year.*)

first surplus reinsurance: The amount first allocated to reinsurers in excess of the original insurer's net retention.

first surplus treaty: In reinsurance, a contract under which the reinsurer shares the risk with the ceding company on a pro rata basis, the proportion being either fixed or varied, according to the class of exposure and the amount the ceding company retains for its own account.

first year: In insurance, refers to various matters during the first year a policy is in force, such as first-year premiums, first-year claims, etc.

first-year premium: Insurance premiums that are due during the first policy year, regardless of whether they are paid annually, semiannually, quarterly, monthly, or weekly. Premiums due after the first year are known as renewal premiums.

first-year-premium problem: In a basic split-dollar plan, the difficulty that sometimes arises because the insured is required to make his or her most substantial contribution in the first policy year. Leveling techniques can be used to lessen this problem.

501(c)(3) annuity: Refers to annuities available to members of tax-exempt organizations under Section 501(c)(3) of the Internal Revenue Code. (*See also: tax-deferred annuity.*)

Five Million Dollar Forum: An organization founded in 1975 exclusively for high achievers in life insurance sales.

five percent rule: In relation to pension funding, a rule entitling the employer to deduct annually an amount not in excess of 5 percent of the compensation of the employees covered under the plan.

fixed amount settlement option: A life insurance settlement option whereby the beneficiary instructs that the proceeds be paid in regular installments of a fixed dollar amount. The number of payment periods is determined by the policy's face amount, the amount of each payment and the interest earned. (*For contrast, see: fixed period settlement option.*)

fixed annuity: An annuity that provides fixed payments during the annuity period. (*For contrast, see: variable annuity.*)

fixed asset: Any property or equipment owned by a company that is used in carrying on its operation and that will not be consumed through use or converted into cash during the current fiscal period.

fixed benefit: In medical plans, a benefit in which the dollar amount does not vary; in contrast to a reimbursement benefit.

fixed benefit retirement plan: A type of retirement plan providing benefits only on a fixed amount or at a fixed percentage—such as 1 percent of monthly salary times the number of years of credited employment; or 25 percent of the employee's average pay over the last few years prior to retirement. (*See also: defined benefit plan.*)

fixed daily benefit: In a health care plan, a stipulated amount of benefit payable for each day of disability or each day of hospital confinement suffered by the insured.

fixed income: Income that remains the same, regardless of changing conditions, such as inflation. An individual living on a fixed pension amount can be said to be living on a fixed income.

fixed period settlement option: A life insurance settlement option in which the number of payments is fixed by the payee, with the amount of each payment determined by the amount of proceeds. (*For contrast, see: fixed amount settlement option.*)

fixed trust: A trust in which the trustee is given no freedom to exercise personal judgment, but must strictly follow the terms detailed in the trust agreement.

fixed-value holdings: An investment with a guaranteed rate of return and with freedom from either speculative hazards or reinvestment problems.

flat: Without interest or service charges.

flat cancellation: The cancellation of a recently written insurance contract, without charge to the insured.

flat commission: In insurance, a standard scale of commissions paid to agents, regardless of the type of exposure and the policy.

flat deductible: In health insurance, an amount of covered expenses payable by the insured before medical benefits begin.

flat dollar benefit: *(See: benefit, flat dollar.)*

flat maternity benefit: In a hospitalization policy, a stipulated benefit that is paid for maternity benefits. The benefit amount is not based on the actual costs of the confinement, but is instead a fixed dollar amount.

flat percentage benefit: *(See: benefit, flat percentage.)*

flat rate: In insurance, a fixed rate not subject to any subsequent adjustment. A reinsurance premium rate applicable to the entire premium income, derived by the ceding company from business ceded to the reinsurer, as distinguished from a rate applicable to excess limits.

flat sum benefit: In a pension plan, an arrangement whereby all participants in the plan, regardless of individual earnings, receive the same benefit amount.

fleet of companies: A number of organizations under common ownership and often under common management.

flexible premium variable life: *(See: variable universal life.)*

following the fortunes: A phrase referring to a clause found in reinsurance contracts, stipulating that once a risk has been ceded, the reinsurer is bound by the same fate as is experienced by the ceding company.

forced loan: A loan that the lender has no power to collect.

forced sale: The act of selling property under compulsion as to time and place. Often, a sale made by virtue of a court order, ordinarily at public auction, for estate tax purposes.

forced sale value: Amount that may be realized at a forced sale. The price that could be obtained at immediate disposal, generally, substantially below fair market value.

foreign: Legally, something originating or headquartered in another jurisdiction, such as another state; not necessarily another country. An insurance company headquartered in another state is called a foreign company, while one located in another country is considered an alien company. (*See also: foreign company* and *alien company.*)

foreign carrier: (*See: foreign company.*)

foreign company: A company is considered a foreign company in any state other than the one in which it is incorporated or chartered. The term may also be applied to an insurance company writing business in a jurisdiction in which it has not been admitted, in which case it may also be referred to as a nonadmitted company. (*See also: alien company.*)

foreign society: A fraternal benefit insurance society operating in a state where it is not chartered and in which its home office is not located.

foreign to occupation: In disability insurance, an underwriting designation which refers to an accident not related to the insured's job or profession.

forfeiture: The loss of a right. In a pension plan, the loss by an employee of the right to amounts paid into a fund by the employer. This may result from termination of employment before the employee acquires vested rights or voluntary withdrawal from a contributory plan, etc.

forfeitures: In employee retirement plans, the nonvested remainders left by terminated employees. In qualified pension plans, forfeitures must be used to reduce employer contributions in subsequent years. In profit-sharing plans, forfeitures may be allocated among remaining participants.

form: In insurance, a document, such as policy, endorsement, rider or application.

formula: The basis for determining the amount of pension to be received or contribution to be made under a retirement plan.

fortuitous: Accidental; unexpected.

fortuitous event: An unexpected, unforeseen event; an accident; something that occurs by chance. Insurance companies provide coverage for fortuitous events or losses.

403(b) annuity: (*See: tax-deferred annuity.*)

403(b) plan: (*See: tax-deferred 403(b) plan.*)

fractional premium: In insurance, a proportionate amount of the annual premium, that is, one-twelfth of the annual premium per month for each month involved. A premium less than the mode premium, usually used when a change in premium date is desired and the premium must be set to cover the tie period between the original payment date and the new one.

fractional vesting: *(See: partial vesting.)*

franchise clause: In insurance, a policy provision covering deductibles and stipulating that no claim will be paid for an amount below a stated limit, with all losses above that amount paid in full. *(See also: deductible.)*

franchise disability income: A collectively renewable form of disability income protection. Similar to individual insurance because each insured receives his or her own policy and chooses the elimination period, benefit period and amount of indemnity.

franchise insurance: *(See: wholesale insurance.)*

fraternal: In insurance, refers to a fraternal benefit society that generally writes fraternal insurance on its members. *(See also: fraternal insurance.)*

fraternal insurance: Life or health insurance protection provided by fraternal benefit societies. Practically all fraternals operate on a legal reserve basis in accordance with special fraternal insurance regulations and under supervision of the state insurance authorities. Before purchasing fraternal insurance, an individual must become a member of the organization.

Fraternal Insurance Counsellor: A designation awarded to fraternal life underwriters associated with fraternal benefit societies that are members of the National Fraternal Congress, who complete the prescribed course of study, pass the FIC examination, and meet the standard requirements established by the Fraternal Field Managers' Association.

fraud: An act of deceit; misrepresentation of a material fact made knowingly, with the intention of having another person rely on that fact and consequently suffer a financial hardship.

free-look provision: A provision in life and health insurance policies that gives the policyowner a stated amount of time (usually ten days) to review a new policy. It can be returned within this time for a 100 percent refund of premiums paid, but cancellation of coverage is effective from date of issue.

freezing past service liability: In pension plans, the practice of estimating the accrued liability for past service and paying into the pension fund only the interest on this amount, instead of fully funding it, thus preventing this liability from increasing. Operates under the assumption that the plan will go on forever.

fringe benefits: Refers generally to benefits, formal or informal, other than salary or wages, provided for employees by employers. (*See also: employee benefit programs.*)

front-end load: In a variable or universal life policy, a term for the expenses deducted from the gross premium before the remaining net premium goes into the cash value account.

frozen assets: Business assets that are not readily salable or that cannot be sold immediately without resulting in serious loss.

frozen initial liability: In a pension plan, a situation where no attempt is made to reduce the initial actuarial liability. The expression may also refer to a method under which funding of accrued liability is contemplated, but in accordance with which the initial accrued liability remains fixed.

full age: The period of life at which a person becomes legally capable of transacting business, usually either 18 or 21 years of age.

full coverage: Insurance that provides for the payment of all insured losses in full.

full disclosure: The requirement that variable universal life prospects be fully informed of the charges and costs provided with all important information about their policies. Also includes the requirement that they be given a current prospectus and that no statements or guarantees be made by the agent regarding cash values of interest rates.

full old-age benefit for worker: Under Social Security, a monthly benefit paid for life to a worker who is fully insured and has reached age 65.

full paid additions: (*See: dividend additions.*)

full preliminary term reserve valuation: A method for determining reserves on life insurance contracts whereby no reserve is accumulated for the first year of the contract's life, with an appropriate adjustment in the subsequent years' reserves. The valuation method makes available to the insurer more funds to meet the high first-year expenses.

full reporting clause: An insurance policy clause providing for a penalty if the insured provided less information than required on the policy application.

full surrender: The right of the policyowner to surrender the policy for its available cash value. However, surrender charges may be imposed by the insurance company. Upon full surrender, coverage stops.

full-time employees: Generally, employees of an employer who work for 1,000 or more hours in a 12-month period, as defined for pension plan purposes in the Employees Retirement Income Security Act (ERISA). (*See also: part-time employees.*)

full vesting: In employee retirement plans, pertains to legally fixed immediate or deferred ownership rights under which all accrued benefits of a participant become vested benefits.

fully funded: In pension plans, refers to the situation in which the funds necessary to meet the financial obligations under the plan are accumulated in a reserve while the plan is in operation.

fully insured: Under Social Security, an individual's status of complete eligibility for benefits. Provides retirement benefits as well as survivor benefits. A fully insured individual has also met one of the requirements for disability benefits.

fully insured plan: In pension plans, one funded entirely through individual insurance contracts issued on the lives of participants. The insurance company products (annuities, retirement income endowment policies, etc.) provide any pre-retirement death benefits and the entire retirement benefit for the employee.

fully paid policy: A life insurance policy on which no further premiums are required. (*See also: paid-up.*)

fund: Money and investments held in trust, or share of insurance company assets, for payment of pension benefits. Any accumulation of money set aside for a specific purpose. Also, to accumulate money necessary to pay pension benefits or to fulfill an agreement, as in a funded buy-sell agreement. To fund each year's benefit in a pension plan means to pay into the fund each year enough to cover the obligations created by the pension plan for that year.

funded: In pension plans, one that has accumulated sufficient funds to meet the future financial obligations of the plan. For example, a pension plan is fully funded if the contributions during the active working lifetime of the employees' retirement benefits are fully paid for. This means that annuities have been bought or sufficient money is available to provide all pensions earned to date. Opposite of an unfunded plan, or pay-as-you-go plan, without prior accumulations of funds.

funded buy-sell agreement: A buy-sell agreement that is able to provide money when needed to execute the agreement. Life insurance is often used for this purpose.

funded pension plan: A pension plan utilizing a systematic prepayment method by the employer to meet the cost of benefits. A plan may be funded by purchasing insurance or annuities under contracts with insurance companies. This is known as an insured plan. Or it may be funded by payment of adequate contributions to a trust, frequently with a bank as trustee, in which case it is known as a self-administered uninsured plan.

funded trust: (*See: life insurance trust.*)

funding: In a retirement plan, the setting aside of funds for the payment of benefits. The money is paid to a trustee or insurance company in advance of the date on which the benefits become payable.

funding, advance: A budgetary arrangement whereby predetermined sums are set aside to provide for the payment of future benefits prior to an anticipated need, such as financing retirement income or a business buy-sell agreement.

funding agency: In a pension plan, an individual or organization that accumulates or administers assets to be used for paying benefits under the plan. Funding agencies may be life insurance companies, corporate fiduciaries, or individuals acting as trustees.

funding, disbursement: In a pension plan, commonly called the pay-as-you-go method; requires no funds to be set aside to provide retirement benefits. All benefits paid to retired employees are paid from the company's gross income and are deducted as a normal business expense.

funding instrument: A contract or agreement that governs the conditions under which assets are accumulated or administered by a funding agency.

funding medium: In a pension plan, the arrangement through which funding methods operate; i.e., a trust agreement; a custodial account; a deposit administration contract; a group annuity contract.

funding method: Manner of accumulating money for future payments.

funding of reserves: In reinsurance, an unadmitted practice under which a ceding company retains funds of the reinsurer equivalent to outstanding loss reserves.

funding standard account: A pension plan funding approach under which a separate account is charged with certain liabilities and credited with certain amounts. The funding standard is satisfied when there is no accumulated funding deficiency, that is, when the balance in the account is zero. (*See also: accumulated funding deficiency.*)

funding, terminal: A type of pension funding method that requires no funds to be set aside for retirement benefits. However, as each employee retires, an immediate lifetime annuity is purchased for that individual. It parallels disbursement funding until retirement. After that, the retired employee is guaranteed benefits for the remainder of his or her life.

funding vehicle: (*See: funding medium and vehicles.*)

funeral or emergency expense benefits: In the life insurance certificates of some fraternal benefit societies, a blank sight draft for a stated amount that can be filled out and cashed immediately upon the certificate's becoming a claim, for use in taking care of sudden emergency or funeral expenses. This amount is later deducted in final settlement of the proceeds of the certificate.

future interest, gifts of: (*See: gifts of future interest.*)

future premiums discounted: In insurance, an arrangement whereby premiums paid in advance may be discounted by a certain percent.

future service: For pension benefit purposes, the period of time beginning with the current date and ending with the anticipated date of an employee's retirement. (*See also: current service.*)

future service benefit: In a pension plan, that portion of a participant's retirement payments to be credited for future years of service.

future service cost: In pension plans, that amount needed to fund pensions for present and future years of participation under the plan.

G

general account: Traditionally, in life insurance companies, the term describing a company's overall investment portfolio. More recently, the separate investment funds upon which the declared rate of return in a universal life policy is based. Also, with variable and variable universal life policies, one of the investment account options that earns a declared rate of return.

general agency: In life and health insurance, an independently owned agency under the control of a general agent, who has a contractual agreement with an insurance company, is paid primarily by commission and pays all or most of his or her own expenses.

general agency system: In life and health insurance, the marketing of insurance through general agents rather than through branch offices.

general agent: In life and health insurance, an individual appointed by the insurer to administer its business in a given territory. The general agent is responsible for building his or her own agency and service force and is compensated on a commission basis, although usually with some expense allowances.

General Agents and Managers Association: An organization of local general agents and managers in a community that generally is affiliated with the General Agents and Managers Conference. The association works to advance common interests of its members and the general public through efforts to raise the level of competence of the life and health insurance field operations by educational means.

General Agents and Managers Conference: A national association of life insurance general agents and managers, affiliated with the National Association of Life Underwriters. Their goal is to find solutions to managerial problems and to provide a forum for exchanging ideas.

General Agents and Managers Conference Management Hall of Fame: An honorary organization founded in 1972 by the board of directors of the GAMC of the National Association of Life Underwriters. Each year, at the annual Life Agency Management Program (LAMP), an outstanding agency builder is inducted at the GAMC Management Hall of Fame Dinner at the annual LAMP meeting.

general expenses: *(See: general operating expenses.)*

general legacy: A gift given by will that is to be paid out of the general assets of an estate and not from a particular source.

general management trust: An investment trust that is not limited to a fixed list of securities from which to select its purchases, but one that permits the trustees to use their own discretion in selecting investments.

general market: In insurance, a broad category of people or businesses having something in common as potential buyers of insurance, such as medical people in general. This compares with specific markets, such as high school teachers, medical doctors, etc. *(See also: specific market.)*

general operating expenses: In insurance, expenses of an insurance company other than commissions and taxes; the administrative costs of running a business.

general partnership: A partnership in which each partner contributes to the business, either in the form of money or services, and also shares in the control and management of the business. Each partner in a general partnership is personally liable for the full amount of partnership indebtedness.

general power of appointment: Authority granted legally to any person by another.

general provisions: *(See: additional provisions.)*

geographical limitations: In insurance, a provision that specifically names geographical areas within which (or outside of which) coverage is not effective.

gift: A transfer of property, made during the donor's lifetime and without payment.

gift causa mortis: A gift made in anticipation of death.

gift in contemplation of death: (*See: contemplation of death, gift in.*)

gift inter vivos: A voluntary transfer of property from one living person to another, without consideration (payment).

gifts of future interest: Gifts that do not pass into the donee's possession or enjoyment until some future date.

gift tax: (*See: federal gift tax.*)

gift tax credit, unified: A unified federal estate and gift tax credit that reduces a taxpayer's gift tax and estate tax on a dollar-for-dollar basis. As of 1987, each taxpayer has his or her own lifetime credit of $192,800 (exempting transfers up to $600,000 from the tax). The credit available at death is that amount less any credit used to reduce gift taxes during the taxpayer's lifetime.

gift tax, federal: (*See: federal gift tax.*)

gift tax marital deduction: An unlimited gift tax reduction for transfer of property from one spouse to another. Use of the gift tax reduction offsets entirely the taxable gift resulting from the transfer. This benefits the donor again at death, since there is no adjusted taxable gift to add into his or her estate tax base.

G.I. insurance: Pertains to a form of Government Issue life insurance for servicemembers in World War I and pre-World War II era. Often used as a general term referring to any government issue life insurance. (*See also: National Service Life Insurance.*)

gimmicks: A negative reference to certain clauses or coverages found in some insurance policies. The inference is that the policyowner is not receiving the same value of coverage that he or she may think is provided by a policy. Also used in reference to clever or unusual means of gaining attention and/or demonstrating a point in marketing.

give: To transfer, yield or bestow something of value to another.

goodwill: An intangible and often major business asset that generally includes such things as the reputations of the owners, the number of satisfied clients, customers, patients, and the continuing influx of new business.

government benefit plans: This phrase covers a broad range of programs: Social Security, Servicemembers' and Veterans' benefits, Civil Service Retirement, Workers' Compensation, Medicare, Medicaid, etc.

grace period: Most life insurance contracts provide that premiums may be paid at any time within a period of generally 30 or 31 days following the premium due date, the policy remaining in full force in the meantime. If death occurs during the grace period, the premium is deducted from the proceeds payable. As a general rule, no interest is charged on overdue premiums if paid during the grace period. In health policies, a period of time (usually 30 days) after the premium due date, the policy remaining in force and without penalty for past due payment.

graded commissions: (*See: commissions, graded.*)

graded death benefits: A life insurance policy provision that provides for death benefits that, in the early years of the contract, are less than the face amount of the policy, but that increase with the passage of time. Most commonly found in juvenile policies issued at age zero or zero plus.

graded premium life insurance: A form of modified life insurance that provides for annual increases in premiums for a constant face amount of insurance during a defined preliminary period, with the purpose of making initial payments more affordable.

graded vesting: In a pension plan, a form of immediate deferred vesting under which an increasing proportion of the accrued benefits of a participant becomes a vested benefit in accordance with a specific formula and requirement (usually in terms of attained age, years of service and/or pension plan membership). This is applicable only if benefits under the pension plan are attributable to specific years of service, or the application of the vesting definition is clearly worked out in the pension plan.

graduated life table: A mortality table where the experience has been smoothed out graphically or by formula.

graduated premium life insurance: (*See: graded premium life insurance.*)

graduated vesting: (*See: graded vesting.*)

grant: A term applied to all transfers of property.

grantee: A person to whom property is transferred.

grantor: One who transfers property.

gratuitous assignment: (*See: voluntary assignment.*)

gripsack general agent: An obsolete term referring to an individual representing one or several insurance companies on a commission basis in an area. The gripsack agent must pay his or her own expenses for travel and office.

gross cost: In a pension plan, that cost that will eventually equal the benefits paid out, plus expenses of administration, less the earnings on any funds set aside for payment of benefits.

gross earnings: Total earnings, before deduction of taxes and expenses.

gross estate: The total of an individual's accumulated wealth at death. It includes such items as home equity, cash and savings, securities, stock, life insurance, land, business interests, notes and accounts receivable, and any personal property.

gross income: (*See: before-tax earnings.*)

gross line: In insurance, that amount of coverage that a company has on a risk without reinsurance. (*See also: net line.*)

gross net premiums: In insurance, gross premiums minus return premiums, but not less reinsurance premiums.

gross premium: In insurance, the net premium (risk factor), plus the expense of operation (loading), less the interest factor (credit); the premium for participating life insurance shown in the rate book. The total amount of premium paid by the policyowner. (*For contrast, see: net premium.*)

gross premium valuation: In insurance, the present value of future gross premiums, minus the present value of future policy benefits and expenses.

gross rates: In insurance, the rates listed in the company's rate book. The gross rate is the net or pure premium, plus a loading for expenses and contingencies.

gross working capital: (*See: current assets.*)

group: A number of people classed together by some common factor: sex, age, place of employment, occupation, location, etc. In group insurance, the collective individuals covered by a master policy.

group accident and health insurance: (*See: group insurance.*)

group annuity: A type of retirement plan designed by insurance companies for a group of persons (usually employees of a single employer), covering all qualifying persons under one contract. Employer contributions (or employer and employee contributions, as the case may be) are determined by the insurance company's actuaries in accordance with the benefits to be offered. Contributions are turned over to the insurance company as specific premiums. The insurance company then guarantees payment of the benefits as they accrue to members of the group who meet the eligibility requirements.

group annuity, deposit administration: (*See: deposit administration group annuity.*)

group annuity plan: A group annuity that is underwritten and administered by an insurance company under a master contract. The retirement benefit consists of a series of units of paid-up deferred annuities, one unit to be purchased each year for each eligible employee.

group application: In group insurance plans, a form signed by the employer that includes schedules of insurance, eligibility requirements, method of premium payment, etc. It becomes part of the group insurance contract.

group certificate: Under a group insurance plan, the document provided to each member of the group, showing the benefits provided under the group contract. (*See also: certificate of insurance.*)

group contract: A contract of insurance made with an employer or other entity, that covers a group of persons identified in reference to their relationship to the entity. These identified individuals may include dependents or other family members. Premiums may be paid entirely by the employer or other entity, entirely by identified individuals, or jointly. Group eligibility for such insurance may be defined or limited by state laws or by insurer underwriting. The group contractual arrangement is used most generally to cover employees of a common employer, employees of the employer-members of a trade association or trusteeship, members of a welfare or employee-benefit association, members of a labor union, members of professional or other association not formed for the purpose of obtaining insurance or debtors. This definition applies to life and health insurance, to annuities, and to some contracts in property/liability insurance.

group credit life and health insurance: Credit insurance written on a group basis. (*See also: credit life insurance.*)

group creditor insurance: Life insurance issued to the creditor on the lives of debtors to pay the amount of the indebtedness in the event of death. Used frequently by lending and other financial institutions to eliminate problems of collection from a deceased's estate.

group deposit administration annuity: (*See: deposit administration.*)

group disability insurance: A health insurance contract issued to cover designated groups having the same employer or common affiliation of interest, and that offers benefits primarily for loss of time and income, although there may be some individual hospital/medical expense coverage as well.

group health insurance: Health insurance provided to members of a group of persons, as employees of one or more employers or members of associations or labor unions. The term is usually used to distinguish this type of health insurance from individual health insurance. One master contract is written to cover the group. (*See also: group life insurance* and *group insurance.*)

group insurance: Insurance protecting a group of persons, usually employees of the same firm. It is based on the principle that the selection process may be applied directly to groups of people, as well as to individuals. If certain general requirements are met, the insurance principles can be applied to groups of nonselected persons. As a rule, the group must have been formed for a purpose other than to obtain insurance; the members must either all be insured or, if premiums are paid in part by the individuals, at least 75 percent must become insured; the amount of insurance for each member of the group must be determined by a formula precluding individual selection or choice by the individuals insured.

group insurance certificate: (*See: certificate of insurance.*)

group insurance, contributory: (*See: contributory group insurance.*)

group insurance, master contract: An insurance agreement between the employer (or any principal recognized by the laws of the various states as eligible to effect a group insurance contract) and the insurance company. This is the agreement that insures the designated employees or group members.

group life insurance: A form of life insurance covering a group of persons generally having some common interest or activity, such as employees of the same company or members of the same union or association. The laws of many states define the types of groups that may be covered and the minimum number of persons who may be defined by the group. Most group insurance is issued using yearly renewable term, without requiring medical examinations.

group life insurance, claims reserves: Reserves established to meet incurred but unreported claims under a group life contract.

group life insurance, contingency reserves: Reserves provided for excess mortality fluctuations and the possibility of castastrophe claims. These reserves differ from policy and claim reserves that are actual liability accounts. Contingency reserves are merely portions of surplus set aside and available in the event that they are needed.

group life insurance, policy reserves: Unearned premium reserves calculated on a net basis. Fundamentally, they equal the pro rata cost of the unexpired period of coverage for which premiums have been collected or are due.

group living arrangement: An arrangement whereby members of a group (such as seniors) reside in private or semi-private bedrooms but share dining room, living room, kitchen and bath. Expenses are usually shared.

group of companies: (*See: fleet of companies.*)

group ordinary life insurance: Level premium ordinary life insurance issued on a group basis.

group paid-up life insurance: A combination life insurance plan under which each employee's annual contribution is used as a single premium to buy a unit of paid-up insurance, while the employer's contribution is used to buy group term coverage. On termination of employment, the employee may take paid-up insurance or receive a refund of contributions or the cash surrender value of the paid-up insurance.

group permanent insurance: A group insurance plan in which the whole life policy purchased provides death benefits to the employee's survivors in the event of premature death. Upon retirement, the cash value can be used to provide income to the employee.

group renewable term insurance: (*See: group life insurance.*)

group retirement income insurance: Level premium retirement income insurance (with $1,000 of death benefit per $10 monthly income) issued on a group basis.

group term policy: The vast majority of group life policies are written using low premium group term insurance. (*See also: group life insurance.*)

group underwriting: Automatic issuance of predetermined amounts of life and/or health insurance to all members of a group.

group valuation: One of a number of different methods used by life insurance companies for determining their policy reserves. Under this method, policies are grouped by age, plan and duration, and the reserve is calculated in total for each group.

guaranteed cash value: In a permanent life insurance policy, the guaranteed amount available to the insured on surrender of the policy according to a table of guaranteed values scaled to the number of years in which the policy is in force. In a universal or variable policy, there is no guaranteed cash value. However, policyowners do have a guaranteed right to borrow or withdraw a designated percentage of accumulated cash value (less possible deferred charges).

guaranteed continuable: (*See: guaranteed renewable contract.*)

guaranteed cost: In insurance, premium charged on a prospective basis, fixed or adjustable on a specified rating basis, but never on the basis of loss experience. Also, nonparticipating insurance. Also, in universal or variable universal life plans, the maximum costs that can be deducted from cash value under the terms of the policy. Contrast this with current costs or charges that may be less.

guaranteed dividend policy: A nonparticipating life insurance policy that promises the payment of an annual dividend of a specified amount. Also known as a coupon policy, it usually contains a sheet of coupons for such dividends, resembling the coupons attached to bonds. The guaranteed dividends are not true dividends in the insurance sense, but are additional benefits for which extra premiums must be charged. The so-called dividends are a series of pure endowments, maturing each year.

guaranteed insurability rider: A rider now offered on most life insurance policies whereby additional insurance may be purchased at specified future times without a medical examination or other evidence of insurability. Rates are based on attained age at time of purchase.

guaranteed interest rate: In permanent life insurance, a term used to designate the minimum annual rate of interest used in calculating policy reserves from year to year, or annual increases in dividend accumulations, or the interest factor in proceeds held under settlement option, or the amount payable under the interest income option, etc. Also refers to the minimum rate credited to cash value in interest-sensitive policies.

guaranteed investment policy: *(See: guaranteed dividend policy.)*

guaranteed issue: *(See: guaranteed insurability rider.)*

guaranteed purchase option: *(See: guaranteed insurability rider* and *new policy option.)*

guaranteed renewable contract: A health insurance contract that gives the policyowner the right to continue coverage by the timely payment of premiums for a substantial period of time, during which period the insurer has no right to make any change in any provision of the contract other than a change in premium rate for classes of insureds. Also referred to as guaranteed continuable.

guaranteed renewable hospital-surgical insurance: Provides for payment of hospital and surgical expenses up to a specified amount and is noncancellable by the company as long as premiums are paid.

guardian or guardian ad litem: A person designated by the court to administer the affairs of a person declared to be legally incompetent, such as a minor. A guardian ad litem is a person designated by the court to handle the affairs of the incompetent in a particular legal proceeding. The guardianship of the person and of the person's property may be placed in separated people.

Guertin Laws: The valuation and nonforfeiture laws regulating insurance companies that have been standard in all states since 1947. (Named for Alfred Guertin, then actuary of the New Jersey Insurance Department and head of the NAIC committee developing the model bill.)

guideline premiums: In universal life policies, the level annual and single premiums calculated on an endowment at 95 basis using guaranteed interest, term costs and loads as defined in the tax law for the purpose of limiting premium payments to qualify under Section 101 of the Internal Revenue Code. In such policies, the minimum premium projected to keep the full coverage in force, based on current assumptions.

H

hazard: In insurance, a specific situation that introduces or increases the probability of a loss-incurring event, as contrasted with the broader term for the cause of possible loss, *peril*. For example, accident, sickness, fire, flood, burglary and explosion are perils. Slippery floors, unsanitary conditions, shingle roofs, congested traffic, unguarded premises, and uninspected boilers are hazards. (*See also: perils.*)

hazard, moral: (*See: moral hazard.*)

head office: (*See: home office.*)

head of household: For income tax purposes, an unmarried person who has dependent children or other dependents (related by blood or marriage) who can be claimed as exemptions. Tax rates for heads of households are generally lower than for single taxpayers.

Health and Accident Underwriters Conference: Association of life insurance companies, now merged into Health Insurance Association of America (HIAA), that carried on research in rating accident and health risks.

health certificate: In life insurance, a signed statement declaring that the health of the insured is not impaired. This must be filed with a request for reinstatement of a lapsed policy. (*See also: reinstatement.*)

health insurance: The name that has been accepted by the insurance industry as the broad term for the branch of insurance that includes all types of disability income, medical expense and acci-

135

dental death coverage. It is also known as accident and health insurance or sickness and accident insurance.

Health Insurance Association of America (HIAA): An association supported by life and health insurance companies and created to provide the research, public relations and legislative base for the promotion of voluntary private health insurance.

health insurance benefits: In health insurance, policy benefits payable as a result of disability from covered sickness or accident. Sickness coverage is rarely written separately, unless the insured also carries an amount of accident insurance with the same company.

health insurance, classifications: (1) Cancelable; (2) optionally renewable; (3) franchise; (4) industrial; (5) group; (6) limited; (7) guaranteed renewable; (8) noncancellable and guaranteed renewable. Health policies that are renewable at the option of the insured, as contrasted with guaranteed renewable policies, are often referred to as commercial policies.

health insurance, group: (*See: group health insurance.*)

Health Insurance Institute: An agency developed by life and health insurance companies to provide for a flow of information between health insurers and the public.

Health Insurance Quality Award: An annual award sponsored by the International Association of Health Underwriters and the National Association of Life Underwriters for equaling or exceeding certain favorable percentages of persistency of health insurance policies written by agents.

Health Maintenance Organization (HMO): Health care centers that stress preventive health care, early diagnosis, and treatment on an outpatient basis. An organized system of health care delivery and financing that provides a broad range of services to a voluntarily enrolled group for a fixed and periodic payment. The HMO participant pays a flat annual premium and is entitled to medical check-ups and routine health care, plus major medical coverage. (*See: prepaid hospital service plan.*)

health plans, corporate: (*See: corporate health plans.*)

health policy: An insurance policy that indemnifies for loss (income and/or expenses) resulting from bodily injury or sickness.

health systems agencies: Federally funded agencies that recommend to state and health planners whether or not to approve proposed hospital additions or acquisitions of major new equipment.

heir: Any person who succeeds to or acquires the estate of a decedent. The term is broadly applied to anyone who receives property from a deceased person's estate.

held in trust: A designation indicating that one person or party is holding property for another person or party until the occurrence of some contingency (such as guardian/trustee holding insurance proceeds until the designated beneficiary attains legal age).

hereditaments: Anything that may be inherited.

highest and best value: The valuation of a closely held business or farm at its fair market value if it were put to its most valuable use. For example, a farm might be valued at the price the land would bring for a shopping center or as a subdivision for new homes, rather than at its actual value as farmland.

high-pressure selling: In insurance sales, encouraging the buyer to purchase insurance without full consideration of needs for insurance and his or her ability to continue payments on the policy, or of using tactics that embarrass or deceive people into buying against their wishes.

high risk: *(See: substandard risk.)*

HMO: *(See: health maintenance organization.)*

home assurance: A concept that recognizes that the traditional role of life insurance in guaranteeing shelter can be applied to all patterns of living, providing both mortgage cancellation and rent continuation coverage. Also used to refer to mortgage insurance alone. *(See also: rent continuation insurance.)*

home health care: Skilled and semi-skilled part-time care received at home. May include nursing care, physical therapy, speech therapy and/or such custodial services as cooking, cleaning and washing.

home office: Generally, the corporate headquarters of an insurance company, where the chief offices of the organization are located.

Home Office Life Underwriters Association: An organization of underwriters in home offices of life insurance companies.

home protector rider: *(See: mortgage insurance.)*

home service agent: *(See: debit agent.)*

home service company: The modern term for insurance companies selling industrial policies using the debit marketing system. *(See also: industrial life insurance.)*

home service ordinary: A monthly premium ordinary life insurance policy, not industrial, with the premiums collected according to the debit system.

honesty clause: *(See: full reporting clause.)*

honorable undertaking: As stated in reinsurance contracts, "This agreement is considered by the parties hereto as an honorable undertaking, the purpose of which is not to be defeated by a strict or narrow interpretation of the language thereof."

honoring: In insurance, the act of paying a claim or meeting an obligation when it is due.

hospice care: Care provided for the purpose of easing the physical and emotional suffering of a sick individual, rather than of curing the illness. This care is available at a hospice facility or at the individual's home.

hospital: An institution for the care and treatment of ill, injured, infirm, mentally abnormal, or deformed persons, with organized facilities for diagnosis and surgery and providing 24-hour nursing service and medical supervision. In some hospital policies, institutions for the treatment of mentally ill persons are expressly excluded from the definition of hospital.

hospital benefits: Health insurance benefits payable for charges incurred while the insured is confined to, or treated in, a hospital, as defined in the policy.

hospital expense insurance: Basic medical expense insurance that provides benefits subject to a specified daily maximum for hospital room and board charges, plus lab, ambulance and operating room costs. Also referred to as hospitalization insurance or basic hospital insurance.

hospital income insurance: A form of disability income insurance that provides a stated weekly or monthly payment while the insured is hospitalized, regardless of expenses incurred. Sometimes called hospital indemnity insurance. *(See also: disability income insurance.)*

hospital indemnities: In health insurance, additional benefits provided under the terms of a policy if the insured is confined in a hospital.

hospitalization insurance: (*See: hospital expense insurance.*)

hospitalization policy: A limited health insurance policy that provides payment only in the event hospital expenses are incurred. If such a policy pays first-dollar benefits but has relatively low limits, it is called a basic hospitalization policy or plan.

hospital miscellaneous benefits: Under a health insurance plan, benefits payable up to a stated maximum for reimbursement of expenses incurred during a period of hospital confinement for such services as x-ray examination, laboratory service, drugs, anesthesia, ambulance service, oxygen and use of the operating room, etc.

hospital room benefits: In health insurance, benefits payable up to a specified daily maximum for the purpose of paying hospital room and board charges.

hospital/surgical expense insurance: Medical expense health insurance that combines basic hospital coverage and basic surgical coverage into one policy.

hour of service: For purposes of retirement plans, an hour for which an employee is directly or indirectly paid by the employer for the performance of duties. An hour of overtime is still counted as only an hour of service, even though the pay for overtime may be higher. Hours during a leave of absence or a vacation with pay are counted.

house confinement clause: A health insurance optional provision requiring that the disabled insured be confined to a house in order to be eligible for benefits. House is expanded to include a hospital, sanitarium, visit to a hospital or office of a physician, or certain activities made at the direction of a doctor for therapeutic purposes.

household: People and things belonging to a house and family; those dwelling under the same roof and composing a family.

HR-10 Plan: (*See: Keogh Act plan.*)

human depreciation concept: The concept that people, like machines, wear out and that, therefore, employers have a moral obligation to assist in the financial security of their retired workers.

human life value: A measure of a person's potential economic value to others. This concept is important in relation to key-executive insurance, as well as to personal insurance in general.

I

identification clause: A clause, formerly included in some health insurance policies that provided that if the insured is physically unable to communicate with relatives and friends, the company will notify them and pay necessary expenses (up to a specified amount) to put the insured in their care.

illegal holding of premiums: In insurance, an agent's handling of collected premium other than as specified by state laws. Consequently, the agent may be accused of embezzlement or of fraudulently converting funds for personal use.

illegal occupation provision: An optional health insurance provision that states that if the insured is injured while engaging in an illegal occupation, the insurance company is not obligated to pay the claim.

illness frequency rate: The number of illnesses suffered by employees per 1,000,000 employee-hours of work on an annual basis.

illness severity rate: The number of days lost due to disabling illnesses or death per 1,000 employee-hours, with 6,000 days charged for death.

immediate annuity: An annuity contract that provides for the first payment of the annuity at the end of the first interval of payment after purchase. The interval may be monthly, quarterly, semiannually or annually.

immediate estate: One of the major characteristics of life insurance in that it is self-completing in the event of the insured's premature death and that it assures the insured's family of a predetermined amount of money when he or she dies.

immediate life annuity: *(See: immediate annuity.)*

immediate vesting: In an employee retirement plan, that form of vesting under which rights to vested benefits are acquired by a participant immediately upon his or her entry into the plan.

impaired capital: In insurance, when liabilities and claims consume a company's surplus, the capital is impaired. Suspension of the right to do business normally follows.

impaired risk: In life and/or health insurance, a person who has an unfavorable health condition, or is exposed to a dangerous occupational hazard that makes him or her substandard. A risk that is substandard, below average or less desirable.

impairment: For life and/or health insurance purposes, an injury, physical ailment, condition or disability that negatively affects a person's risk rating and possibly insurability.

impairment of capital: In insurance, a condition to which the surplus account of a stock company has been exhausted, so that it must invade the capital account to meet liabilities.

impairment rider: A rider attached to a health insurance contract that waives the insurance company's liability for all future claims on a pre-existing condition.

imperfect trust: *(See: executed trust.)*

implied authority: Authority that, while not specifically granted to the agent in the agency agreement, the agent can assume he or she has through common sense. Authority that is apparently necessary for an agent's ability to carry out day to day or routine responsibilities.

implied consent: In the selling situation, the concept that unless a prospect explicitly disagrees with what is presented or said, his or her agreement may be assumed.

implied contract: A legally binding contractual agreement in which the parties speak by their actions rather than by their oral or written words. An insurance contract is not an implied contract because every condition is included in the policy. *(See also: entire contract clause.)*

implied trust: A trust raised or created by implication of law; a trust implied or presumed from circumstances.

implied warranty: In insurance, an expression, not in writing, that conditions exist that comply with a warrant which has been established as part of the contract. (*See also: warranties and representations.*)

inadmitted asset: Any asset that may not be included in assets reported by an insurance company to the state insurance examiners. These inadmitted assets are presumed to have little value to meet claims in case of liquidation.

inchoate: Not yet completed. In reference to contracts, they are inchoate until they have been executed by all parties.

incidental life insurance protection: For purposes of Section 403(b) of the Internal Revenue Code, death benefits under an annuity contract that do not exceed 100 times the contract's monthly retirement benefit or cash accumulation.

incidents of ownership: For insurance purposes, the right to exercise any of the privileges in the insurance policy (change beneficiary, withdraw cash values, make loans on the policy, make assignment, etc.).

includible compensation: For purposes of determining maximum contribution limits of nontaxable retirement income plan contributions, the amount of compensation received from an employer and includible in gross income, exclusive of any amount contributed by the employer.

income: The money a person or company has coming in from any source. Income is made up of the amount received from both personal and investment earnings, as well as realized capital gains.

income bond: (*See: retirement annuity.*)

income continuation agreement: In professional partnerships, an agreement may provide that, after a partner's death, his or her estate will receive a stated income or a percentage of profits for a certain period of time. According to the weight of authority, a partner's gross estate includes the value of such a provision at his or her death.

income, earned: (*See: earned income.*)

income-earning ability: The ability of an individual to earn an income or wage. The three major threats to income-earning ability are death, disability and old age, all of which may be protected against by life and health insurance.

income, fixed: (*See: fixed income.*)

income, gross: (*See: before-tax earnings.*)

income insurance: A term used to describe the payment of life insurance proceeds in periodic installments rather than in a lump sum. (*See also: settlement options.*)

income policy: A life or endowment insurance policy that provides specified monthly amounts in the payment of proceeds, rather than payment of a lump sum. Sometimes used with reference to an annuity contract.

income protection: In insurance, protection against loss of earnings (usually due to disability). (*See also: disability income.*)

income provider plan: (*See: family maintenance policy.*)

income settlement options: (*See: settlement options.*)

income statement: One of three major kinds of financial statements used by businesses. It is primarily a flow report that lists a company's income or revenues and its expenses for a certain period of time in order to summarize a company's financial operations. (*See also: balance sheet* and *statement of changes in financial position.*)

incompetent: One who is incapable of managing his or her legal and financial affairs because of mental deficiency or failure to have yet attained legal age.

imcomplete: For insurance purposes, the status of an application lacking certain information necessary for underwriting or classifying the risk.

incontestability: An insurance policy provision whereby the insurer, after the policy has been in effect for a specified period, gives up the right to dispute a claim. Ordinary policies are usually incontestable after having been in effect for two years; weekly premium, usually after one year.

incontestable clause: A life and health insurance policy provision that states that the insurance company may not contest payment of benefits (assuming premiums have been paid) after a specified period, usually one to three years after issue. This, in effect, gives the insurance company time to determine if there have been any misrepresentations made on the application.

increase: In insurance, an accounting term meaning a surplus of new business and renewals after subtracting the chargeable lapses.

increase in hazard: An increase in an insured's risk beyond the intent of the insurance company when the original policy was issued. For instance, once insured at a lower rate, the policyowner may take up a more hazardous hobby or line of work, or may develop an impairment, raising the level of risk for the insurer.

increasing loan values: (*See: emergency fund.*)

increasing term insurance: Term life insurance coverage that increases in face value each year (or certain period) from the date of policy issue to the date of expiration. (*For contrast, see: decreasing term insurance and level term insurance.*)

incubation period: (*See: probationary period.*)

incur: To become liable for an actual loss or expense.

incurred but not reported: A phrase referring to losses that have occurred, but have not yet been reported to the insurer or reinsurer.)

incurred claim: In insurance, a situation where payment may be demanded under the provisions of the policy.

incurred expenses: Expenses paid or to be paid.

incurred losses: Losses occurring within a fixed period, whether or not adjusted and paid during the same period. In insurance, obtained by adding to losses paid during a given year those losses still outstanding at the end of the year, less losses outstanding at the beginning of the year.

incurred loss ratio: In insurance, the percentage of losses incurred to premiums earned.

indemnify: To restore to the victim of a loss, in whole or in part, by payment, repair, or replacement to his or her original financial condition; to make an insured financially whole again, but not to an extent that there is profit from the loss.

indemnity: Payment of an amount to offset all or part of an insured loss. The insured is indemnified for a specified loss or part thereof. Not synonymous with benefits. (*See also: benefits.*)

indemnity period: The time during which a loss is totally or partially covered. In a health insurance plan, for example, disability income payments are ordinarily limited to a specified indemnity period that may be relatively brief or it may be as long as the insured's lifetime.

indemnity reinsurance: A type of reinsurance contract characterized by a series of independent transactions in which the ceding insurer transfers its liability with respect to individual policies, in whole or in part, to the reinsurer.

indeterminate premium: Refers to term policies where the actual premium charged may be lower than the guaranteed premium stated in the policy. Policies with indeterminate premiums generally make reference to the *guaranteed* (or maximum) premium that can be charged, and the *current* (or lower) premium, based on the current and projected mortality and/or investment experience.

individual account plan: Either a defined contribution pension plan or a profit-sharing plan that provides an individual account for each participant and whose benefits are based solely upon the amount contributed to the participants' accounts and any income, expenses, gains and losses, and any forfeitures of other participants' accounts that may be allocated to the remaining participants' accounts.

individual annuity: (*See: retirement income policy.*)

individual benefit statement: Under an employee retirement plan, the total accrued benefit and the vested benefit.

individual contract health insurance: A contract of health insurance, made with an individual, that covers the insured and, in medical expense policies, may cover specified members of his or her family. In general, any health insurance contract except group or blanket contracts.

individual contract pension trust: A pension plan under which a trust is created to buy and hold title to individual insurance or annuity contracts for employees covered by the plan. The trust receives the premium payments from the employer and transmits them to the insurance company, receiving in return the individual policies. The insurance company generally will pay the benefits directly to the employees, but payment also may be made from the insurance company to the trust for transmittal to the employees.

individual insurance: An individual life or health insurance policy purchased on an individual basis (as distinct from group and blanket insurance.) Sometimes called personal insurance.

individual life insurance: An individual life insurance contract that usually covers only one insured, but that sometimes covers several people, such as the members of a family through the use of riders. The term is often used to distinguish this type of life insurance from group life insurance.

individual method: In pension plans, a kind of projected benefit cost method that is characterized by the assumed allocation of the actuarial cost in respect to each employee individually. The total actuarial cost is generally separable as to the various participants, meaning that costs are individually calculated for each employee or are calculated by group methods in such a way as to produce essentially the same total result as though it were individually calculated.

individual policy pension trust plan: A type of pension plan frequently used for groups of less than 50 people, administered by a trustee who is authorized to purchase individual policies or annuity contracts for each participant in the plan. The policies usually provide both life insurance and retirement benefits.

individual practice association: One of two basic kinds of health maintenance organizations, in which medical services are provided by independent practitioners who work out of their own offices and who are compensated on a fee-for-service basis. An IPA is usually sponsored by a medical care foundation or a medical society. (*See also: health maintenance organization* and *prepaid hospital service plan.*)

individual projected benefit cost method: In pension plans, a benefit cost method characterized by the assumed allocation of the actuarial cost in respect to each employee individually, generally as a level amount or as a percentage of earnings, over all or part of his or her period of service, period of coverage under the plan, or over some other appropriate period uniformly applied. Under individual cost methods, the total actuarial cost is generally separable as to the various participants (i.e., costs are individually calculated for each employee or are calculated by group methods in such a way as to produce essentially the same total result as though individually calculated.)

individual proprietorship: An unincorporated business, owned and operated by an individual. He or she is subject to full liability, and all income to the business is taxed as personal income. Also known as sole proprietorship.

Individual Retirement Account (IRA): A personal, qualified retirement account in which an individual may accumulate contributions up to a certain sum each year for retirement income. Such accounts may also be established by purchasing individual retirement annuities from an insurance company or by purchasing individual retirement bonds issued by the federal government. Contributions may or may not be deductible, depending on the individual's income and/or coverage under an employee-sponsored retirement plan. Regardless, funds accumulate on a tax-deferred basis. (*See also: IRA.*)

inducement by misrepresentation: (*See: twisting.*)

industrial accident: (*See: accident, industrial.*)

industrial group: A group eligible for group insurance as employees of one employer; contrasted to an association group. (*See also: association group* and *group.*)

industrial health insurance: Health insurance providing small amounts of benefits, with premiums due weekly or monthly and collected by a home service agent. (*See also: weekly premium insurance* and *industrial life insurance.*)

industrial increase: (*See: weekly premium increase.*)

industrial insurance: Sometimes referred to as debit or home service insurance, small amounts of insurance issued on individual lives with weekly or monthly premiums payable to a home service agent who collects the premium at the individual's home. A medical examination is usually not required. (*See also: industrial health insurance, industrial life insurance* and *weekly premium insurance.*)

industrial life insurance: Often called debit or home service insurance, life insurance issued on individual lives from birth to age 70 in small amounts. Weekly or monthly premiums are collected at the individual's home by a home service agent. Usually, no medical examination is required. (*See also: home service company* and *industrial insurance.*)

inevitable accident: An accident that can neither be foreseen nor prevented. (*See also: fortuitous event.*)

infant: A person under legal age. Contracts made by infants are not enforceable against them and may be repudiated later. Special state statutes alter the above generalization and provide that certain infants may contract for life insurance.

inflation factor: A loading to provide for future increases resulting from inflation in medical costs and loss payments.

in-force business: In insurance, policies that are on the books of a company. Life or health insurance for which premiums are being paid or for which premiums have been fully paid. The term usually refers to the face amount of a life insurer's portfolio of business; in health insurance, it refers to the premium volume of an insurer.

Information Retrieval Index: A vertical filing system devised by the MDRT for published articles relating to life insurance.

inheritance: That which is legally transferable to an heir; a legacy.

inheritance, estate of: An estate that may descend to heirs.

inheritance tax: Tax levied upon the right to transmit property at death, imposed upon and measured by the share each heir receives. Since it is levied on the right to succeed to a deceased person's property, it is sometimes called a succession tax. This latter term is common in Canada.

initial death benefit: In flexible feature life insurance policies, the original face value of the policy; the specified amount. (*See also: specified amount.*)

initial expenses, excess: (*See: excess initial expenses.*)

initial liability, frozen: (*See: frozen initial liability.*)

initial premium: In life and health insurance, the first premium, generally payable with the application or upon delivery of the policy. In group insurance, especially health, an amount paid at the inception of an insurance contract that permits adjustments to be made based upon future experience.

initial reserve: In life insurance, the reserve amount determined at the beginning of the policy year. It equals the preceding year's terminal reserve, plus the annual net premium.

initial term insurance: *(See: interim term insurance.)*

injury: Damage or hurt done or suffered. In health insurance, an injury refers to bodily damage sustained by accident.

injury independent of all other means: An injury resulting from an accident and not from an illness.

inpatient: A person who is admitted to a hospital as an overnight (or longer) patient. Services provided by a hospital, or health benefits payable when a patient is legally admitted to a hospital facility.

inquiry blank: In life and health insurance, a form submitted to the company by an agent for the purpose of determining whether or not the company will give authority to have an applicant medically examined. A form used by agents to query the underwriting department to determine the general attitude respecting a specific impaired risk.

inquiry form: *(See: inquiry blank.)*

inside limits: In health insurance, the upper benefit limit that is intended to impose reasonable limits on covered expenses in order for them to be considered *customary and reasonable*. A major medical plan, for instance, may limit the daily hospital room benefit to $115, or x rays to $600 per claim.

insolvency clause: In reinsurance, a clause that holds the reinsurer liable for its share of loss assumed under the treaty, even though the primary insurer is insolvent.

inspection: In insurance, the independent checking on facts about an applicant or claimant, usually by a commercial inspection agency.

inspection bureau: With respect to insurance, a private organization in the business of investigating risks for insurance companies.

inspection receipt: In life and health insurance, a receipt obtained from an applicant when a policy (upon which the first premium has not been paid) is left with him or her for further inspection. It states that the insurance is not in effect and that the policy has been delivered for inspection only.

inspection report: In life and health insurance, the report of an investigator containing facts required for the insurance company to make a decision on an application for new insurance or for reinstatement of an existing policy. (*See also: commercial inspection report.*)

installment amount option: (*See: fixed amount option.*)

installment deferred annuity: In life insurance, an annuity in which the annuitant pays into the annuity fund over a period of time, after which (usually starting immediately) annuity payments begin coming back to the annuitant and continue for life.

installment pay-outs: In business, a buy-sell agreement funding technique that involves spreading payments for a deceased owner's interest in the business over a period of years.

installment premiums: In insurance, premiums paid for on other than a single premium basis, such as annually, semiannually, quarterly, etc.

installment refund annuity: An annuity that assures the continuation of payments to the annuitant for life and thereafter (if necessary) until the annuitant and his or her beneficiary have received total payments equaling no less than the purchase price of the annuity.

installment settlement: In life insurance, a series of periodic payments of proceeds instead of payment in a lump sum. Any of the income settlement options in a policy. A policy clause allowing the beneficiary to choose to receive proceeds in installments.

installment time option: (*See: fixed period settlement option.*)

Institute of Life Insurance: An industry-sponsored national life insurance organization responsible for building the public image of life insurance through a variety of programs.

institutional investors: Institutions whose investments constitute a highly important part of their overall operations, although they are formed primarily for purposes other than investment. Life insurance companies and mutual funds and pension funds are institutional investors.

insurability: In life and health insurance, all conditions pertaining to an individual that affect his or her health, susceptibility to injury, as well as life expectancy. These factors are considered in determining the amount of risk. If the risk is too high, the insurance company will refuse coverage, as the individual is considered to be uninsurable by that company's underwriting standards.

insurability option: (*See: guaranteed insurability rider.*)

insurable interest: The interest arising when one person has a reasonable expectation of benefiting from the continuance of another person's life or of suffering a loss at his or her death. In life insurance, a person generally is considered to have an unlimited insurable interest in himself or herself. However, a person must have an insurable interest in another person at the time of application in order to insure the other's life. Where no insurable interest exists, policies obtained by one person on the life of another are not enforceable at law since they are considered contrary to the public policy.

insurance: Protection, through specified money compensation or reimbursement for loss, provided by written contract against the happening of specified chance or unexpected events. The transfer of risk that results when one party, for a consideration, agrees to reimburse another for loss caused by designated contingencies. The first party is called the insurance company; the second, the insured; the contract, the insurance policy; the consideration, the premium; the property in question, the risk; and the contingency in question, the hazard or peril. The term assurance, common in England, is ordinarily considered identical to, and synonymous with, insurance.

insurance abstract: (*See: abstract, insurance.*)

insurance account: (*See: debit.*)

Insurance Accounting and Statistical Association: An organization of statisticians and accountants of life insurance companies.

Insurance Advertising Conference: An association of intercompany individuals who administer the advertising programs for their respective insurance companies.

insurance age: (*See: attained age.*)

insurance carrier: (*See: insurance company.*)

insurance commissioner: (*See: commissioner.*)

insurance company: As commonly used, any corporation, association or fraternal benefit society engaged primarily in the business of furnishing insurance protection to the public. (*See also: insurance.*)

insurance consultant: (*See: agent.*)

insurance contract: The legally binding unilateral agreement between an insurance company and a policyowner. (*See also: contract of insurance* and *insurance policy.*)

insurance counselor: (*See: agent.*)

insurance coverage: The total dollar amount of life insurance carried by an individual. In health insurance, often used to indicate what is covered and the extent or amount of coverage.

insurance, credit life: (*See: credit life insurance.*)

insurance department: A division of the state government that has supervisory responsibility over insurance matters and the regulation of insurance companies and agents doing business within its borders.

Insurance Economic Society of America: An organization established for the study of all forms of social insurance and to disseminate information to enlighten the public. Members strive to bring about a unified opinion and cooperative effort of all men and women in the insurance business, maintain insurance as a free enterprise, and develop research work involving studies of the insurance business and certain phases of compulsory social insurance.

insurance examiner: A representative of a state insurance department who audits and examines the financial records of insurance companies.

Insurance Hall of Fame, The: An institution created to honor people who have made outstanding contributions to the insurance industry. Selections are made on a global basis.

insurance history: A record of an individual's personal insurance in force, as well as the story of a person's experience with previous insurance companies.

insurance in force: In life insurance, the total face amount of contracts in force.

Insurance Institute of America: A society of individuals interested in improving education in the area of insurance.

insurance interest: Any interest in an individual, for insurance purposes, of such a nature that his or her death might cause monetary loss to the beneficiary or some other party. (*See also: insurable interest.*)

insurance policy: The printed form prepared by an insurance company to serve as the contract between the policyowner and the company. The policy sets forth all conditions and terms of the agreement. (*See also: insurance contract.*)

insurance poor: A belief held or comment often made when an insured carries so much insurance and pays so much in premiums that there is not enough money left to live on comfortably.

insurance premium: The designated amount of money payable by the insured to the insurance company that is required to keep the contract in force.

insurance program: In life and health insurance, a unified plan that coordinates the needs, policies and settlement options available to carry out the aims and objectives of a client.

insurance rate: The ratio of the premium to the total amount of insurance carried, usually expressed in dollars per $100 or per $1,000 of coverage.

insurance register: A policyowner's personal record or file of important data about insurance carried; dates of purchase, amounts of premiums, expiration, companies, etc.

insurance regulation: Government requirements and restrictions imposed on insurance companies. Since insurance is a business that can affect the financial security of vast numbers of people, government regulation (setting of rates, standards, operating and licensing requirements, etc.) is deemed essential. It is a primary function of insurance regulation to maintain the financial solvency of all insurance companies. In the U.S., the role of regulation is assumed by the states.

insurance reserves: The present value of future claims, minus the present value of future premiums. Reserves are balance sheet accounts set up to reflect actual and potential liabilities under outstanding insurance contracts. There are two main types of insurance reserves: premium reserves and loss (or claim) reserves.

insurance risk: In life and health insurance, a general term denoting the hazard involved in insuring a person or group. The premium or cost of insurance is based upon the relative risk or hazard involved.

insurance risk, pure: (*See: mortality risk.*)

insurance salesperson: (*See: agent.*)

Insurance Service Association of America: A society of insurance agents whose goal is the exchange of information and interchange of business.

insurance superintendent: (*See: commissioner.*)

insurance with other insurers provision: An optional provision in individual medical expense health insurance policies that limits double payment of benefits when the insured has more than one policy covering the same loss. The insured is to receive one settlement for each claim, so as not to profit from the loss.

insured: In life and health insurance, the individual or group covered by the contract of insurance.

insured additional: A person, other than the original named insured, who is protected under a life or health insurance contract.

insured buy-sell agreement: A buy-sell agreement funded by life and/or disability income insurance. (*See also: funded buy-sell agreement.*)

insured installment redemption: A buy-sell agreement funding device whereby the business receives the insurance proceeds and uses them to retire the decedent's business interest on an installment basis.

insured named: In a life or health insurance contract, the person identified as the insured in the policy.

insured pension plan: A pension plan in which the benefits are at least partially insured by an insurance company. Such plans provide a death benefit to beneficiaries if the employee dies before retirement.

insured percentage: (*See: coinsurance percentage participation.*)

insured plan: (*See: insured pension plan.*)

insured status: When determining Social Security benefits, an eligible worker is either fully insured or currently insured or both, depending on his or her year of birth and the quarters of coverage he or she has been credited with. Insured status determines the benefits the worker and/or dependents can receive.

insurer: The company underwriting the insurance and assuming the risk.

Insurers Public Relations Council: An organization comprised of insurance company senior public relations professionals. The purpose of the Council is to provide a forum for these people to discuss, on an industry-wide basis and from a corporate viewpoint, mutual operating problems and activities, as well as to share experiences and foster professional development.

insuring agreement: *(See: insuring clause.)*

insuring clause: In an insurance policy, a clause that defines and describes the scope of the coverage provided and the limits of indemnification. The insuring clause states the policy's intent and contains the insurance company's promises.

integrated deductible: In superimposed major medical plans, a deductible amount between the benefits paid by the basic health insurance plan and those paid by major medical. All or part of the integrated deductible may be absorbed by the basic plan.

integrated plan: An employee retirement income plan that builds retirement benefits, according to an approved Treasury Department formula, on a superstructure of Social Security benefits.

intentional injury: An injury resulting from an intentional act. Self-inflicted injuries are not covered under the terms of an accident policy.

interest: The rent paid for borrowed money or received for loaned money. A person's share of ownership in property or a business, etc. *(See also: insurable interest.)*

interest accrued: Interest earned but not yet payable.

interest-adjusted cost method: In life insurance, a method of comparing costs of similar policies by using an index that takes into account the time value of money due at different times through interest adjustments to the annual premiums, dividends and cash value increases at an assumed interest rate.

interest, compound: *(See: compound interest.)*

interest, exact: The interest that is computed on the basis of 365 days of the year.

interest, excess: (*See: excess interest.*)

interest factor: One of three factors taken into consideration by an insurance company when calculating premium rates. This is an estimate of the overall average interest that will be earned by the insurer on invested premium payments.

interest only option: In life insurance, a settlement option under which all or part of the proceeds of a policy are left with the insurance company for a definite period at a guaranteed minimum rate of interest. The principal remains with the company for a specified period of time. Interest may be paid (usually subject to certain minimums) annually, semiannually, quarterly or monthly—or, in some cases, may be added to the proceeds.

interest option: (*See: interest only option.*)

interest rate: That percentage of a principal sum earned from investment or charged upon a loan.

interest-sensitive whole life: A traditional whole life policy with fixed premiums and traditional nonforfeiture values where a retrospective fund is accumulated out of the premiums, less loads and term costs plus interest. Though the policy's cash value earns a guaranteed minimum rate of return, it may actually earn more depending on the company's investment experience. The cash value of the policy is the greater of the fund less surrender charges and the traditional cash values.

interim binder: (*See: binding receipt.*)

interim dividend: A dividend paid in advance of the full or regular dividend.

interim term insurance: Term life insurance issued to an applicant for a period of 30 or 60 days, after which time the insurance company either issues a permanent insurance policy or rejects the application. This is one form of interim insurance. (*See also: conditional premium receipt.*)

interinsurance exchange: (*See: reciprocal insurance.*)

intermediary: In reinsurance, a broker who negotiates contracts of reinsurance on behalf of the reinsured. These transactions normally take place with those reinsurers that recognize brokers and pay them commissions on reinsurance premiums ceded.

intermediate: In disability insurance, a type of disability less than total. Also, a claim report or notice of the condition of a continuing disability. (*See also: partial disability.*)

intermediate care: Occasional nursing and rehabilitative care, under a doctor's order and performed under the supervision of skilled medical personnel.

intermediate disability: (*See: partial disability.*)

intermediate notice: In disability insurance, a report, required by many insurance companies, informing the company regarding the progress of a continuing disability. Also called second preliminary notice.

intermediate nursing facility: A health facility licensed by the state and often certified by Medicare and/or Medicaid to provide intermediate care.

intermediate policy: In life insurance, a contract combining certain characteristics of the weekly premium policy and the ordinary life contract. It is usually written for $500 or for additional amounts in multiples of $100. Premiums are collected at the homes of the policyowners. The rates are slightly lower than on weekly premium policies, the latter usually being written for smaller amounts. The term is now rarely used.

Internal Revenue Code Section 501(c)(3) organizations: (*See: Section 501(c)(3) organizations.*)

International Association of Health Underwriters: Association of agents and related personnel in the health insurance industry.

International Claim Association: An organization of people who work in the area of settling insurance claims.

interpolated terminal reserve: A reserve fund that an insurance company uses to cover its liability in a particular policy. It is used in determining the value of certain life insurance policies for gift tax purposes.

interview, fact-finding: (*See: fact-finding interview.*)

inter vivos trust: A trust established to serve some function while the grantor is still alive. A testamentary trust, on the other hand, operates only upon the grantor's death and is created in his or her will.

intestate: One who dies leaving no will. Also, the condition of dying without a will.

intoxicants and narcotics provision: In individual health insurance policies, an optional provision which states that the insurance company will not cover any losses suffered by the insured while intoxicated or under the influence of drugs not prescribed by a doctor.

inventory: An accounting of the separate items comprising an assembled property, such as an estate. An agent may suggest an inventory of a client's estate when determining insurance needs or making an analysis for estate planning purposes.

investment account: A separately managed cash value investment fund (usually a mutual fund) into which variable and variable universal life insurance policyowners allocate the premiums and cash value. Policies generally have several of these accounts, each with its own investment objective and degree of risk.

investment income: The return received by businesses and individuals from their investment portfolios, including interest, dividends, rent income, and realized capital gains.

investment manager: In an employee retirement plan, a fiduciary (other than a trustee or a plan's named fiduciary) who manages, acquires, or disposes of a plan's assets.

investment portfolio: A list detailing the securities owned by a person, business or mutual fund. Most insurance companies carry a broadly varied investment portfolio. Also refers to the equity-based accounts in variable and other interest-sensitive products.

investment year interest rate: *(See: investment year method of dividend calculation.)*

investment year method of dividend calculation: Any dividend calculation method that recognizes differences in earned interest rates depending upon the year in which the investment is made. *(For contrast, see: portfolio method of dividend calculation.)*

involuntary bankruptcy: Bankruptcy proceedings begun by the petition of a creditor who seeks to settle the affairs of a debtor.

involuntary trust: A trust established by the doctrines of equity for the purpose of administering justice in the most efficient manner when there is no intention of the parties to create a trust relation.

IRA (Individual Retirement Account):   A personal qualified retirement account or annuity through which an individual may accumulate tax-deferred dollars up to a certain sum or percent of income each year for retirement income. Contributions may or may not be tax deductible, depending on the individual's income and coverage under an employer-sponsored plan. Regardless, earnings accumulate on a tax-deferred basis. (*See also: individual retirement account.*)

IRA account: Like an IRA annuity, the IRA account receives contributions, called deposits, each year from an individual and may be arranged with an insurance company or any of several other types of funding media (bank savings accounts, CDs, bonds, mutual funds, etc.) that meet the requirements. (*See also: individual retirement account.*)

IRA annuity: Issued by a life insurance company, a fund, built by premium payments, investment increments, etc., for retirement purposes. An IRA annuity may be created by an individual retirement annuity contract or an individual endowment insurance contract. (*See also: individual retirement account.*)

IRA bond: One of several IRA investment vehicles (*see also: IRA annuity* and *IRA account*); a bond specially issued by the federal government under the provision of the Second Liberty Bond Act, with interest compounded semiannually. (*See also: individual retirement account.*)

IRA certificate: Certificate issued for funds placed in an IRA time deposit account. (*See also: individual retirement account.*)

IRA investment vehicle: Any one of a number of vehicles used for the purpose of accumulating assets in an IRA and for the maintenance of the assets' integrity.

IRA rollover account: The qualified IRA account resulting when funds are transferred from one IRA vehicle to another or from some other qualified plan (pension, profit sharing, etc.) to an IRA if the individual's participation in such other plan is terminated. The transfer takes place on a tax-free basis. (*See also: individual retirement account.*)

IRA time deposit: A time deposit open account for IRA purposes, with Federal Reserve Board-determined exceptions. (*See also: individual retirement account.*)

irregular premium: In insurance, the fractional or proportionate premium paid to change the regular premium due date from one month or season of the year to another.

irrevocable beneficiary: A beneficiary designation that cannot be changed by the insured without consent from the beneficiary.

irrevocable trust: A trust that cannot be terminated by the donor (grantor). If funded with income-producing property, it can offer both estate tax and income tax savings to the donor.

issue: In insurance, a term applying to the insurance company's act of approving and forwarding new policies to the agent for delivery to applicants. Also used with reference to offspring or descendants.

issue age: (*See: age at issue.*)

issue date: (*See: date of issue.*)

issued business: In life and health insurance, contracts actually written by the insurance company, paid for, but not yet delivered to or accepted by the insured.

issue department: In life and health insurance, the department within a company that prepares policies and keeps records.

issue limit: In insurance, the maximum amount of coverage a company is willing to extend on a given risk.

J

joint and full survivor annuity: An annuity that pays an income jointly to two individuals. Upon the death of one, the same income continues to the survivor for life. When the survivor dies, payments stop.

joint and one-half survivor annuity: An annuity that pays an income jointly to two individuals. Upon the death of one, one-half of the income continues to the survivor for life.

joint and several: A legal term meaning that all signers of an obligation are bound jointly, as well as each of them individually, for the full amount of the debt.

joint and survivorship annuity: (*See: annuity, joint and survivor.*)

joint and survivorship option: In life insurance, a contract option that permits policy proceeds to be paid out as a joint and survivorship annuity.

joint and two-thirds survivor annuity: An annuity that pays an income jointly to two individuals. Upon the death of one, two-thirds of the income continues to the survivor for life.

joint annuity: An annuity that is paid to two named persons until the first one dies, at which time the annuity ceases.

joint control: A life insurance policy provision that states that a person, persons or organization other than the insured, usually the beneficiary, has a joint right with the insured to the exercise of the rights, powers, benefits, privileges and the options of the policy.

joint field work: A situation where two insurance agents or an agent and supervisor make prospecting and sales calls jointly.

Commissions on sales may or may not be shared on some predetermined basis, depending on company, agency, or individual procedures.

joint insurance: A life insurance contract that covers two or more lives and provides for the payment of the proceeds at the death of the first insured, at which time the policy automatically terminates, with no remaining coverage for the survivors.

joint insured: One whose life is insured by a joint insurance contract. (*See also: joint insurance.*)

joint interests: A right or title or legal share in an asset, business or other property held by two or more persons.

joint liability: Liability that rests upon more than one person.

joint life and survivorship annuity: (*See also: annuity, joint and survivor.*)

joint life annuity: (*See: annuity, joint life.*)

joint life insurance: (*See: joint insurance.*)

joint life policy: (*See: joint insurance.*)

jointly owned property: Property owned jointly by two or more parties, the full value of which is generally includible in the estate of the first owner to die. However, if a husband and wife are the only joint owners, only one-half the value will be includible in the estate of the first owner to die.

joint return: The form for, or method of, filing income tax returns whereby married couples combine their incomes, deductions, exemptions, tax computations, etc. This is optional, but in some cases results in lower federal income taxes, as compared with filing separately. (A surviving spouse with dependent children may generally file a joint return for two taxable years after the death of his or her spouse.)

joint tenancy: Undivided ownership interests in property that are vested in two or more people, with the right of survivorship. When one dies, that person's interest passes to the surviving tenant or tenants rather than to the deceased tenant's heirs. An estate shared equally by two or more parties, with the survivor obtaining complete possession.

judgment rates: In insurance, rates established by the underwriter based on his or her experience and somewhat arbitrary decision, with or without the application of a formal set of rules.

jumbo risk: An insurance contract with exceptionally high limits, such as $250,000 or more.

jumping juvenile policy: Juvenile insurance, sometimes called an *estate builder policy*, on which the face amount automatically increases, usually by five times the original face amount when the child reaches a predetermined age. No additional premium is required when the amount increases. (*See also: estate builder policy.*)

junior partner: In general, a person who has a minority ownership interest in a partnership. For Keogh plan purposes, a self-employed person who has an ownership interest of 10 percent or less in a partnership.

juvenile: A person below the age of 16 or 18, as the law of the state decrees.

juvenile insurance: Life insurance policies written on the lives of minors within specified age limits, generally with the parents or grandparents as the policyowners and premium payors.

K

Keogh Act (or HR 10): The Self-Employed Individuals Tax Retirement Act, originally passed by Congress in 1962 and since amended several times, enabling self-employed individuals to establish and fund tax-favored individual retirement plans similar to those available to corporations.

Keogh (or HR 10) Act plan: A plan under the Self-Employed Individuals Tax Retirement Act, that permits a self-employed individual to establish a formal retirement plan and obtain tax advantages similar to those available under qualified corporate pension plans.

Kerr-Mills Act: (*See: Medicaid.*)

key-employee insurance: (*See: key-executive insurance.*)

key-executive insurance: Protection of a business firm against the financial loss caused by the death or disability of a vital member of the firm. A means of protecting a business from the adverse results of the loss of individuals possessing special managerial or technical skill or experience. Often referred to as key-employee insurance.

key-man insurance: A term formerly used, but now generally called key-executive insurance. (*See also: key-executive insurance.*)

kit, sales: In insurance, a portfolio or traveling case equipped with manuals, forms, applications, and various other sales aids (such as advertising, charts, diagrams, estate plans, and other related material) to help an insurance agent make a more efficient sales presentation.

L

LAMP: Life Agency Management Program. The annual convention of the General Agents and Managers Conference, usually held in April of each year.

lapse: Termination of an insurance policy because of nonpayment of premiums or, in the case of variable and universal life policies, the depletion of cash value below that amount needed to keep the policy in force. In life insurance, the term sometimes means nonpayment before the policy has developed any nonforfeiture value, being called *termination* if premium failure occurs after nonforfeiture value develops or *surrender* if cash value is withdrawn.

lapsed legacy: Property willed to another, but that becomes a part of the general estate because the planned recipient (the legatee) predeceased the testator. (*See also: legacy.*)

lapsed policy: A policy whose coverage terminated.

lapse rate: The rate at which policies terminate through failure of insureds to continue paying either scheduled or minimum premiums, usually expressed as a ratio of lapses during a given period of time to the total number of policies of that type issued.

lapse ratio: The ratio of the number of life insurance contracts lapsed without value or surrendered for cash within a given period to the number in force at the beginning of the period.

last payment, date of: (*See: date of last payment.*)

last survivor annuity: (*See: annuity, joint and survivor* and *survivorship annuity.*)

last survivor insurance: Life insurance on two or more persons, the proceeds being payable upon the death of the last insured.

lawful heirs: Those individuals having a legal right to a decedent's estate.

law of large numbers: A component of the law of probabilities that states that the larger the size of the group, the more accurately the loss experience of that group can be predicted. This is one of the main principles involved in determining actuarial tables for insurance purposes.

laws of descent and distribution: State laws concerning the manner in which property and other assets are to be distributed upon an individual's death in the absence of a valid will, and stipulating who has a right to portions of the estate.

lay underwriter: Home office representative who evaluates a risk based upon known probability and statistics, as well as evaluation of the human element. Not a medical doctor, the lay underwriter nonetheless generally has a thorough knowledge of medical risks.

Leading Producers Round Table: An organization of agents who qualify for membership annually (or on a life basis) by producing certain high levels of health insurance premium volume in a year. Sponsored by the International Association of Health Underwriters.

ledger cost: A method of expressing the cost of a life insurance policy over a period of years. First, the dividends, if any, are subtracted from the gross premiums. Then, the cash surrender value is subtracted. Remaining is the ledger cost for the given period.

legacy: A disposition of personal property or money by will. There are several types of legacies: specific or demonstrated legacy, paid from specified property or funds; general legacy, a specific amount payable out of general assets; residuary legacy, a gift of all personal assets and otherwise disposed. Legacy and bequest are equivalent terms.

legacy, demonstrative: (*See: demonstrative legacy.*)

legacy, general: (*See: general legacy.*)

legacy, specific: (*See: specific legacy.*)

legal action provision: A mandatory health provision that states that the policyowner must allow 60 days after submitting the proof of loss forms before taking legal action, and if the policyowner sues, such action must occur within three years.

legal asset: An asset held by the executor of an estate and subject to all debts under common law.

legal capacity: The ability to enter into a legal contract, i.e. being of legal age, sane, not a convict or enemy alien. Only such an individual is considered a legally competent party.

legal guardian: An adult charged with administering the legal affairs of a minor person.

legal investments: Approved classes of investments to which savings banks, trust funds and insurance reserves are limited by law, as being within the prudent and safe range. Examples of such legal investments include United States government obligations, certain municipal bonds, high grade railroad and public utility bonds, real estate first mortgages, etc.

legal liability: *(See: liability.)*

legal list: *(See: legal investments.)*

legal reserve: The amount of money that must be maintained by a life insurance company each year for future claims and the increased risk as the insured's age advances. Standards are established by the insurance laws of the various states.

legal reserve life insurance: A method of insuring lives by contracts backed by definite reserve accumulations that are computed by formulas defined and regulated by state law.

legal reserve life insurance company: A life insurance company that maintains the reserves required by the jurisdiction within which the company operates.

legals: *(See: legal investments.)*

legatee: One who is designated to receive a legacy.

letter of administration: Written authority granted by a probate court to the administrator who will act for the estate of one dying without a will or who succeeds an executor who dies before the administration of an estate is concluded.

letter of determination: *(See: determination letter.)*

letter of indemnity: A legally binding contract whereby one party agrees to reimburse another for loss resulting upon the occurrence of a stated event.

letter of license: Written permission by a creditor, informing a debtor to proceed as directed to avoid bankruptcy.

letter, pre-approach: (*See: pre-approach letter.*)

letters testamentary: Written authority granted by a probate court to the executor of a will to act for the estate.

level annual premium funding method: A method of accumulating money for payment of future pensions, under which the level annual charge for a particular benefit is determined for each age. This level annual charge is payable each year until retirement, so at that time the benefit will be fully funded.

level cost: A pension cost method based on an actuarial formula designed to produce a constant year-to-year accrual of normal cost, either in amount of percentage of payroll or other index, if (a) the experience conforms with the actuarial assumptions and (b) there are no changes in the plan or the employee group for which cost accruals are assumed.

level premium: A life insurance premium that remains fixed throughout the life of a policy and yet makes possible, by means of an accumulating reserve, the payments of all death claims as they occur in a given group.

level premium insurance: (*See: level premium plan.*)

level premium plan: The plan of insurance (used by all regular life insurance companies) under which, instead of charging an annually increasing premium that reflects the increasing chance of death, an equivalent level premium is payable. The plan involves the accumulation of reserves arising out of the excess premiums paid in the earlier years and the depletion of those reserves to supplement inadequate premiums in the later years.

level premium reserve: (*See: active life reserve.*)

level rate: (*See: level premium.*)

level term insurance: Term life coverage on which the face value remains unchanged from the date the policy comes into force to the date the policy expires. (*For contrast, see: decreasing term insurance* and *increasing term insurance.*)

liabilities: With respect to an insurance company's liabilities, the company's immediate or contingent policy obligations, unpaid claims, funds left under settlement options, assigned surplus, and miscellaneous debts.

liabilities, current: *(See: current liabilities.)*

liability: The condition of being bound by law to do something that may be enforced in the courts. An obligation, usually financial. The probable cost of meeting an obligation.

liability, contingent: *(See: contingent liability.)*

liability, freezing past service: *(See: freezing past service liability.)*

liability, frozen initial: *(See: frozen initial liability.)*

liability insurance, employer's: *(See: employer's liability insurance.)*

license: With respect to insurance, certification, issued by the appropriate state department of insurance policies, that an individual is qualified to sell insurance for the period stated (usually one or two years), and renewable upon application without the necessity of the applicant's undergoing the original qualifying requirements.

lien plan: A plan for issuing coverage on substandard risks, under which a standard premium is paid but less than the full face amount of the policy is payable if death occurs within a certain period of years. Also, a plan under which an impairment of the insurance company's assets is offset by pro rata liens against policies, to be deducted from the face amount when paid as a claim.

Life Agency Management Program: *(See: LAMP.)*

life annuity: *(See: annuity, life.)*

Life Communicators Association (LCA): An international professional organization of men and women employed by life insurance companies as communications practitioners in advertising, sales promotion, internal company communications and public relations.

life conservation: A reference to efforts to preserve human life, such as through research, legislation, and appeals to society. Also used with reference to keeping life insurance policies in force; the opposite of lapse.

life contingencies: Contingencies or influencing circumstances involving the duration of life of an individual or a group of individuals. Also, the term frequently refers to the method of actuarial calculation using the probabilities of life and death.

life estate: A freehold interest in land, the duration of which is confined to the life of one or more persons or contingent upon certain happenings. The individual's (and heirs') right to the property ceases at his/her death.

life expectancy: The average duration of the life remaining to a number of persons of a given age, according to a mortality table. The term *life expectancy* should not be confused with *probable lifetime*. The latter refers to the difference between a person's present age and the age at which death is most probable, i.e., the age at which most deaths occur. (*See also: probable lifetime.*)

life expectancy term insurance: A special policy type, issued at each individual age at the required premium for that age's expectation of life. As an example, with a standard life expectancy at age 24 of 43 additional years, the policy would be issued as *term to age 67*, with the insurance expiring if the insured lives beyond that age.

life income: A pension or annuity guaranteeing the recipient an income for life upon attaining a certain age. Also, an arrangement providing income for life.

life income option: One of the settlement options under which the proceeds of a life insurance or annuity policy may be applied to buy an annuity payable to the beneficiary for life—often with a specified number of payments certain or a refund if payments do not equal or exceed premiums paid.

life income with period certain option: A life insurance proceeds settlement option providing a fixed number of monthly installments in a guaranteed amount to be paid whether the named beneficiary lives or dies.

life insurance: The transfer of part of the financial loss due to death of an insured person to an insurance company. The risk insured against is the death of a particular person (known as the insured), upon whose death within a stated term, or whenever death occurs if the contract so provides, the insurance company agrees to pay a stated sum or income to the beneficiary.

Life Insurance Advertisers Association: An organization made up of advertising personnel from the home offices of insurance companies. Frequently referred to as LIAA.

Life Insurance Agency Management Association: An organization, now known as the Life Insurance Marketing and Research Association that, through research, seeks solutions to the problems of administering the agency force of a life insurance company.

Life Insurance Association of America: An organization that serves as the legislative relations arm of a large segment of the life insurance business.

life insurance company: An organization chartered by the state for the purpose of furnishing life insurance protection and annuities. Many life insurance companies are also chartered to issue health insurance.

life insurance, credit: (*See: credit life insurance.*)

life insurance for charitable giving: One of the uses of life insurance, offering a way for an individual to leave part or all of his or her estate to a charitable organization upon death. There are many possible plans, the simplest being to purchase an insurance policy and designate the organization as beneficiary.

life insurance for children: (*See: juvenile insurance.*)

life insurance, graded premium: (*See: graded premium life insurance.*)

life insurance, group: (*See: group life insurance.*)

life insurance, industrial: (*See: weekly premium insurance.*)

life insurance, legal reserve: (*See: legal reserve life insurance.*)

life insurance, limited payment: (*See: limited payment policy.*)

Life Insurance Marketing and Research Association (LIMRA): An organization—previously known as the Life Insurance Agency Management Association—founded by life insurance companies in the U.S. and Canada to study common problems of marketing and agency management through research and development and exchange of ideas. Member companies represent nearly 90 percent of the life insurance in force in the U.S. and Canada.

Life Insurance Medical Research Fund: A fund created and maintained by member life insurance companies and devoted to improving the general health in communities.

life insurance, ordinary: (*See: ordinary insurance.*)

life insurance, permanent: (*See: ordinary insurance.*)

life insurance, primary purpose: To provide an immediate estate and/or income for the dependents of the policyowner in the event of the early death of the insured or to provide funds to a business enterprise to liquidate an owner's interest upon death or to replace, with money, the value of a key individual.

life insurance, straight: *(See: ordinary insurance.)*

life insurance, term: *(See: term insurance.)*

life insurance trust: A trust for the purpose of distributing life insurance proceeds. Life insurance companies usually cannot act as trustees or guardians, nor exercise discretion in making payments to beneficiaries. In some cases, it is advisable to have policy proceeds paid to a designated trustee and distributed under the terms of a trust agreement, thereby permitting greater flexibility in the distribution of the proceeds. Such an arrangement constitutes an unfunded life insurance trust. Under a funded life insurance trust, the trustee is given not only control over the policy proceeds but also securities or other property to provide funds out of which to pay the premiums.

life insurance trust, contingent: *(See: contingent life insurance trust.)*

life insurance, whole life: *(See: whole life insurance.)*

Life Insurers Conference (LIC):   An organization that provides for exchange of information on management problems among the member life insurance companies. Member companies are either home service or combination companies, selling weekly premium insurance, monthly debit ordinary insurance, etc.

Life Office Management Association (LOMA):   An organization serving the life insurance industry through education programs related to administrative and technical procedures within a company or agency.

life paid-up at age ( ):   A form of limited payment life insurance that provides protection for the whole of life, with premium payments stopping at the indicated age and thus paying up the policy. For example, if a 45-year-old man bought a life paid-up at age 65 policy, he would pay premiums for 20 years and receive coverage for life.

life table: A tabulated statement presenting mortality and survivor characteristics of a given population.

life table, graduated: *(See: graduated life table.)*

lifetime disability benefit: A payment to help replace income lost by an insured for as long as total disability lasts.

lifetime exemption: Prior to the Tax Reform Act of 1976, the value of gifts, in excess of the $3,000 per year per donee annual exclusion allowance that an individual could make during his or her life that were exempt from gift tax under the Internal Revenue Code, was a lifetime limit of $30,000 per donee. The Tax Reform Act of 1976 eliminated this and imposed a flat rule that all gifts above $3,000 are included in the gross estate.

lifetime insurance: (*See: whole life insurance.*)

lifetime maximum benefit: Under major medical policies, the maximum dollar benefit that each insured and each insured dependent is entitled to receive for the aggregate of expenses incurred for all diseases or injuries suffered during his or her lifetime. Also known as aggregate amount.

lifetime policy: In health insurance, a noncancellable, guaranteed renewable policy. Also, policies that pay loss of income indemnities for the lifetime of the insured. In life insurance, the term may mean a whole life policy.

lifetime transfers: The giving or transfer of property from one individual (the donor) to another (the donee) during the donor's lifetime. In order for the transfer to be treated as a gift, it must be voluntary, complete, and without full or adequate consideration. (*See also: living gift.*)

life underwriter: This term can apply either to an agent who sells life insurance at the field level or to a home office employee whose job it is to evaluate the risk an insurance company is being asked to undertake. (*See also: agent or underwriter.*)

Life Underwriters Association: An organization of insurance sales representatives of life insurance companies working to promote the interests of the institution of life insurance, improve prospecting and selling techniques, and protect the interests of all life underwriters.

Life Underwriters Association of Canada (LUAC):   A national organization for agents, having local associations throughout Canada. Executive offices located in Don Mills, Ontario.

Life Underwriters Association Training Course (LUATC):   A two-year, on-the-job, sales training course sponsored by the Life Underwriters Association of Canada for the benefit of its members.

Life Underwriters Political Action Committee: (*See: LUPAC.*)

Life Underwriter Training Council (LUTC):   An institutionally supported organization, headquartered in Washington, D.C., that conducts training programs for life insurance agents, using local agents as instructors.

limit, aggregate: The maximum amount that an insurance company will cover during the contract period.

limitations: Exceptions to coverage and limitations of coverage as contained in an insurance contract.

limitations, geographical: (*See: geographical limitations.*)

limited form: (*See: limited policies.*)

limited health insurance policy: A health insurance policy that provides protection only against specifically designated accidents or illnesses.

limited income option: A settlement option under which the proceeds of a life insurance policy are payable in installments, either for a fixed period or for a fixed amount.

limited life policy: A policy that only pays benefits for death resulting from certain specified causes rather than from any cause. For instance, a policy that protects an insured from accidental death only will not pay benefits for death resulting from illness.

limited partnership: A business partnership consisting of one or more general partners and one or more limited partners. A limited partner contributes capital to the business, but has no active, hands-on control or management of the business and is generally liable for partnership indebtedness only to the amount of his or her capital contribution.

limited payment policy: A life insurance policy that provides for payment of the premium for a period of years less than the period of protection provided under the contract.

limited policies: Health insurance policies that restrict benefits to specified accidents or diseases, as compared to broad form policies. Examples of limited policies are travel policies, dread-disease policies and ticket policies. (*See also: broad form policies* and *limited health insurance policy.*)

limited portfolio method of dividend calculation: (*See: investment year method of dividend calculation.*)

limit, excess: (*See: excess limit.*)

limit of liability: (*See: limit of risk.*)

limit of risk: The maximum amount a life insurance company is willing to insure under a given form of contract on any particular life.

limits: In life insurance, the maximum and minimum amounts that the insurance company will insure one life at various age levels with respect to various types of insurance. In health insurance, ages below or above which the insurance company will not issue a new policy or above which it will not continue a policy in force. The term also refers to the maximum amount of benefit payable for a given situation or occurrence.

limits, contribution: (*See: contribution limits.*)

LIMRA: (*See: Life Insurance Marketing and Research Association.*)

line broker, excess: (*See: excess line broker.*)

line, gross: (*See: gross line.*)

Linton yield: (*See: traditional net cost comparison method.*)

liquid assets: Cash or other assets that readily can be converted to cash.

liquidating dividend: When a business is being settled or liquidated, a prorated distribution of property to owners, creditors, depositors and other lawful claimants.

liquidation: The using up of a fund previously created; the conversion of holdings into cash.

liquidity: The characteristic of being readily convertible into cash.

litigation: The act of carrying on a lawsuit.

living gift: A transfer of property from one individual to another during the donor's lifetime. It can be a means of reducing estate shrinkage and estate transfer costs if it is bona fide, absolute and complete, and not a mere subterfuge attempting to put the apparent legal title in the beneficiary's name while the donor in reality retains control over any benefits from the property during his or her life.

living motives: Gifts made during the lifetime of the donor for purposes of benefiting the donor and/or donee during the donor's lifetime, and not solely to save death taxes or for benefits to begin after the donor's death. An example of a living motive is a desire to make members of the family, particularly children, financially independent.

living test: A concept used in determining the appropriateness of a life insurance plan. Not only must coverage provide a death benefit, but if the insured lives, a workable plan must create consistent accumulation of cash, offer a competitive rate of interest, and deliver no fewer than a specified number of dollars at a given time in the future, to provide an income adequate to live on. (*See also: death test.*)

living trust: A trust created to take effect during the lifetime of the grantor; also called an inter vivos trust.

Lloyds Association: An association comprised of individuals who band together within an organization to assume risks. Each person is responsible only for the share of the risk he or she assumes. There are a limited number of such associations in the United States.

Lloyds broker: One who has authority to negotiate insurance contracts with the underwriters on the floor at Lloyds. (*See also: Lloyds of London.*)

Lloyds of London: An English institution within which individual underwriters accept insurance risks. Lloyds provides the support facilities for such activity but is not in itself an insurance company.

loading: In insurance, the amount added to net premiums (risk factor minus interest factor) to cover the company's operating expenses and contingencies. The loading includes the cost of securing new business, collecting premiums, and general management expenses. Precisely, it is the excess of the gross premiums over net premiums.

loading charge: In life insurance, the additional charge for overhead costs added to the net premium. This charge is required by actuarial tables to cover mortality and interest factors. In the case of open-end investment companies (mutual funds), the charge made at the time of purchase to cover overhead, such as commissions.

loading, expense: (*See: expense loading.*)

loan: In life insurance, money loaned at interest by the insurance company to a cash value insurance policyowner on the security of the cash value of his or her policy contract. (*See also: automatic premium loan provision* and *loan value.*)

loan, exhaust: (*See: exhaust loan.*)

loan, fiduciary: An unsecured loan.

loan, forced: (*See: forced loan.*)

loan value: In life insurance, a specified amount that can be borrowed from the insurance company by the policyowner, using the cash value of the policy as collateral. In the event the policy matures with the debt either partially or fully unpaid, then the amount borrowed, plus any accrued interest, is deducted from the face amount and the balance is paid to the beneficiary.

locked-in vesting: That form of vesting in a contributory pension plan under which the participant may not withdraw contributions after benefits attributable to employer contributions have vested, except possibly upon disability or with tax penalty.

lodge system of insurance: (*See: fraternal insurance.*)

LOMA: (*See: Life Office Management Association.*)

longevity: Length of life. The major factor in the calculation of the premium for an annuity.

long term: In life insurance, refers to a straight term policy providing coverage for a long period of time and frequently having accumulating cash values. Life expectancy (term to expectancy) that is written for a term of years extended to the end of the policyowner's life expectancy.

long-term disability: A disability having a relatively long duration, usually two or more years. Also, a form of group disability insurance paying benefits for more than the customary 13 to 26 weeks; more commonly, benefits of five years' duration or more, again depending on terms of reference.

long term disability income policy: A health insurance policy that pays long term disability income benefits (usually more than two years).

loss: In insurance, to be financially harmed. The basis of a claim for indemnity under an insurance policy. The amount for which the insurance company becomes liable on the occurrence of the event insured against.

loss constant: A flat sum or amount included in the premium of a risk too small for experienced ratings to be applied. It is generally associated with workers' compensation insurance.

loss conversion factor: An amount added to the actual losses to provide for the expenses incurred in handling of claims. It is normally associated with a retrospective rating plan of workers' compensation insurance.

loss department: That office of an insurance company that pays and handles claims. Some companies call this department the benefits department because it handles policyowners' benefits.

losses incurred: The total losses, whether paid or not, sustained by the insurance company during a given period.

losses paid: A summary of claims paid.

loss of benefits: Under Social Security, benefits may be lost or reduced (often on a dollar-for-dollar basis) if the person receiving them earns an income in addition to receiving Social Security benefits. The amount of loss depends on the extent of outside earnings.

loss-of-income benefits: Benefits paid because the insured is disabled and unable to work. Also referred to as disability benefits.

loss of income concept: The idea governing the disability income policy that provides qualified individuals with a total disability benefit—plus a variable, long-term partial benefit. The amount of partial benefit is related to the actual amount of the insured's income loss, if any.

loss-of-income insurance: Policies that provide benefits to help replace an insured person's income loss caused by an illness or accident. (*See also: disability income insurance.*)

loss-of-occupation concept: The idea incorporated in the type of disability income policy that provides qualified individuals with a monthly benefit based on the inability of the insured to perform the duties of his or her regular occupation.

loss-of-sight-or-limbs benefit: An extra benefit provision in some policies, whereby a benefit is payable for the loss of sight or limbs.

loss-of-time benefits: (*See: loss-of-income benefits.*)

loss-of-time insurance: (*See: disability income insurance.*)

loss outstanding: The sum of losses an insurance company carries in the form of claims not yet settled. The amount of loss for which the insurance company is liable and that it expects to pay in the future.

loss payable clause: The policy provision that provides for payment of a loss by the insurance company to someone other than the insured.

loss ratio: The percentage of losses in relation to premiums.

loss ratio, written-paid: The ratio of losses paid to premiums written by the insurance company during a specific time interval.

loss report: The document detailing the facts of the claim filed by the agent. A claim report.

loss reserve: The estimated liability for unpaid insurance claims or losses that have occurred as of any given valuation date. Usually includes losses incurred but not reported, losses due but not yet paid, and amounts not yet due.

loss retention: *(See: deductible.)*

lump sum: Payment of the entire proceeds of a life insurance policy at one time. This is the method of settlement provided by most policies, unless an alternate settlement is elected by the policyowner before the insured's death or thereafter by the beneficiary before receiving the payment.

lump-sum death benefit: Under Social Security, a benefit designed to help defray funeral expenses and paid at the death of all covered individuals who are either fully insured or currently insured. The payment is made to the surviving widow or widower of the deceased. If there is no surviving widow or widower, payment is made to the funeral director or to the person who paid the funeral expenses. The lump-sum death benefit equals three times the PIA (Primary Insurance Amount) of the deceased individual, up to a certain maximum amount.

LUPAC: Life Underwriters Political Action Committee. A committee of the National Association of Life Underwriters that promotes legislative and political causes that it deems to be in the best interests of NALU members and the insurance industry as a whole.

LUTC: *(See: Life Underwriters Training Council.)*

M

major hospitalization insurance: A type of medical-expense health insurance that provides benefits for most hospitalization expenses incurred, up to a high limit, subject to a large deductible. Such contracts may contain internal maximum limits and a percentage participation clause (sometimes called coinsurance clause). Distinguished from major medical in that it pays benefits only when the insured is hospitalized.

major medical expense insurance: A health policy designed to help offset the heavy medical expenses resulting from catastrophic or prolonged illnesses or injuries. Generally, it provides benefit payments of 75–80 percent of all reasonable and customary medical expenses above the deductible amount that is paid by the insured, up to the maximum limit of liability and within the time period provided by the policy. (*See also: comprehensive major medical insurance.*)

major medical plan, calendar year: (*See: calendar year major medical plan.*)

malingering: Feigning a disability in order to collect insurance benefits, especially following a recovery from a covered disability.

malpractice: Professional misconduct, negligence or lack of ordinary skill in the performance of a professional act. Such action renders a person liable to suit for damages.

malpractice insurance: A form of liability coverage on a professional person for the defense of suits instituted against him or her for malpractice and/or to pay damages assessed by a court, usually up to a specific maximum limit.

Management Hall of Fame: (*See: General Agents and Managers Conference Management Hall of Fame.*)

manager: Common title for the head of a life and/or health insurance agency operated as a branch of the home office, as opposed to being operated as a general agency. The manager is a home office employee, generally compensated by salary and allowances, often plus incentive bonuses.

manager, branch: (*See: branch manager.*)

mandatory valuation reserve: In life insurance, a reserve which, by state law, a company is required to hold to offset any declines in the valuation of securities listed as admitted assets.

manual: In life and health insurance, a field book containing rates, classifications and underwriting rules for a particular insurance company. (*See also: rate manual.*)

manual rates: The cost of a unit of insurance or bond protection of the various kinds of insurance or bonds, as published in pertinent manuals. Rates developed by the use of a recognized rating plan.

manual rating: In insurance, the calculation of the premium rate from a manual classifying the types on a general basis, such as by industries, without reference to the particular conditions of an individual case.

marital deduction: For federal estate and gift tax purposes, a deduction for gifts and bequests to spouses that is unlimited in amount, except for certain terminable interests in property. (*See also: gift tax marital deduction.*)

marital deduction, gift tax: (*See: gift tax marital deduction.*)

market: (*See: general market, specific market,* and *thin market.*)

market price: With respect to assets (stocks, bonds, debentures, real estate, etc.) the price actually paid or the price considered to be obtainable in the open market under current conditions.

market value: The value of assets (stocks, bonds, debentures, real estate, etc.) based on a current market valuation.

marshaling of assets: A court-ordered rule for the distribution of equity of a debtor's property among creditors that requires that each creditor exhausts his or her immediate rights to permit all others to be paid if possible. Thus, in the case of a liquidating partnership, the firm creditors must first exhaust the firm assets, and personal creditors the personal assets of the partners, before either group crosses over to reach the other remaining assets.

Massachusetts trust: A type of business organization under which the control and management, as well as the legal title of the assets, of a business are in the hands of a trustee or group of trustees, while the ownership and equitable title to the assets of the business are in beneficiaries whose ownership is evidenced by trust certificates.

master contract: (*See: master policy.*)

master file: The active working file of an insurance company that contains all the billing and current status information for each policy.

master plan: A standardized form of qualified retirement plan, with or without a trust, administered by an insurance company or bank acting as the funding medium for purposes of providing benefits on a standardized basis. A master plan requires that the sponsoring organization both fund the benefits and administer the plan. The plan must be submitted to the IRS for approval.

master policy: The contract of insurance issued to the employer, association, or other named group under a group insurance plan that contains all the terms, conditions and benefits of the agreement. Individual employees participating in the group plan receive individual certificates that state the benefits but usually not all the details of the plan contained in the master policy.

material fact: In insurance, vital information required to make an underwriting decision. A statement of something that is done or exists is of such importance that disclosure (or failure to disclose) would alter an underwriting decision or loss settlement.

maternity benefit: A medical expense health insurance benefit that covers all or a portion of the costs arising from pregnancy and childbirth. In individual health policies, maternity benefits are often excluded from coverage unless purchased with additional premium.

maternity benefit, flat: (*See: flat maternity benefit.*)

mature: In life insurance, the time when a policy becomes payable. A whole life policy matures upon the death of the insured or when its cash value equals its cash value (usually at age 100). In either case the face amount becomes payable. Also, the status of a bond when it reaches the date on which it is redeemable for its full maturity value.

maturity date: In life insurance, that date upon which a policy endows and becomes payable if the insured is still living. Also, the stated date on which a bond is redeemable for its full maturity value.

maturity dividend: In a participating life insurance policy, an extra dividend paid when a policy matures other than by death, as, for instance, a 20-year endowment.

maturity value: The proceeds payable on an endowment contract at the end of the specified endowment period or payable on a life insurance contract at the last age of the mortality table, if the insured is still living at that time. The maturity value of a traditional whole life policy generally is the same as the face amount of the policy and is equal to the reserve value of the contract on its maturity date. With universal life, variable life and other interest sensitive products, the maturity value may be substantially greater than the specified or initial face amount. The actual amount payable by the company may also be increased by dividend additions or accumulated dividend deposits or decreased by outstanding loans or withdrawals of cash value. Also, the stated value of a bond on its maturity date.

maximum average indexed monthly earnings: Regarding the calculation of Social Security benefits, an average earnings base determined by indexing credited earnings of a worker in terms of average earnings in a current year (per formula) and used to determine the amount of benefits when eligibility for benefits arises after 1978 (except that the pre-1979 method is used in 1979 through 1983 for retirement benefits only, if it produces higher benefits) if the worker has maximum taxable earnings in all computation years, that would give him or her maximum indexed earnings. (*See also: maximum average monthly wage.*)

maximum average monthly wage: Regarding the calculation of Social Security benefits, an average earnings base used to determine the amount of benefits when eligibility for benefits arises before 1979 (and in 1979 through 1983 for retirement benefits only, if it produces higher benefits than the post-1978 method), if the worker has had maximum taxable earnings for a sufficient number of years. (*See also: maximum average indexed monthly earnings.*)

maximum disability policy: A form of noncancelable disability income insurance that limits the insurance company's liability for any one claim, but not the aggregate amount of all claims.

maximum probable loss: In insurance, the largest loss expected in a risk under *normal* circumstances.

maximum wage base: The maximum annual income level on which Social Security taxes are paid and credited for benefit calculation purposes.

McCarran Act: (*See: Public Law 15.*)

MDRT: (*See: Million Dollar Round Table.*)

mean reserve: In insurance, the average of the initial reserve and the terminal reserve, computed as of the middle of the policy year; one-half the sum of the initial and terminal reserves. This is the legal reserve, the policy value that the insurance company is required by law to maintain. (*See also: legal reserve.*)

Medicaid: A joint state and federal welfare program, administered by states and subsidized by federal government grants, under which specified medical expenses are paid for low income, needy people who qualify. Generally, those who qualify are persons whose income and resources are below the limits set by state law. Technically referred to as Title XIX benefits because Medicaid is the 19th addition to the 1935 Social Security Act. (*For contrast, see: Medicare.*)

medical attendance: Treatment or care by a legally qualified physician.

medical care insurance: (*See: medical expense insurance.*)

medical care plans: A form of group insurance. (*See also: medical expense insurance.*)

Medical Impairment Bureau: Previous name for the Medical Information Bureau. (*See also: Medical Information Bureau.*)

medical examination: In life and health insurance, the physical examination of a proposed insured, usually conducted by a licensed physician or other qualified medical personnel, the results of which become part of the application, and are attached to the policy contract. The so-called nonmedical in reality is a short-form medical report and is filled out by the agent. Various company rules, such as amount of insurance applied for or already in force, age of applicant, sex, past physical history, data revealed by inspection report, etc., determine whether the examination shall be medical or nonmedical.

medical examiner: In life and health insurance, a doctor who examines applicants or claimants on behalf of, and as an agent for, the insurance company.

medical expense, blanket: (*See: blanket medical expense.*)

medical expense insurance: One of two major categories of health insurance (the other being disability income insurance), these policies cover the out-of-pocket medical costs that result from accident and sickness. The reimbursed expenses generally include hospital, doctor, surgery and dental charges. Types of coverage include *basic* and *comprehensive*. (*For contrast, see: disability income insurance.*)

Medical Information Bureau (MIB):   A service organization that collects medical data on life and health insurance applicants and stores this information for exchange among member insurance companies. Its purpose is to guard against fraud and concealment by helping the companies uncover pertinent health facts about new applicants.

medical inspection report: (*See: commercial inspection report.*)

medical insurance: Health insurance that provides payment for medical, surgical and/or hospital expenses. (*See also: medical expense insurance.*)

medical report: In life and health insurance, an information document completed by a physician or other approved examiner and submitted to an insurance company to supply medical evidence of insurability, or lack of insurability. It also includes a report of such information provided the company in relation to a claim.

Medicare: Title XVIII to the Social Security Act, a federally financed plan of medical expense health insurance for persons who qualify, primarily those over age 65. Part A, Medicare Basic Hospital Insurance, is completely paid by the federal government out of mandatory payroll taxes for social security. Benefits are predominantly hospitalization daily room and board coverage and some home health care provision. Part B, Supplemental

Medical Insurance, is financed equally by the recipient and by the federal government. Benefits are similar to a basic medical plan with some surgical coverage, equipment rental, etc.

Medicare Supplement Insurance (Medigap): Private insurance issued to fill in coverage gaps not met by Medicare.

Medigap: (*See: Medicare Supplement Insurance (Medigap).*)

medium, funding: (*See: funding medium.*)

merchandising aids: Any of an assortment of charts, brochures, pamphlets or other visuals that an agent may employ to assist him or her in selling activities.

merit rating: (*See: experience rating.*)

military service provision: A clause in some life and health insurance policies excluding losses suffered as a result of an individual's military participation. Most life insurance policies issued today have no military service clause.

Million Dollar Round Table (MDRT): An association of life insurance agents who qualify by selling at least a specified minimum face amount of life insurance (meeting certain qualification standards) in a calendar year. This requirement is adjusted annually based on increases in the cost-of-living indices.

minimum amount policy: A life insurance policy sold only in a minimum face amount or above, usually with a reduction in rate over the same form of coverage written in amounts below the minimum.

minimum compensation level: That amount of compensation an employee must earn before being eligible to participate in an employee benefit plan.

minimum deposit insurance: (*See: financed insurance.*)

minimum deposit policy: A cash value life insurance policy having a first-year loan value that is available for borrowing immediately upon payment of the first-year premium.

minimum indemnities: In accident or health insurance, minimum lump-sum benefits payable for specified losses, such as loss of fingers or toes, fractures, dislocations and sprains.

minimum pension: The minimum benefit amount payable under a pension plan. If the pension provided by formula is below a specified amount, the employer will automatically provide an additional amount to bring the pension up to this level.

minimum premium: With universal life and other flexible-premium policies, the smallest amount of premium the insurance company requires to be paid in the policy's first year. Also known as the planned annual premium or guideline premium.

minimum rate: A class rate for low hazard risks.

minor: An individual having not yet attained full legal age, which is usually defined as 18.

minor beneficiary: A beneficiary under the legal age and thus not considered competent to give a valid receipt. A legal guardian must be appointed to accept benefits on behalf of the minor beneficiary.

miscellaneous expenses: Sometimes called ancillary benefits, usually hospital charges other than room and board, including such items as x-rays, drugs, laboratory fees, etc.

misnomer: A wrong name.

misrepresentation: A false statement as to a past or present material fact made in an application for insurance intended to induce an insurance company to issue a policy it would not otherwise issue. Also refers to the actions or words of an agent who misrepresents a policy's terms, dividends, etc.

misstatement of age: Giving the wrong age for oneself in an application for insurance or for a beneficiary who is to receive benefits on a basis involving life contingency. Also, a provision in most life and health policies setting forth the action to be taken if a misstatement of age is discovered after policy issue.

mixed company: A company having capital stock, but providing in its charter that the policyowners shall share in the control of the company and in the distribution of surplus according to some definite arrangements. Most mixed companies issue both participating and nonparticipating policies.

mode of payment: The frequency with which premiums are paid (annually, semiannually, etc.).

mode premium: (*See: mode of payment.*)

modification, experience: (*See: experience modification.*)

modified coinsurance: A coinsurance agreement in life reinsurance under which the ceding insurance company retains and maintains the entire reserve, with the annual increase in the reserve (adjusted for interest) being transferred to the ceding insurance company by the reinsurer at the end of the year.

modified life: Whole life insurance with reduced premiums payable during the first few years (usually three to five) that are only slightly higher than the rate for term insurance. Thereafter, the annual premium is higher than that for a comparable whole life policy.

modified preliminary term: A modified reserving system that permits part, if not all, of the first year's net premium on a life insurance policy to be used to meet first-year acquisition costs and claim expenses, and that requires that part of the renewal loadings be added to the policy reserve accumulation.

modified premium: Any premium that is altered from the regular premium for similar life policies, such as the premium for a modified life policy.

modified refund annuity: (*See: annuity, modified refund.*)

modified reserve: Any reserving system that is altered from the full level premium reserve system.

modified split-dollar plan: A split-dollar life insurance plan which has been changed from the typical plan, usually in order to overcome problems caused by the substantial first-year premium ordinarily required by the insured employee or to maintain a level amount of insurance. (*See also: basic split-dollar plan* and *split-dollar insurance.*)

modified whole life: (*See: modified life.*)

money-purchase benefit: A type of pension plan under which contributions by both the employer and the employee are fixed as flat amounts or flat percentages of the employee's salary. Either at retirement or as contributions are paid, a benefit is provided for the employee of whatever amount the accumulated contributions or current contributions will produce for him or her, according to the premium or actuarial tables adopted. (*See also: defined contribution plan.*)

money-purchase pension plan: A qualified pension plan under which the employer is committed to make an annual contribution. From these contributions, an actuarial projection is made to determine the benefits an employee will receive at retirement.

monopolistic state fund: A state or provincial workers' compensation insurance plan that prohibits the writing of this type of coverage by private carriers.

monthly account: In insurance, a monthly accounting form required from the agent of a combination company in order to account for the premiums on monthly debit ordinary policies collected from the policyowners on the business in the agent's register.

monthly bank check: (*See: bank check plan.*)

monthly debit ordinary (MDO): Ordinary life insurance sold on a monthly premium basis, with premiums collected by the home service agent.

monthly debit ordinary status card: A computer-generated card showing the status of MDO business in force and lapsed.

monthly income contract: A combination of permanent life insurance and a decreasing term insurance rider designed to pay the face amount of the contract at the date of death and a specified monthly income to beneficiaries until a specified date, usually 10, 15, or 20 years from the date of issue of the contract. (*See also: family income policy.*)

monthly life income: (*See: annuity.*)

monthly reducing term: (*See: mortgage protection insurance.*)

morale hazard: A hazard arising from indifference to loss because of the existence of insurance. Different from moral hazard.

moral hazard: The effect of personal reputation, character, associates, personal living habits, financial responsibility, and environment, as distinguished from physical health, upon an individual's general insurability. Different from morale hazard.

moral risk: In life and health insurance, financial worth and moral condition as reviewed by a study of habits, environment, mode of living and general reputation that an underwriter must take into consideration in determining whether an applicant for insurance is a standard insurable risk. This information is usually obtained from inspection reports.

morbidity: A term that refers to sickness. (*See: morbidity tables (rates).*)

morbidity, expected: (*See: expected morbidity.*)

morbidity tables (rates): A collection of data used to estimate the amount of loss due to disability resulting from accident or sickness. These figures are used to determine health insurance rates. Similar to the mortality table used in life insurance computation.

mortality: In insurance, the relative incidence of death as measured within a given age group.

mortality, anticipated: (*See: mortality, estimated.*)

mortality, estimated: The mortality assumed in advance of actual experience for a given group over a given period, usually for an insured group for a coming year, as contrasted to that actually experienced and measured at the end of the assumed period.

mortality, expected: (*See: mortality, estimated.*)

mortality experience: The rate at which participants in a pension or insurance plan have died or are assumed to die. Also, the financial effect of the actual deaths that have occurred on the operation of a plan.

mortality, experienced: The actual mortality experienced, usually in an insured group, as contrasted to that estimated or anticipated.

mortality factor: One of the basic factors needed to calculate basic premium rates. It utilizes mortality tables in attempting to determine the average number of deaths at each specific age that will occur each year.

mortality rate, age adjusted: The incidence of death standardized for a given age in order to be useful for comparisons between different populations or within the same population during varying periods of time.

mortality rate, age specific: The ratio of deaths in a specified age group to the population of the same group during a specified period of time.

mortality rate, cause specific: The ratio of deaths from a specified cause in any given group for a given period of time.

mortality rate, crude: The ratio of total deaths to total population during a given period of time, unadjusted by age, sex or other factors.

mortality, rate of: The ratio of the number of deaths in a given group in a year's time to the total number in the group exposed to the risk of death.

mortality rate, specific-cause-of-death: *(See: mortality rate, cause specific.)*

mortality risk: The risk of death. The risk carried by a life insurance company and sometimes called the pure insurance risk. The degree of risk is the difference between the policy reserve (usually equal to the cash value of a permanent life policy) and the face amount of the policy.

mortality savings: The savings occurring when actual mortality losses are less than the amount calculated from the mortality table used.

mortality table: A listing of the mortality experience of individuals by age and sex used to estimate how long a male or female of a given age is expected to live. The mortality table is the basis for calculating the risk factor, which in turn determines the gross premium rate.

mortgage cancellation insurance: *(See: mortgage insurance.)*

mortgage disability insurance: A specific type of disability income insurance that pays benefits (often directly to the mortgage holder) during a total disability of the insured, or until the mortgage is paid up.

mortgage fund: A fund created by life insurance upon the event of a homeowner's death. *(See also: mortgage insurance and home assurance.)*

mortgage insurance: One of the basic uses for life insurance, so called because many family income earners leave insurance for the specific purpose of paying off any mortgage balance outstanding at their death. Many companies have designed special policies for this purpose. Insurance is generally made payable to a family beneficiary instead of to the mortgagee. *(See also: home assurance.)*

mortgage protection insurance: A kind of decreasing term insurance designed so the amount corresponds directly to the loan amount and length of time remaining on a mortgage. If the insured dies during the mortgage period, the insurance company pays the balance remaining on the mortgage to either the beneficiary or the mortgage company.

mortgage redemption insurance: (*See: mortgage insurance.*)

mortuary dividend: (*See: postmortem dividend.*)

mothers-fathers benefit: A Social Security benefit provided for an eligible widow or widower at any age while caring for a child eligible for a child's benefit. The benefit to the parent ceases when the child reaches age 18, unless the child is disabled.

motivating stories: In a sales interview, personal stories told by an agent to illustrate and emphasize the importance of adequate insurance coverage or of the uses of a particular plan.

multi-employer pension: A plan covering workers of two or more financially unrelated employers. Pension contributions are paid into a common fund, with benefits payable to all retired workers from the pooled assets of the fund. Employees may transfer from one participating employer to another without losing earned pension credits.

multi-line: A term used to denote an insurance company, agency or agent in the business of selling and servicing more than one type of insurance, usually life insurance and property/casualty insurance.

multiple benefits: In life or health insurance, benefits that may be doubled, tripled, or even quadrupled under certain conditions. Most commonly known as accidental death benefit or double indemnity, whereby the policy pays double the face amount if the insured dies as the direct result of an accident.

multiple employer trust: Several small groups of individuals that need life and health insurance but do not qualify for true group insurance, banded together under state trust laws to purchase insurance at a more favorable rate. Often referred to as a trust group.

multiple funding: A means of providing retirement benefits through the use of a separate fund in addition to life insurance cash values. (*See also: conversion fund (supplemental).*)

multiple indemnity: A life insurance provision stating that some or all of the benefits under a policy will be increased by a stated multiple in the event that a specific peril occurs (such as double or triple indemnity on life insurance payable for accidental death.)

multiple life policy: A life insurance policy taken out on the lives of three to five persons, with benefits payable upon the death of each person, except the last one to survive.

multiple line: (*See: multi-line.*)

multiple protection insurance: A combination of term and whole life coverage that pays some multiple of the face amount of the basic whole life portion (say $10 per month per $1,000) through-out the multiple protection period (such as to age 65).

must calls: In insurance, refers to names of people in an agent's prospect file he or she must be sure to contact during a particular week or month.

mutual benefit association: An organization offering benefits to members on a plan under which no fixed premiums are paid in advance; instead, assessments are levied on members to meet specific losses as they occur. (*See also: assessment insurance.*)

mutual company: A life insurance company that has no capital stock or stockholders, is owned by its policyowners, and is managed by a board of directors chosen by the policyowners. Any earnings in addition to those necessary for the operation of the company are returned to the policyowners in the form of policy dividends. (*For contrast, see: stock company.*)

mutual fund: An investment company that raises money by selling its own shares to the public and investing the proceeds in other equities and/or securities, with the value of its shares fluctuating with the investment experience of its portfolio. Investment companies are of two types: (1) open-end, commonly called mutual funds, in which capitalization is not fixed and more shares may be sold at any time, and (2) closed-end, in which capitalization is fixed and only the number of shares originally authorized may be sold.

mutual funds: Mutually owned funds invested in diversified equities and/or securities. Shareholders are issued certificates as evidence of their ownership and participate proportionately in the earnings of the fund.

mutual insurance company: (*See: mutual company.*)

mutual investment trust: (*See: mutual fund.*)

mutualization: The process of converting a stock insurance company to a mutual insurance company, accomplished by having the company buy in and retire its own shares.

N

naked trust: *(See: dry trust.)*

named insured: In a life or health insurance contract, the person or persons, organization, firm, or corporation specifically named as the insured(s) in the policy.

named perils: The insured events or occurrences named in a policy; the only causes of loss for which the insurance company will pay benefits. Contrasts with a policy that insures all perils except those specifically excluded.

narrow market: *(See: thin market and specific market.)*

NASD exam: Conducted under the sponsorship of the National Association of Securities Dealers, exams required of all individuals intending to deal in securities markets. Agents selling variable products must be NASD registered.

National Association of Insurance Brokers, Incorporated (NAIB): Voluntary association of insurance brokers organized for the exchange of information and recommendations to state legislatures.

National Association of Insurance Commissioners (NAIC): An association of state insurance commissioners active in solving insurance regulatory problems and in the formation and recommendation of model legislation and regulations. The aim is to achieve state-to-state uniformity so that insurance marketing on a national basis is simplified.

National Association of Insurance Commissioners Model Code: A set of rules proposed by the NAIC in 1975 to establish minimum standards and guidelines to assure full and truthful disclosure to the public of all material and relevant information in the advertising and promotion of life insurance products.

National Association of Life Companies (NALC): A voluntary association of smaller and newer life insurance companies, organized for the exchange of information and ideas.

National Association of Life Underwriters (NALU): A national organization for life insurance agents, with state and local associations throughout the country. NALU sponsors sales congresses and seminars, promotes high ethical standards, participates in community service projects and supports legislation that it deems to be in the best interests of agents, the industry and the public. Executive headquarters are in Washington, DC.

National Association of Securities Dealers (NASD): An association whose members consist of brokers and dealers handling over-the-counter securities and mutual funds. The association resulted from special legislation passed by Congress in 1938 (the Maloney Act) for the purpose of regulating the over-the-counter market.

National Fraternal Congress (NFC): A national organization of fraternal benefit societies joined together for cooperative information and action on affairs of common interest. Executive headquarters are in Chicago.

national health insurance: Any system of socialized health insurance benefits covering all or nearly all citizens, established by federal law, administered by the federal government, and supported or subsidized by taxation. Medicare and Medicaid are examples of national health insurance programs.

National Insurance Association, Incorporated (NIA): An intercompany association of insurance companies, specializing in black individual and business risks formed for the exchange of information and ideas on common problems.

National Management Award (NMA): An award of the General Agents and Managers Conference given to agency heads meeting prescribed performance standards.

National Quality Award (NQA): Presented jointly by NALU and LIMRA to agents who have placed a minimum required number of life insurance policies with a 13-month persistency rate of 90 percent or better.

National Safety Council: A nonprofit organization chartered by Congress in 1913. Made up of thousands of industry members nationwide, the purpose of the Council is the dissemination of safety education materials.

National Sales Achievement Award (NSAA): Sponsored by the NALU, a sales volume award for life insurance agents.

National Service Life Insurance (NSLI): Life insurance created by Act of Congress in 1940 to provide life insurance policies for individuals on active service with military forces. The forerunner of today's Servicemen's Group Life Insurance (SGLI), issuing term insurance to each member of the armed forces. (*See also: Servicemen's Group Life Insurance.*)

natural death: Death by means other than accident, murder or suicide.

natural group: For purposes of group insurance coverage, a natural group is defined as one organized for some purpose other than obtaining less expensive group insurance, and must have been in existence for a satisfactory period of time (usually two years) before its members are eligible for a group insurance program.

natural premium: The premium that is sufficient to pay for a given amount of insurance from one premium date to the next. A policy issued on this basis is called a yearly renewable term policy, and the net natural premium rate for it is called a yearly renewable term rate. The premium advances each year with the age of the insured. The yearly renewable term plan is usually impracticable, since at the older ages few persons can afford or are willing to pay the necessary premiums.

necessaries: With reference to the contracts of infants, things that are proper and suitable to the person according to his or her circumstances and situation in life.

need: One of the qualifying requirements for an insurance prospect. He or she must have a genuine need for insurance.

negligence: Legally, a failure to use that degree of care that an ordinary person of reasonable prudence would use under the given circumstances. Negligence may be constituted by acts of omission, commission, or both.

negligence, gross: Reckless, wanton and willful misconduct where the standard of due care of a reasonable, prudent person has been ignored by such a wide margin that it reflects an indifference to the natural and probable consequences to a degree that it almost amounts to an intentional act.

negotiable instrument: A written promise or request for payment of a certain sum of money to order or to bearer. A negotiable instrument is freely transferable, though, often by assignment or endorsement.

net amount at risk: The difference between the face amount of an insurance contract and the reserve.

net cost: A term ordinarily referring to the actual cost of insurance to a policyowner in a mutual company after the policy dividends are deducted from the premiums deposited. Since there are no dividends on nonparticipating policies, the net cost of such policies is equal to the total premiums paid. In determining the true net cost (sometimes called net ledger cost) of a life insurance policy over a period of years, allowance should also be made for the cash surrender value at the end of the given period. (*See also: net premium.*)

net earnings: Revenue from operating sources, after deduction of the operating expenses, maintenance, uncollectible revenues, and taxes applicable to operating properties or revenues, but before deduction of financial charges and generally before deduction of provisions for depreciation and retirements.

net gain from operations: The sum insurance companies account for in their convention statements as net gain from operations after dividends to policyowners, excluding capital gains and losses. Often, this sum figure is arrived at after deducting reserves in excess of the statutory requirements, which deductions might well be considered surplus charges, rather than operating expenses.

net income: The balance remaining after deducting from the gross income all operating expense, maintenance, taxes and losses, excepting interest or other financial charges on borrowed or other capital.

net increase: In insurance, issued or new business paid for, plus reinstatements, minus lapses and cancellations.

net interest earned: Average interest earned by an insurance company on its investments after investment expense, but before federal income taxes.

net level premium: The pure mortality cost of a life insurance policy from age of entry to maturity date; derived by dividing the net single premium for the policy by the present value of an annuity due of one for the premium-paying period.

net level premium reserve: The reserve needed to cover a net level premium. Generally speaking, the level premium system of paying for a long-term life or health policy involves overpayment in the early years and underpayment in the latter years.

net line: Gross line on an individual risk, less all reinsurance ceded. Also, the maximum amount of loss on a particular risk to which an insurer or reinsurer will expose itself without reinsurance or retrocession.

net loss: The amount of loss sustained by an insurance company after all claims have been met.

net lump-sum distribution: In a qualified retirement plan, the adjusted total taxable amount, minus the adjusted minimum allowance when the entire benefit or vested amount is distributed in a single payment.

net natural premium: (*See: natural premium.*)

net premium: In insurance, (1) premium paid, minus agent's commission; (2) the original premium, minus any returned premium; (3) the net charge for insurance cost only, minus expenses or contingencies; (4) a participating premium, minus dividends paid or anticipated.

net premium rate: The insurance premium rate that, with interest, will produce a fund sufficiently large enough to pay the total of all benefits becoming payable under the policies concerned—that is, a premium that provides for the payment of claims only, with no allowance for expenses. It is the amount of the premium before loading for expense.

net premiums, gross: (*See: gross net premiums.*)

net profits: A term broadly used to describe only the profits remaining after including all earnings and other income or profit and after deducting all expenses and charges of every character, including interest, depreciation, and taxes.

net rate: The actual rate paid by a policyowner for a participating insurance policy after dividends have been deducted from the total premiums paid. In a nonparticipating policy, the rate stated in the rate book.

net retained line: (*See: net line.*)

net retention: (*See: net line.*)

net surplus: Earnings remaining with a business after all operating expenses, taxes, interest and dividends have been paid. Surplus would exist before dividends are deducted; net surplus, after deducting dividends.

net taxable estate: Adjusted gross estate, less any allowable marital, orphan's or charitable deduction.

net worth: Value of a business calculated by subtracting its total liabilities from its total assets. Also referred to as the book value of a business.

new business: A term describing the amount of new insurance policies issued by an insurance company during a particular period of time.

new business commission register: A list furnished by some insurance companies to the agent, reporting the transactions affecting his or her commissions.

new money interest rate: (*See: investment year method of dividend calculation.*)

new policy option: An option to purchase additional insurance at the end of an extra protection period, regardless of health or occupation. Commonly referred to as guaranteed purchase option.

newspaper policies: Limited accident policies, usually purchased through a newspaper as a part of a subscription.

New York interest: Interest computed by the exact number of days in a month, rather than by use of a 30-day month, etc.

next of kin: One or more persons in the nearest degree of relationship to another person. Legally, those related by blood, as opposed to those related by marriage.

NFC Mortality Table: National Fraternal Congress Table of Mortality, prepared in 1898 for fraternal insurance in order to establish better mortality and lapse experience.

1937 Standard Annuity Table: An annuity table constructed on the assumption that women on the average outlive men by five years. Based on this assumption, it used a five-year set back for women.

nominator: In insurance, one who provides a referred lead, that is, gives the name (often with qualifying information) of a prospective buyer of insurance or a prospective recruit.

nominator's clause: (*See: payor insurance.*)

nonadmitted assets: In insurance, assets by general accounting standards that do not qualify under state law for insurance reserve purposes, such as furniture, fixtures, bonds in default, certain securities, etc.

nonadmitted carrier: (*See: nonadmitted company.*)

nonadmitted company: A company not licensed to do business in a particular state. Also called an unauthorized company. (*For contrast, see: admitted company.*)

nonadmitted reinsurance: Reinsurance for which no credit is given in the ceding company's annual report, because the reinsurer is not licensed to do business in the ceding company's jurisdiction.

nonassessable contract or policy: A policy that limits the liability of policyowners to the amount of premiums paid. The policyowners cannot be assessed additional premiums or amounts.

nonassignable contract or policy: A policy that the owner cannot legally assign to a third party.

noncan: (*See: noncancelable health insurance policy.*)

noncancellable disability insurance: Usually, disability insurance that may be continued at the option of the insured to a specified age, such as to age 60. Disability insurance that may not be canceled by the carrier during the period for which the policy is written, e.g., one year.

noncancellable health insurance policy: A health policy that the insured has the right to continue in force (by the payment of premiums as set forth in the contract) for a substantial period of time, during which period the insurance company has no unilateral right to make any change in any provision or cancel the policy. Both the premium and renewability are guaranteed. Also called noncancellable and guaranteed renewable.

non compos mentis: Not sound in mind.

nonconfining sickness: An illness that prevents the insured from working, but does not confine the insured to his or her home, a hospital, or a sanitarium.

noncontributory plan: Any employee plan or program of insurance (usually group) in which the employer pays the entire premium and the employer-insured contributes no part of the premium.

noncontributory retirement plan: Any plan or program of employee retirement benefits for which the employer pays the entire cost.

nonconvertible term insurance: A term policy that may not be converted to a permanent policy.

nondeductible: An item or amount that cannot be deducted for tax purposes. In health insurance, nondeductible describes the type of coverage that has no deductible amount; the insurance pays benefits starting with the first dollar of covered expense.

nondisabling injury: An injury that does not prevent the insured from the degree of activity or employment specified in the contract to qualify for total or partial disability benefits. A disability income policy may contain a provision for a small benefit in case of such injury, such as medical costs up to 25–50 percent of one month's disability benefit payment.

nonduplication of payments (or benefits): A provision in some health insurance policies specifying that benefits will not be paid for amounts reimbursed by other insurance companies or for which no reimbursement is legally required. In group insurance, usually called coordination of benefits (COB).

nonearned income: Income acquired other than from working at an occupation. Investment returns, for instance, are nonearned income. (*See also: unearned income.*)

nonforfeitable: A vested benefit, payable to a participant or a beneficiary under an immediate or deferred benefit retirement plan that unconditionally belongs to a participant of the plan and that is legally enforceable against the plan.

nonforfeiture options or provisions: In life insurance, refers to privileges allowed under terms of the contract after cash values have been created. Four privileges exist: (1) surrender for full cash value; (2) loans up to full amount of cash value; (3) paid-up policy for amount of insurance, which cash value, as a single premium, will buy at net rates; (4) term insurance for full face amount of original policy for as long a period as cash value will pay net premiums. (*See also: nonforfeiture values.*)

nonforfeiture values: Those values or benefits in a life insurance policy that by law, the policyowner does not forfeit, even if he or she chooses to discontinue payment of premiums; usually cash value, loan value, paid-up insurance value, and extended term insurance value. (*See also: nonforfeiture options or provisions.*)

noninsurable risk: A risk that cannot be measured actuarially or for which the chance of loss is so high that insurance cannot be written against it.

noninsurance: A situation in which no financial preparation (including self-insurance) has been made for meeting losses.

noninsured plans: Retirement plans that are not guaranteed through insurance or annuity contracts. Instead, an uninsured plan would generally use such funding vehicles as government bonds, face-amount certificates, mutual fund shares, etc.

non-ledger assets: Assets due and payable in the current year but not yet received and, hence, not yet entered on the bookkeeping ledger.

nonliquid assets: Assets that are not readily convertible into cash. Such assets cannot easily be used to help defray estate administration costs. Examples include residences, automobiles and furnishings.

nonmedical: The term applied to the medical portion of a life insurance application that accepts a health questionnaire completed on the applicant over his or her signature and does not require a medical examination.

nonmedical insurance: Life insurance issued on a regular basis without requiring the applicant to submit to a medical examination. In deciding to issue the policy, the company relies on the applicant's own answers to questions regarding his or her physical condition, and on personal references or inspection reports.

nonmedical report: A form completed by the applicant, giving certain information as to health, etc., required by an insurance company for issuance of insurance when a medical examination is not required.

nonoccupational insurance: Health insurance that covers off-the-job accidents and sickness, also referred to as unemployment compensation disability insurance. A policy that does not cover disability resulting from injury or sickness that is covered by workers' compensation insurance.

nonpar: *(See: nonparticipating life insurance* and *guaranteed cost.)*

nonparticipating fund: That proportion of the assets of a stock insurance company selling participating insurance that is equal to the sum of the liabilities of the nonparticipating operations and surplus allocated to the nonparticipating operations.

nonparticipating fund ratio: In life insurance, the ratio of the nonparticipating fund to the total funds of the company in a stock company selling participating life insurance.

nonparticipating life insurance: Life insurance that does not pay policy dividends and under which the policyowner is not entitled to share in any divisible surplus of the company. Any profits from the excess of the premium over the costs of insurance accrue to stockholders; stockholders also absorb any losses. Generally, the premiums for nonparticipating contracts are lower than for comparable participating contracts, although the net cost may be higher after it is in force for some years. *(For contrast, see: participating insurance.)*

nonparticipating stock company: A stock company currently issuing only nonparticipating life insurance. Such a company may also have a block of participating business in force if it once sold participating insurance or for other reasons.

nonprobate property: Property that does not pass under the decedent's will (or under the local intestacy laws), such as joint tenancy property and life insurance proceeds. Nonprobate property is not included in the decedent's estate for tax purposes.

nonprofit corporation: A corporation organized solely for charitable, educational, humanitarian, or other such limited purposes and not as a profit-making business. A major advantage of a qualified nonprofit corporation is exemption from income taxes; however, it is liable for other taxes to the extent the corporation has income-yielding property or operations. Also known as not-for-profit corporation

nonprofit insurance company: A corporation organized under special state laws to provide hospital, medical, or dental insurance on a nonprofit basis.

nonproportional insurance: Life reinsurance whereby the reinsurer makes payments to the ceding company only after the ceding company's claims exceed a preset aggregate loss limit.

nonproportional reinsurance: A form of life reinsurance under which the reinsurer makes claim payments to the ceding company when the ceding company's claims exceed a predetermined aggregate loss limit, as distinguished from cases where the reinsurer participates in paying claims proportionate to those made by the ceding company on each policy reinsured.

non-prorating policy: An insurance policy in which the benefits stipulated in the policy will be paid whether or not the insured changes his or her occupation.

nonqualified assets: Property that does not qualify for the federal estate or gift tax marital deduction.

nonqualified deferred compensation plan: A pension plan that fails to meet or was not intended to meet the qualifications set forth in Section 401(a) of the Internal Revenue Code of 1954.

nonqualified pension plan: A pension plan not meeting the requirements of the Internal Revenue Code, presently Sections 401 through 405. This type of plan is disadvantageous taxwise, although in a given instance it may have offsetting advantages.

nonrecurring expense: An unusual expense or loss that is unlikely to be repeated.

nonrefund annuity: An annuity providing the annuitant with a fixed income for life, but stipulating that upon the death of the annuitant no further payments will be made.

nonrenewable contract: An agreement or policy written for a specific period and purpose and that does not contain an option to be renewed for successive terms. (*For contrast, see: renewable and convertible term* and *renewable term insurance.*)

nonresident: An individual who does not reside within a specified geographic boundary (e.g., a state).

nonresident agent: An agent licensed in a state or territory in which he or she is not a resident

nonstock corporation: A type of nonprofit corporation, such as religious, charitable, mutual insurance or municipal corporations, in which members hold no stock.

nontransferable: A contract in which the benefits or any of its value cannot be sold, assigned, discounted or pledged as collateral for a loan or as security for the performance of an obligation or for any other purpose, to any person other than the insurance company.

nonwaiver agreement: In insurance, a stipulation by the insurance company that investigation and determination of the value of a claim does not constitute an admission that the insurance company has assumed liability.

nonworking spouse: Designation given to a husband or wife who receives no earned income.

noon clause: The provision in some insurance contracts stating at what time the insurance coverage starts (usually noon standard time in the time zone of the insured).

no refund annuity: (*See: annuity, life.*)

no right of withdrawal: Refers to money placed in a retirement income plan that the intended income recipient cannot receive or withdraw until the determined time, usually retirement.

normal cost: In insurance, the current year's premium based on the level annual premium. In retirement and qualified pension plans, the deposit requirement, based upon the date the participant first became, or the date he or she would have become, eligible to participate.

normal retirement age: The designated age or time of retirement stipulated under provisions of a specific plan.

normal retirement benefit: The greater of an employee's early retirement benefit from a plan or the benefit payable at the time of his or her normal retirement age. The value of the benefits is determined without regard to medical and/or disability benefits.

not-for-profit corporation: (*See: nonprofit corporation.*)

notice of claim provision: A mandatory health insurance provision stating that the policyowner must submit written notice of a loss to the insurance company within twenty days, or as soon after that period of time as is reasonably possible.

notice of expiration: (*See: expiration notice.*)

notice to company: In insurance, written notice to the insurance company of the occurrence of an event on which a claim is to be based.

not taken: In insurance, a policy that has been issued but not accepted or paid for by the prospective policyowner and, therefore, is returned to the insurance company without ever having been in force.

no value: With respect to insurance policies, one that is out of benefit and has no monetary value remaining.

null and void: Of no legal or binding force.

numerical rating: A life insurance underwriting method for determining the extra rate to be charged a substandard insured. Standard is rated 100. Various impairments are assigned different numerical values. The sum of 100 plus the value(s) of the ratings of the impairments indicates the table to use in determining the rate of the policy.

nurse fees: (*See: nursing expense provision.*)

nursing expense provision: In health insurance, provides per diem benefits to the insured if that individual requires nursing care. The nurse generally must be a private duty registered nurse (RN) and not a member of the insured's immediate family.

nursing home insurance: A medical expense health insurance policy offered primarily to senior citizens to provide residential and/ or convalescent nursing home care. The NAIC bill, accepted by most states, requires that a nursing home policy that covers only convalescent care, must have that limitation stated clearly on the face of the policy.

nursing home provision: In health insurance, provides benefits of some specified amount if the insured is confined to a nursing home when no longer needing inhospital care.

O

objections: With respect to the selling of insurance, questions or concerns raised by prospects during the agent's presentation—sometimes validly, sometimes as a means of evasion. (*See also: objections in the interview* and *objections to the interview.*)

objections in the interview: In insurance selling, concerns or negative statements expressed to the agent by the prospect regarding the agent's recommendations. (*See also: objections.*)

objections to the interview: In selling insurance, objections raised by the prospect to granting the agent an interview.

obligatory treaty: In insurance, a reinsurance contract under which the business covered by the contract must be ceded by the ceding company in accordance with specific contract terms and must be accepted by the reinsurer.

occupational accident: An accident arising out of or occurring in the course of one's employment and caused by hazards inherent to or related thereto.

occupational classification: Groupings of occupations by equivalent degrees of inherent hazard to which they are subject. Various systems of classifications are used by different insurance companies for purposes of underwriting and rating health insurance policies in particular.

occupational disease (or sickness): Impairment of health not caused by accident, but by exposure to conditions arising out of or in the course of one's employment.

occupational hazard: A danger inherent in the insured's line of work.

occupational injury (or sickness):   An injury or sickness arising out of, or in the course of, one's employment.

occupational manual: A book listing occupational classifications for various types of work.

occupational policy: In insurance, a plan that insures a person against both off-the-job and on-the-job accidents or sicknesses.

Occupational Safety and Health Act (OSHA):   A federal law, originally enacted in 1971 that mandates specific health and safety standards in places of employment. Inspections revealing violations can result in fines and corrective measures.

Occupational Safety and Health Administration (OSHA):   The branch of the Department of Labor responsible for administration of the Occupational Safety and Health Act.

occupational sickness: *(See: occupational disease (or sickness).)*

occupation provision: *(See: change of occupation provision.)*

occurrence: In accident or health insurance, an accident or sickness that results in an insured loss.

odds: The probable number of incidents of a given occurrence in a statistical universe or representative sample, expressed as a ratio to the probable number of nonoccurrences. *(See also: probability.)*

offer: In insurance terminology, the applicant's signing and submitting a written application for life insurance, accompanied by the first premium. *(See also: offer and acceptance.)*

offer and acceptance: As applied to life and health insurance, (1) the offer may be made by the applicant through signing of an application, submitting to a physical examination, and prepaying the first premium. Policy issuance and delivery, as applied for, constitute acceptance by the company. Or (2) the offer may be made by the company, where no premium payment has been submitted with application and medical. Premium payment on the offered policy then constitutes acceptance by the applicant.

offeree: One to whom an offer is made.

offeror: One who makes an offer.

office, branch: *(See: branch office.)*

Old Age and Survivors Disability Insurance: The actual name for Social Security, a United States federal system of social insurance benefits for aged workers and their eligible family members, eligible surviving family members of deceased workers, and disabled workers and their eligible family members, set up by the 1935 Social Security law, with compulsory participation for all eligible persons, and with benefits and contribution rates determined by schedule and/or formulas provided by Congress.

Old Age and Survivors Insurance: The retirement and death benefits under U.S. Social Security.

old-age benefit for spouse of worker: Under U.S. Social Security, a monthly benefit paid to the wife or husband of an individual who is receiving old-age benefits, provided the spouse has been married to that individual for at least one year (or if they are the natural or adoptive parents of a mutual child).

Old Age Security: In Canada, the equivalent to U.S. Social Security. Provides a monthly pension for all persons over age 65 who meet residency requirements. It is financed out of federal general tax revenues, with no contributions from individuals. Benefits reportable for income tax purposes.

older age policy: In health insurance, medical care policy issued to persons 65 years of age or over to supplement government-sponsored programs such as Medicare.

old line: A term without precise meaning, but generally applied to nonfraternal insurance companies operating on a legal reserve basis. A legal reserve fraternal is not usually called old line unless it gives up its lodge system and moves under the regular insurance code of the state rather than the special section for fraternals. (Origin of the term is in doubt but seems to have developed usage at the time of competition between the new fraternal and commercial insurance companies to connote the fact that the fraternals were newcomers.)

old line company: A life insurance company that sells insurance on a level premium, legal reserve basis.

old line legal reserve: Refers to legal reserve companies selling commercial life insurance, as opposed to fraternal insurance.

old line life: Legal reserve insurance companies writing insurance with standard premiums, as opposed to assessment insurance available through fraternal benefit societies.

140 percent rule: In employee retirement plans, a rule stating that, when an individual is a participant in both a defined benefit plan and a defined contribution plan maintained by the same employer, the sum of the defined benefit plan fraction and the defined contribution plan fraction for any one year may not exceed 1.4 (which translates into 140 percent). This fractional amount was revised by TEFRA in 1982, which sets the aggregate limit at 1.0 or 100 percent.

one-year term dividend option: *(See: fifth dividend option.)*

onus (onus propondi): The burden of proof.

open account: *(See: open debit.)*

open agency: *(See: open debit.)*

open certificate: In insurance, a policy under which the rates and policy provisions may be changed. Fraternal benefit societies are required by law to issue this type of certificate. *(See also: open policy.)*

open cover: In insurance, a reinsurance facility under which risks of a specified category may be declared and insured.

open debit: A life or health insurance debit territory or book of business currently without an agent. Most commonly refers to home service insurance.

open-end policy: *(See: open certificate.)*

open-end question: In a sales interview, a question that elicits an opinion from the prospect or that requires more than a simple yes or no response.

open policy: An insurance contract on a specified risk or group of risks, in which the amount and terms are not specified, and under which reports of individual amounts insured and periods of coverage are made to the insurance company by the insured. More properly called open certificate. *(See also: open certificate.)*

operating expenses, general: *(See: general operating expenses.)*

operations: In insurance, the normal activities of an insurance company or agency in the course of conducting its business.

option: A choice between two or more courses of action. In life insurance, a choice of methods of receiving or applying policy dividends, nonforfeiture values, death benefits, or cash values, etc. Under pension plans, this often refers to choices available to participants, such as that of retiring before normal retirement age on an actuarially reduced pension or of choosing some other type of annuity actuarially equivalent to the normal type which they would otherwise receive under the plan.

optional benefit: In insurance, an additional benefit offered by the company, which may be included in a policy at the applicant's request, usually for an additional premium. Waiver of premium and accidental death benefit riders are examples of optional benefits.

optional indemnities: *(See: elective indemnities.)*

optionally renewable contract: In health insurance, a contract in which the insurance company reserves the right to terminate the coverage at any anniversary date or, in some cases, at any premium-due date, but does not have the right to terminate coverage between such dates. It can be renewed at the option of the insurance company.

optional modes of settlement: *(See: settlement options.)*

optional paid-up insurance: In life insurance, one of the guaranteed nonforfeiture options in a policy, under which the cash reserves of the policy are used to buy single premium paid-up insurance at the attained age.

optional provisions: *(See: Uniform Provision Law.)*

optional settlements: *(See: settlement options.)*

option, dividend: In life insurance, an option whereby the insured is given a choice as to how policy dividends are to be applied or paid.

option, fifth dividend: *(See: fifth dividend option.)*

option, interest: *(See: interest only option.)*

option, nonforfeiture: *(See: nonforfeiture options or provisions.)*

options, dividend: *(See: dividend options.)*

options of payment: *(See: settlement options.)*

ordinary agency: A life insurance agency handling mainly ordinary life insurance. *(See also: ordinary insurance.)*

ordinary agent: A term used to distinguish those life insurance agents not involved in personally collecting premiums from their home service counterparts. The opposite of ordinary agent is home service agent, debit agent, combination agent or industrial agent, all of whom are involved directly in premium collection.

ordinary annuity: *(See: annuity.)*

ordinary insurance: One of the three main categories of life insurance (ordinary, group and industrial). Ordinary life insurance consists of permanent (whole life, endowment, universal life, variable universal life and other interest-sensitive cash value plans) and temporary (term) types of coverage.

ordinary insurance account: In a combination life insurance company, the amount of ordinary insurance in force in the account of an agent.

ordinary insurance company: An insurance company that issues mainly ordinary life insurance and does not issue home service or industrial policies.

ordinary life insurance: *(See: ordinary insurance.)*

ordinary life insurance, group: Level premium ordinary life insurance issued on a group basis.

ordinary life pension trust: A trust-funded pension plan that provides death benefits through the purchase of ordinary or whole life insurance contracts for covered employees. The trust pays premiums on the insurance coverage until the employee reaches retirement age. The trust also accumulates, in an auxiliary fund, the additional sums necessary to purchase the retirement benefits of the plan for the employees, using the paid-up value of the life insurance policy for each employee as part of the purchase price of the annuity.

ordinary life—whole life—straight life: These three terms are synonymous and are applied to the type of life insurance policy that continues during the whole of the insured's life and provides for the payment of amount insured at death, or at age 100 if the insured is still living at that age.

ordinary register: In insurance, a record book in a combination company or agency, containing data on the ordinary policies in an agent's account.

original age conversion: *(See: conversion, original age.)*

orphan: In insurance terminology, a policy or policyowner not being actively serviced by the selling agent. This could be because the selling agent has been transferred, moved to the home office, left the company, died, retired, etc.—or because the policyowner has moved from where the policy was purchased to another city or part of the country.

other insurance: In health insurance, the existence of one or more other contracts covering the same interests and perils as the one for which application is or has been made. If duplicating other insurance exists, benefits are paid proportionately from all policies so the insured does not realize a profit from the loss.

other insurance clause: A provision found in almost every insurance policy, except life (and sometimes health) insurance contracts, stating what is to be done in case any other contract of insurance provides the same coverage or covers essentially the same thing. (*See also: nonduplication of payments (or benefits).*)

outpatient: A person who receives care at a clinic or hospital without being admitted to that facility as an overnight or resident patient.

outstanding business: In life and health insurance, business issued but not yet placed in force by payment of the first premium.

outstanding claims account: (*See: funding of reserves.*)

outstanding premiums: Insurance premiums due but not yet collected.

oustanding receipts: In insurance, receipts held in file, either at the home office or collection office, awaiting payment of premiums due.

over-age insurance: Health insurance issued at ages above those for which such insurance is usually issued, mainly above 65. (*See also: older age policy.*)

overall property tax limitation: A constitutional or statutory limitation on the total amount of taxes that may be levied for all purposes against any parcel of real estate within one year, such overall limit to be a fixed percentage of the true value of the property. It is so called to distinguish it from the limitations on separate portions of the real estate tax now in effect in nearly all states.

overhead: Charges of a fairly fixed nature that do not vary with the volume of sales activity. Charges for electricity, water, heat, insurance, rent, and some taxes are overhead items.

overhead expense policy: A form of disability income insurance designed to pay specified, ongoing business expenses during the owner's disability.

overhead writing: The practice by an insurer of accepting business from a broker or agent other than an agent who has an exclusive territorial agreement.

overinsurance: An excessive amount of insurance carried by an insured, which might create a temptation, to cause loss deliberately or to prolong disability or hospital stay. Insurance companies place provisions in some health policies to limit liability in situations of overinsurance.

overlapping insurance: Coverage from two or more policies or insurance companies, that duplicates coverage of certain hazards or risks, at least in part.

over-line: The amount of insurance or reinsurance exceeding the insurer's or reinsurer's normal capacity, inclusive of automatic reinsurance facilities. Also, a commitment by an insurer or reinsurer above and beyond its normal facilities or capacity.

overloading: Selling an individual more insurance than his or her insurable worth justifies or for an amount of premium greater than the applicant's ability to pay.

overriding commission: Commission paid to a general agent, special agent, agent, or manager in addition to the commission paid the agent or broker who secures the application or renewal of the contract.

over-the-counter selling: In insurance, a nonagency system of marketing whereby the insured obtains insurance by going directly to the insurance company. Savings bank life insurance departments and certain direct writers engage in over-the-counter selling.

overwriting: (*See: overriding commission.*)

owner: In life and health insurance, the person designated as the owner of the policy, with all rights contained in the policy. The owner is so designated on the policy application and may or may not be the insured. Also referred to as the *policyowner* or *policyholder.*

owner-employee: With respect to Keogh or HR 10 plans, a self-employed person who is a sole proprietor or who owns more than a 10 percent interest in a partnership.

ownership insurance: A policy in which all rights are vested in a corporation or person other than the insured. Business insurance is a common type of ownership insurance.

ownership of expirations: A company agreement, ordinarily found in the life and health fields, stating that certain details of a policy (such as expiration) will not be revealed to any other agent or broker except the originating agent, thus permitting the original agent to contact the client for renewal or extension of a policy.

ownership provision: A provision stating that the policy may be owned by a person other than the insured. This is frequently applicable to business life insurance, or to juvenile life insurance during the insured's early years.

owner waiver of premium benefit: In life insurance, a rider attached to a juvenile policy in which the insured is not the owner that waives future premiums upon the death of the owner or during a period of total disability of the owner prior to a specific age of the insured child, e.g., 21. (*See also: payor insurance.*)

P

package policies: Insurance policies offering several coverages (such as mortgage protection, juvenile insurance, etc.) included in one contract.

paid additions, full: (*See: dividend additions.*)

paid business: A term used to describe new life or health insurance that has been issued, upon which the first premium has been paid, and that is in force.

paid expenses: (*See: expenses paid.*)

paid for: (*See: paid business.*)

paid for credit: In insurance agency accounting, the amount assigned to each policy in determining production and compensation.

paid-in-advance: In life insurance, premiums that are paid before they become due, usually at a discount.

paid-up: A policy on which no future payments are to be made and under which the company is held liable for the benefits provided under the terms of the contract. A life insurance policy upon which no further premiums are due, but that continues to remain in force.

paid-up additions: A dividend option stating that the policyowner may obtain full-paid additional insurance by using policy dividends on a net single premium basis at the insured's attained insurance age.

paid-up insurance: (*See: paid-up policy.*)

paid-up life insurance, group: (*See: group paid-up life insurance.*)

paid-up policy: Insurance on which the policyowner has completed payments, but that has not yet matured. This may be either (1) reduced paid-up insurance provided under the nonforfeiture provision; (2) a limited payment policy under which all premiums have been paid; or (3) a policy on which accumulated dividends are applied to pay the net single premium required to pay up the difference between the policy's reduced paid-up insurance and its face amount.

paid-up values: In life insurance, one of the nonforfeiture values of a permanent policy. At any time, the policyowner may stop making premium payments and use the cash value built up in the contract to buy a reduced paid-up policy.

par: (*See: participating insurance.*)

parent company: In insurance, the senior company in an insurance group or a fleet of insurance companies.

parent's benefit: Under Social Security, a monthly benefit, beginning at age 62 paid to each eligible parent of a deceased, fully insured worker, if the parent was at least 50 percent dependent upon the worker at the time of the worker's death.

parent-subsidiary group: A group of two or more companies where the parent company owns at least 80 percent interest in the subsidiary corporation or partnership or 100 percent interest in a subsidiary sole proprietorship. The parent may be incorporated or unincorporated.

partial disability: In health insurance, an illness or injury that prevents an insured from performing a significant part, but not all, of his or her occupational duties. Disability income policies often provide partial disability benefits. (*For contrast, see: total disability.*)

partial vesting: In an employee retirement plan, immediate or deferred vesting under which a designated portion of the accrued benefits of a participant become vested. This is only applicable if benefits under the plan are attributable to specific years of service or if the application of the vesting definition is clearly worked out in the plan.

partial withdrawals (surrenders): In variable universal life insurance policies, the policyowner's right to remove a portion of the accumulated cash value. Partial withdrawals may incur a surrender charge and/or a processing fee.

participant: In an employee benefit plan, any employee or former employee who is eligible to receive benefits from the plan or whose beneficiaries may be eligible to receive benefits from the plan. Also, any member of a group plan or employee welfare plan as defined by ERISA.

participating insurance: A plan of insurance, often issued by mutual companies, under which the insured receives a portion of the surplus of the company, called dividends. The dividends represent the difference between the premiums charged and the actual costs (reflecting claims, expenses, earnings, etc.) experienced during the period for which the premiums were charged. *(For contrast, see: nonparticipating life insurance.)*

participating profits: In a stock life insurance company selling participating policies, the participating branch's share of net gain from operations before dividends to participating policyowners are paid.

participating spread: In insurance, the excess of the premium rate for a participating policy over the premium rate for an otherwise comparable nonparticipating policy.

participating surplus: In life insurance, the portion of a stock company's surplus allocated to the participating branch.

participation: Generally refers to membership in an employee benefit plan. It is frequently used in connection with contributory pension plans. Although all employees may be covered by a plan in the sense that they may eventually be entitled to participate, some may not participate because they have not yet met the age or service eligibility conditions or, if participation is voluntary, because they do not wish to contribute.

partnership: A form of doing business that enables two or more people to strengthen their own effectiveness by working together as co-owners of a business. It recognizes each partner's assets and talents, and ties together individual skills, sales ability, production knowledge, capital, etc., into a single, productive enterprise.

partnership entity: The partnership considered as an entity and not in terms of its individual part owners.

partnership entity plan: A buy-sell agreement providing that upon the death of a partner, the partnership will purchase that person's share of the business, and the deceased partner's estate will sell its share to the partnership. The premiums for insurance funding an insured plan are payable by the partnership out of income and any cash value of the insurance.

partnership, general: *(See: general partnership.)*

partnership insurance: *(See: business insurance* and *buy-sell agreement.)*

part-time employees: Legally and for purposes of benefits, refers to those employees who work less than 1,000 hours for an employer in a calendar year. Such employees need not be included in qualified retirement plans.

party-in-interest: With respect to an employee benefit plan, any individual who works with the plan and serves as a fiduciary, counsel or who is an employee of an employee benefit plan; or any person providing service to such a plan; or the employer who establishes such a plan; or an employee organization whose members are covered by such a plan; or an owner of 50 percent or more of a company that establishes an employee benefit plan. The term also includes relatives of the above group and any employee, officer, director, or a 10 percent or more shareholder of an employer that establishes an employee benefit plan.

passive trust: A trust in which the trustee has no active duty to perform.

past service: With respect to an employee retirement plan, service rendered prior to the adoption of the plan for which retirement benefit credit will be given. *(See also: current service.)*

past service benefit: In an employee retirement plan, retirement benefit credits that are provided by the employer and are for all or part of the individual's years of service with the company prior to the adoption of the plan. Also, that portion of a participant's retirement benefit that relates to the period of credited service before the effective date of the plan.

past service costs: In an employee retirement plan, the amount required at a particular time to meet all future benefits provided under the plan and not funded by future normal costs and employee contributions with respect to the employees covered by the plan at that time.

past service credits: In an employee retirement plan, retirement benefit credits provided for years of an employee's service before the plan was adopted. Such credits may be limited to a specified number of years before the plan became effective.

past service funding: In an employee retirement plan, a method of funding the past service liability in the plan, with the cost sometimes amortized over a period of years. The employer may not deduct more than one-tenth of the original liability in any one year for income tax purposes.

past service liability: In an employee retirement plan, the cost of providing retirement benefits for service rendered prior to the adoption of the plan. The cost, which is determined actuarially, will depend upon the age and years of service of the working force and upon the number of years of past service that are credited under the plan, as well as other factors.

past service liability, freezing: *(See: freezing past service liability.)*

pay: In life insurance, abbreviation for *payment* as in *20-pay life policy.* Also, compensation, which may be defined in a variety of ways. For example, under a unit credit pension plan, the employee's compensation and service are generally explained as a certain percent of pay per year of credited service irrespective of the percentage used, the definition of pay will make a considerable difference in the dollar benefit result.

pay-as-you-go funding: *(See: current disbursement and funding, disbursement.)*

pay-as-you-go plan: With respect to an employee retirement plan, an informal term referring to a plan in which the employer pays benefits out of current income as they become due. There is no advance funding.

payee: The recipient of a payment.

payee clause: In insurance, a clause in the contract providing for payment of loss to a person or class of persons.

payee, contingent: *(See: contingent beneficiary.)*

payment, ex gratia: *(See: ex gratia payment.)*

payment of claims provision: A mandatory health insurance policy provision that states to whom the insurance company must pay any claims.

payments, deferred: *(See: deferred payments.)*

payment to the estate: In life insurance, designating the insured's estate as a policy beneficiary, as opposed to designating an individual or organization. This practice eliminates many of the tax advantages available for insurance proceeds.

payor: In life and health insurance, the person who pays the premiums on a policy. Also, the applicant for or in a juvenile life policy.

payor benefit: (*See: payor insurance.*)

payor insurance: In life insurance, an optional coverage available with certain juvenile policies upon payment of an extra premium; it provides for the waiver of future premiums in event the person responsible for the payment of the premiums dies or is disabled before (1) the policy on the child becomes fully paid or matures as a death claim or as an endowment or (2) the child reaches a specified age. (*See also: payor provision.*)

payor provision: In a juvenile life insurance policy a provision that provides that, in the event the payor (usually a parent of the insured child) dies or becomes totally disabled, the policy becomes paid-up or the premiums are waived until the insured reaches a certain age.

payroll audit: With respect to insured employee benefit plans, an examination of the insured's payroll records by a representative of the insurance company to determine the premium due on a policy.

payroll deduction: In insurance, an arrangement whereby premiums on employees' insurance are deducted directly from the workers' wages and forwarded to the insurance company by the employer. Also used to indicate similar handling of employee contributions to an employee benefit plan.

payroll deduction insurance: (*See: salary allotment insurance.*)

payroll savings life insurance: (*See: salary allotment insurance.*)

pecuniary legacy: A bequest of a sum of money or of an annuity. It may or may not specify the fund from which it is to be drawn.

penalty tax: In certain qualified retirement plans, a tax imposed on excess contributions made above an approved limit, as in a Keogh plan or an IRA.

Pen Ben: (*See: Pension Benefit Guaranty Corporation.*)

pension: An income paid by an employer and/or the government (say, Social Security) to a worker who has retired because of age or disability.

pension annuity: (*See: retirement annuity.*)

Pension Benefit Guaranty Corporation: A nonprofit corporation within the Department of Labor, set up to insure participants in, and beneficiaries of, covered plans against the loss of benefits arising from a premature termination of a retirement plan.

pension benefit plan, employee: (*See: employee pension benefit plan.*)

pension committee: In an employee pension plan, a designated group having supervisory authority over the operation of the plan within the organization. May be composed solely of management representatives or may also include union representation.

pension, disability: (*See: disability pension.*)

pension funding: (*See: funding.*)

pension, normal cost: Under a pension plan, the normal costs for operating and maintaining the plan for any year. This is the actuarially determined cost, considering; (1) if the plan has been in effect from the beginning of service of each of the present participants; (2) the costs of prior years have been paid; and (3) all assumptions as to interest, mortality, time of payment, etc., have been fulfilled.

pension plan: A plan established and maintained by an employer to provide retirement benefits to employees with favorable tax treatment for the employer and the employees. Frequently funded by insurance plans. Sections 401 through 419 of the Internal Revenue Code established requirements for a qualified plan and set forth the tax treatment thereof.

pension plan, aggregate cost method: (*See: aggregate method.*)

pension plan, compensation: (*See: compensation.*)

pension plan, defined benefit: (*See: defined benefit plan.*)

pension plan, defined contribution: (*See: defined contribution plan.*)

pension plan, deposit administration: (*See: deposit administration plan.*)

pension plan, disability retirement benefits: (*See: disability retirement benefits.*)

pension plan, funded: (*See: funded pension plan.*)

pension plan, insured: (*See: insured pension plan.*)

pension plan, money-purchase: (*See: money-purchase pension plan.*)

pension plan, past service costs: (*See: past service costs.*)

pension plan, past service credits: (*See: past service credits.*)

pension plan, qualified: (*See: qualified pension plan.*)

pension plan, retroactive disapproval: (*See: retroactive disapproval.*)

pension plan, self-administered: (*See: self-insured pension plan.*)

pension plan, self-insured: (*See: self-insured pension plan.*)

pension plan trustee: If a pension plan is self-administered, the employer must irrevocably part with his or her contribution by giving the funds to an independent entity, usually a trustee, who administers the plan. Funds must be invested; benefits must be paid to beneficiaries under the terms of the plan; funds may have to be borrowed to meet claims; and property other than securities must be managed and operated. The trustee accounts to the creator of the trust, usually the employer, and to the trust beneficiaries.

pension pool: A pension plan in which a number of employers create a common pension fund so that employees changing places of employment have no difficulty transferring accrued pension rights.

pension trust: A trust set up to fund a pension plan, frequently used for small groups, administered by trustees who are authorized to purchase individual level premium policies or annuity contracts for each member of the plan.

pension trust, exempt: (*See: exempt pension trust.*)

pension trust fund: A fund consisting of money contributed by the employer and, in some cases, the employees to provide pension benefits. Contributions are paid to a trustee (either corporate or individual) who invests the money, collects the interest and earnings, and disburses the benefits under the terms of the trust agreement. A pension trust may be wholly self-administered (*See also: self-administered trusteed plan*), or the plan may be partially insured, with benefits purchased from an insurance company by the trustee, often as each participant retires.

pension trust, multiple plan: A diversified pension system consisting of separate plans for different groups of employees. One plan may be for persons on salary; another for workers of a particular union; another for company executives. All plans, however, are part of a single system.

per capita: Literally, *by the person.* In life insurance, for reasons of distributing proceeds to beneficiaries, per capita means designated individual share in the proceeds on an individual basis. (For insurance, if three primary beneficiaries are designated, each will receive one-third; should one die, the two remaining will each receive one-half.) (*For contrast, see: per stirpes.*)

percentage benefit, flat: (*See: benefit, flat percentage.*)

percentage participation: (*See: coinsurance percentage participation.*)

percentage tables, extra: (*See: extra percentage tables.*)

percentage vesting: (*See: partial vesting.*)

per diem: Per day; on a daily basis.

per disability major medical plan: Major medical coverage providing a benefit for each illness or sickness, with a deductible amount applicable to each. Once applied, the deductible is not again taken prior to the termination of the benefit period.

peril: The cause of a loss. In life insurance, peril refers to death; in health insurance, it is accident or sickness. Also, a broad, generic term, under which specific situations giving rise to loss may be classified as hazards. (*See also: hazards.*)

period certain: (*See: annuity certain.*)

periodic reviews: A concept employed by some life agents to keep up to date regarding changing circumstances of clients; a method of keeping in touch with clients at birthdays, policy anniversaries or other significant dates. It usually involves at least an annual review with the client about his or her changing insurance situation.

period of eligibility: (*See: eligibility period.*)

permanent and total disability: A disability that presumably prevents the insured from ever performing any work for compensation, or engaging in any occupation in which the insured might reasonably be expected to engage, in view of his or her station and physical and mental capacity.

permanent disability: A long-range disability that will last for an indefinite indeterminable period of time.

permanent insurance: Any form of life insurance in which the insured has the guaranteed right to keep the policy in force as long as he or she pays the premium. Also refers to any life insurance policy that builds cash value. (*For contrast, see: term insurance.*)

permanent insurance, group: (*See: group permanent insurance.*)

permanent partial disability: An injury or sickness causing a partial disability from which there is no recovery. Primarily a workers' compensation insurance term.

permanent partial disability benefits: Benefits paid for a disability that impairs earnings capacity, but that does not involve total inability to work.

permanent total disability: Total disability from which a person is not expected to recover. When used as a definition of disability qualifying for insurance benefits (usually in life insurance waiver-of-premium provision), the disability is stipulated as permanent if it persists for a specified number of months, usually six. Definitions found in disability income policies will vary.

permanent total disability benefits: Payments to an individual who is totally unable to work or who qualified under a specific policy. Such compensation may be limited to a maximum time or a maximum amount, but if unlimited may continue for life. A workers' compensation insurance term.

per risk excess reinsurance: Reinsurance in which the retention and amount apply per risk rather than per accident, per event, or on an aggregate basis.

persistency: The staying quality of life insurance policies. High persistency means that a high percentage of policies remain in force to the end of a specified period of coverage. Low persistency means that a high percentage of policies lapse because of nonpayment of premiums.

personal hazard: (*See: moral hazard.*)

personal injury: Bodily harm.

personal insurance: (*See: individual insurance.*)

personal life insurance trust: A trust arrangement whereby proceeds of the insured's life insurance policies go into a trust, with the trustee designated as beneficiary of the policies. Upon the death of the insured, the proceeds are paid to the trustee, who manages and disburses the funds according to the terms of the trust instrument. This is often useful in estate planning.

personal observation prospecting: The habit, developed by the agent, of seeing people in terms of their potential insurance needs, of being aware of and looking for new names and prospects in everyday activities.

personal producing general agent (PPGA): In life insurance, an agent or general agent whose contract provides for compensation both from business personally written and that written by subcontracted agents. Traditionally, PPGAs do little recruiting and contracting of new, inexperienced agents. It is not unusual for one or more experienced producers to be under subcontract as agents.

personal property: In a broad and general sense, everything subject to ownership that does not come under the definition of real estate or real property. Refers to possessions of a personal and movable nature, as opposed to immovable objects, such as houses or lands. (*For contrast, see: real property.*)

per stirpes: Literally, *by the branch.* Under this legal designation, the death proceeds of a life insurance policy are divided equally among the named beneficiaries. The share of any deceased named beneficiary is then distributed to his or her living descendants. (*For contrast, see: per capita.*)

physical examination: In life and health insurance, an examination given by a doctor for the underwriting of an insurance policy. (*See also: medical examination.*)

physical examination and autopsy provision: An insurance provision that states that the insurance company has the right to require a physical examination of the insured or an autopsy on a deceased insured (if not prohibited by state law). The purpose of this provision is to allow the insurance company to protect itself from fraudulent claims, or to determine if the cause of a loss was an accident or sickness, or if drugs or alcohol contributed to a loss.

physical hazard: That type of hazard that arises from the physical characteristics of an individual (e.g., impediments of hearing or sight). It may exist because of a current condition, past medical history, or physical condition present at birth.

physical impairment: In life and health insurance, a physical defect that makes an applicant a below-average risk.

physically impaired risk: In life and health insurance, a person having a physical impairment or disease that may affect his or her acceptability as a risk.

physician's expense policy: A medical expense health plan that reimburses the policyowner for the cost of a physician's services (other than surgical). Commonly referred to as a basic medical policy.

placed business: In life and health insurance, policies whose applications have been examined and the policies issued and delivered to the policyowners, who have paid the first premiums.

plan description: When starting or revising a pension plan, the administrator must file a form with the Department of Labor, giving information on what the plan provides and how it operates, including eligibility requirements for participation and benefits, provisions for nonforfeitable pension benefits, circumstances resulting in disqualification, ineligibility, loss and denial of benefits, and remedies for redress of claims denied.

plan, excess: In pension plans, one designed around the benefits of Social Security, using the Social Security benefits as a base income. (*See also: minimum compensation level.*)

plan, formal: In employee benefit plans, one set forth in writing, under which contractual and legally enforceable rights pass on to the participating employees.

plan, funded: In employee retirement plans, one in which funds are deposited to provide for retirement benefits.

plan, informal: A retirement system in which the employer has no legal obligation and the employee has no legal rights. Such plans have no standard of benefits to be paid and have no special method of funding, nor are they qualified to receive tax-favored treatment.

plan, insured: A retirement plan under which some kind of benefits are guaranteed by an insurance company. It does not imply that there is an element of life insurance connected with the plan.

plan, offset: An employee retirement plan designed to reduce each employee's standard benefit by a portion of the Social Security benefits he or she receives.

plan, qualified: An employee retirement plan under which contributions made by the employer are deducted from taxable income, and that provides that the deposits made for employees' future benefits are not to be considered as taxable income to them for the year in which they are made.

plan sponsor: An employer that establishes or maintains a benefit plan for employees; or an employee organization that establishes or maintains a plan for the employees; or in the case of a plan established and maintained by two or more employers, the committee or board of trustees who establish or maintain the plan.

plan summary: In a qualified retirement plan, a written summary of the plan, usually in the form of an employee booklet, which the plan administrator is required by law to supply if the plan has one or more employees as participants.

plan summary booklet: *(See: plan summary.)*

plan termination insurance: *(See: Pension Benefit Guaranty Corporation.)*

plan, unfunded: *(See: pay-as-you-go plan and funding, disbursement.)*

plan, uninsured: Any pension plan that is not maintained or handled through insurance products.

plan, unqualified: Any retirement plan that does not meet the qualifications for special tax advantages as set forth in the Internal Revenue Code. Such a plan provides only those deductions that are allowed in the course of normal business operation.

plan year: In a retirement plan, a calendar, policy or fiscal year on which the records of the plan are kept.

pledge: The posting of property, such as the cash value of a life insurance policy, to a creditor as security for a debt. The pledge is valid only as long as the creditor has possession of the property.

point-of-sale: In insurance, literally, when the agent is making a presentation to a prospect. Also refers to sales aids, such as visuals, charts and proposals used by an agent in an interview.

policy: In insurance, the written contract or agreement between the insurance company and the policyowner. The policy, including all endorsements and attached papers, constitutes the entire contract of insurance. (*See also: contract* and *insurance policy.*)

policy accumulation: (*See: accumulation, policy.*)

policy anniversary: In insurance, the anniversary of the date of issue of a policy, as shown in the policy schedule.

policy assignment: (*See: assignment.*)

policy change provision: A life insurance provision stating that the policyowner has the right to change his or her coverage from a term policy to a permanent, cash value policy, such as whole life, without providing evidence of insurability. To protect the company against adverse selection, evidence of insurability is required to change coverage from a permanent policy to a term plan.

policy date: In insurance, the date on which coverage becomes effective, as shown in the policy.

policy delivery: (*See: delivery of policy.*)

policy dividend: In participating insurance, the return of unused premium to the policyowner. It represents the difference between the gross premium charged and the actual costs of running the business and paying claims. Policy dividends are not guaranteed and are not taxable, since they are actually a return of premium.

policy fee: A small annual charge (sometimes a one-time charge) to the policyowner, in addition to the premium, to cover the costs of policy administration (premium collection and tax payments).

policyholder: The person or organization having rightful possession of a policy, irrespective of ownership rights or life insured. (*See also: policyowner.*)

policy loan: In life insurance, a loan made by the insurance company to the policyowner, with the cash value of the policy assigned as security for the loan. One of the standard nonforfeiture options.

policyowner: In insurance, the person who has ownership rights in an insurance policy and who may or may not be either the policyholder or the insured. (*See also: policyholder.*)

policy period: In insurance, the length of time during which the policy contract provides protection. Also called policy term.

policy plans: All the various insurance plans offered by an insurance company, as described in the rate book or manual published by the company.

policy proceeds: In life insurance, the amount payable in a single sum (if so elected) to the beneficiary or policyowner under a policy at death, surrender or maturity. However, the policy proceeds generally may be applied under the policy's settlement options to provide income rather than a single lump sum.

policy register: A record maintained by an insurance company for noting the issuance of, and accounting for, all of its policies.

policy reserve method: In life insurance, a method of accounting for insurance cash values, policy loans and premiums. This method shows a policy worth more than its cash value because the initial cost of the contract purchases benefits for the policyowner that extend beyond the end of the current accounting period. Also known as accrual basis method.

policy reserves: The funds that an insurance company is required by law to hold specifically for the fulfillment of its policy obligations. Reserves are calculated so that, together with future premiums and interest earnings, they will enable the company to pay all future claims. (*See also: reserve* and *active life reserve.*)

policy schedule: (*See: schedule policy.*)

policy summary: In insurance, an outline summary of a policy's provisions and financial make-up, provided by the agent to the insured (or prospective insured) to explain the policy. Some states require the agent to provide each applicant with a policy summary.

policy, surrendered: (*See: surrendered policy.*)

policy term: In insurance, the period of coverage provided by a policy. Also called policy period.

policy valuation: (*See: valuation.*)

policy value: (*See: reserve.*)

policy year: In insurance, that 12-month period extending from one policy anniversary to another.

policy year experience: In insurance, experience on business that became effective during a given year, irrespective of when the loss payment may actually have taken place. Reinsurance experience calculated with all applicable premiums and losses assigned to the experience year in which each reinsured policy becomes effective.

pool: Group of insurance companies joining together to share certain risks on an agreed-upon basis.

pooled investment: A pension plan arrangement whereby a corporate trustee invests and administers a group of plans in the form of a single unit, thus reducing costs and increasing investment opportunities through diversifications.

poor risk: (*See: substandard risk.*)

portability: A character of group insurance plans in which the employee can continue the insurance protection by assuming premium payments if he or she leaves the firm prior to retirement; or an employee under a pension plan with one employer could continue to have the same (or better) benefits with another employer with no loss of coverage time. Also, applies to the flexible nature of individual insurance policies; the insured can take the coverage wherever he or she goes.

portfolio: The securities in which the assets of an individual, a company (including an insurer), or a plan are invested; this term also applies to the reinsurance held by an insurance company. In a variable universal life policy, refers to the investments within a given cash value investment account.

portfolio interest rate: (*See: portfolio method of dividend calculation.*)

portfolio method of dividend calculation: In participant life insurance policies, a method whereby dividends are calculated based on the average interest rate earned on total portfolio of investments. (*For contrast, see: investment year method of dividend calculation.*)

post-contract-selection: (*See: post-selection.*)

post-dated check plan: A premium-paying arrangement under which the policyowner gives the insurance company a series of checks, each dated ahead of the date mode premiums fell due for a year or more, the company cashing each check on the specified date.

postmortem dividend: In life insurance, a dividend allotted after the death of the insured and constituting a pro rata portion of the dividend that would have been payable at a later date if the insured had lived.

postponement: A rejection or declination of an application for insurance, with an offer to consider at a later date.

post-retirement funding: In employee retirement plans, the sometimes used practice of funding benefits of employees who are at or near retirement at the time of a plans' inception or liberalization, by spreading the employer's cost over a period extending five to ten years beyond the employee's retirement.

post-selection: A management term referring to the process of measuring a new agent's early indicators of success and terminating the agent contract if there is reason to believe that adequate sales results will not be forthcoming. Sometimes called post-contract-selection as opposed to precontract-selection.

power of agency: The body of law concerning the responsibility and authority of an insurance company's agents that determines what he or she can and cannot do and what the company's liability is for the actions of that agent. These powers are usually specifically listed in the agency contract in three categories: apparent authority, implied authority and express authority.

power of appointment: Authority granted to one person (called the donee) to appoint a person or persons who are to receive an estate or an income from a fund, after the testator's death, or the donee's death, or after the termination of an existing right or interest.

power of appointment, general: (*See: general power of appointment.*)

power of attorney: Authority given one person (or entity) or act for and obligate another according to the instrument creating the power. In reciprocal insurance, power given by each subscriber to the individual (or corporate) manager (called attorney in fact) to exchange insurance for the grantor with other subscribers.

pre-approach: In insurance, contact made by an agent to prospects, or potential prospects, by letter or other communication, to approach the prospects on the most favorable basis possible.

preauthorized check plan: In insurance, a simplified method of paying premiums monthly. Policyowners authorize the insurance company to draw automatically one check per month in the amount of their premiums on their bank checking accounts.

precatory trust: One in which words employed in a will or other instrument do not amount to a positive command or to a distinct testamentary disposition, but are terms of entreaty, request, recommendation, or exception.

pre-contract orientation: (*See: pre-induction training.*)

pre-contract selection: In agent recruitment, a management process whereby prospective agents are carefully screened and their potential for success evaluated before they are offered a contract. (*See also: pre-induction training.*)

pre-contract training: (*See: pre-induction training.*)

preexisting condition: In health insurance, an injury, sickness or physical condition that existed before the policy effective date. Most individual policies will not cover a preexisting condition; most group policies will.

preexisting injuries or sickness clause: (*See: preexisting condition.*)

preferred risk: In life insurance, a person whose physical condition, occupation, mode of living, and other characteristics indicate an above average life expectancy. (*For contrast, see: standard risk.*)

preferred risk policies: In life and health insurance, policies warranting a lower premium charge on the basis of rigid selection. Certain classes may be selected, such as business or professional people, for example, where the mortality or morbidity experience is expected to be better than average.

pre-induction training: Also called pre-contract training or pre-contract orientation, that training given to a prospective life/ health insurance agent prior to becoming a full-time agency associate. Included is the study of licensing courses and other material geared to knowledge and skills development, plus activities designed to prepare for the career or eliminate the candidates. (*See also: selection.*)

preliminary application: (*See: inquiry blank and trial application.*)

preliminary term insurance: Term insurance attached to a newly issued permanent life insurance policy extending term coverage for a preliminary period of one to 11 months, until the permanent insurance becomes effective. If an age change occurs during the preliminary term period, the rate of the regular permanent policy is based on the advanced age. The purpose is to provide full life insurance protection immediately, but to delay the start of the larger permanent insurance premium and the anniversary to a later date.

preliminary term reserve system: A concept whereby the entire first-year premium is used for first-year expenses, and the reserves are made up after the first year by using part of the renewal loadings to supplement the net premiums. (*See also: modified preliminary term.*)

preliminary term reserve valuation, full: (*See: full preliminary term reserve valuation.*)

premature death: In life insurance terminology, death of the insured occurring when the family is normally relying on the earnings of the insured for support. Death that occurs other than in retirement years when one's major responsibilities are fulfilled.

premature distribution: With respect to an IRA or Keogh plan, any type of payment of a benefit from the plan in a taxable year ending prior to the date on which the owner of the IRA or Keogh plan attains age 59$\frac{1}{2}$ (except in the event of the owner's death or disability).

premium: The periodic payment required to keep a specific insurance policy in force. Though "premium" and "rate" are sometimes used interchangeably, technically, *rate* is the amount charged for a given unit of coverage and *premium* is the total of the unit rates for a given policy.

premium, advance: (*See: deposit premium* and *advance premium.*)

premium, annuity: Technically not a valid term since, in insurance terminology, the word "premium" is properly used in the legal sense only in connection with life insurance contracts. The proper term with respect to an annuity is purchase payment.

premium base: (*See: subject premium.*)

premium card: In insurance, the policy history card showing all pertinent data and a record of premium payments. In companies using data processing systems, this is now obsolete.

premium clause: In an insurance policy, the clause specifying the amount of premium owed each period by the policyowner. (*See also: premium mode.*)

premium contact, critical: (*See: critical premium contact.*)

premium, critical: (*See: critical premium.*)

premium deposit: An accumulation of premium paid by the insured prior to the due date. The deposit may include accrued interest.

premium discount: In life insurance, a discount (based on projected interest to be earned) allowed on premium paid in advance of the premium due date

premium discount plan: A plan that provides for a percentage reduction on premium based upon the size of the premium.

premium due date: With respect to insurance, the date upon which premium payment is due. In life and health insurance, this exact date is especially important in that it involves the grace period determination and policy lapse.

premium, earned: The amount of the premium earned by the insurance company because time has passed. That portion of an advance premium for which the company has already delivered coverage.

premium estimated: The conditional premium subject to final adjustment upon assessment of the necessary underwriting facts.

premium extension agreement: In insurance, an arrangement whereby the premium due date is extended by depositing a partial payment, which will be forfeited if the balance of the premium is not paid before the end of the extension period.

premium, extra: (*See: extra premium.*)

premium, financed: (*See: financed premium.*)

premium, fractional: (*See: fractional premium.*)

premium, gross: (*See: gross premium.*)

premium loan: In life insurance, a loan against the cash value of a policy, made to pay premiums. Frequently referred to as an automatic premium loan, a provision found in many life policies. (*See also: automatic premium loan provision.*)

premium, minimum: The lowest consideration for which an insurance company will insure a risk for a specified period. Also, the smallest premium that a company will accept. In universal and variable universal life plans, this is the minimum amount needed to keep the policy in force during an initial period, such as the first one or two policy years.

premium mode: The frequency of premium payments due, as selected by the policyowner. Typical premium modes are annual, semi-annual, quarterly, or monthly (or weekly in industrial insurance).

premium, net: *(See: net premium.)*

premium notice: A statement sent by the insurance company or one of its agencies informing the insured that the premium on a policy is due.

premium payment period: Under a limited payment life insurance contract, the number of years during which premiums are payable. For example, a 20-pay life policy has a 20-year premium payment period. Also, the period of time during which premiums are payable for any insurance policy.

premium protection rider: In life insurance, a provision sometimes added to a policy (often an educational or juvenile policy) to ensure the payment of all premiums in the event of the premium payor's death.

premium, provisional: *(See: deposit premium.)*

premium, pure: In insurance, the amount of premium needed to pay claims as they occur, sometimes including claim expense.

premium rate: The price per unit of insurance coverage, generally presented as a cost per thousand dollars of coverage. *(See also: rate.)*

premium receipt: The receipt given to a policyowner by the insurance company upon payment of a premium.

premium receipt book: In combination, or home service insurance, the policyowner's official receipt for premiums paid on weekly premium policies.

premium receipt, conditional: *(See: conditional premium receipt.)*

premium refund: A life insurance policy provision, effective for a specified period in the event of the insured's death, guarantees payment to the beneficiary of the principal sum plus all premiums paid to date of death. The amount reverts to principal sum only if the insured lives beyond specified period. Sometimes written as a special policy form; sometimes added by rider to a standard policy. A premium refund is generally guaranteed if the policy is returned during an initial ten-day inspection period. *(See also: premium return.)*

premium reserves: A reserve calculated to reflect the liability of the insurance company for losses that have not yet occurred, but for which the premiums have been paid. Essentially, the pro rata unearned premium reserve.

premium return: (1) Insurance premium returned to the policyowner as a result of cancellation, rate adjustment, or calculation that an advance premium is in excess of actual premium. (2) A life insurance provision (usually a rider) that agrees to pay the beneficiary, in addition to the face amount, an amount equal to premiums paid to date if death occurs prior to a stated date or end of a stated period, such as 20 years. A form of increasing term insurance. (3) A provision in a health insurance contract that, in the event claims during a stated period of time do not exceed a certain percentage of the premium paid, a benefit equal to the sum of premiums paid or some percentage thereof (such as 80 percent) will be paid the policyowner.

premiums, deferred: (*See: deferred premiums.*)

premiums discounted, future: (*See: future premiums discounted.*)

premiums, gross net: (*See: gross net premiums.*)

premiums in force: In life and health insurance, the sum total of premiums payable in a year on all policies in force.

premium, single: A single, discounted lump-sum payment in full for a life insurance or annuity contract at its issue.

premiums written: The total amount of premiums on contracts written by an insurance company, usually within a given period, say, during a particular month or year.

premium tax: A state tax collected from an insurance company and assessed as a percentage of the premiums paid to the company by policyowners residing in the state.

premium, unearned: In insurance, that portion of a premium applicable to the unexpired part of the policy period.

premium valuation, gross: (*See: gross premium valuation.*)

prepaid application: An insurance application that is accompanied by the first premium payment.

prepaid expense: An expense paid before the accounting period to which it is attributable.

prepaid hospital service plan: The common name for a health maintenance organization (HMO), a plan that provides comprehensive health care to its members, who pay a flat annual fee for services. (*See also: health maintenance organization (HMO).*)

prepaid premium: An insurance premium paid prior to the due date.

prepayment of premiums: In insurance, payment by the insured of future premiums, through paying the present (discounted) value of the future premiums or having interest paid on the deposit.

prepayment plans: A term referring to health insurance plans that provide medical or hospital benefits in service rather than dollars, such as the plans offered by Blue Cross and Blue Shield.

present value: The amount of money that if invested at a specified rate of interest, will, at a given future time accumulate to a specified sum.

price discrimination: (*See: discrimination.*)

price-earnings ratio: The ratio of the price per share of a firm's stock to the firm's earnings per share.

prima beneficiary: (*See: beneficiary, primary.*)

primary: In life insurance, a term that usually refers to the first beneficiary. In the reinsurance field, usually refers to the nouns "insurer," "insured," "policy," and "insurance," meaning respectively: (1) the insurance company that originates the business, i.e., the ceding company; (2) the policyowner insured by the primary insurer; (3) the initial policy issued by the primary insurer to the primary insured; (4) the insurance covered under the primary policy issued by the primary insurer to the primary insured.

primary beneficiary: In life insurance terminology, the beneficiary specifically designated by the insured as the first in priority to receive policy proceeds.

primary cover: In health insurance, coverage from the first dollar, perhaps after a deductible, as distinguished from an excess cover. (*See also: excess insurance.*)

primary insurance amount (PIA): Under U.S. Social Security, the worker's full retirement benefit at age 65 or disability benefit. Benefits at other than retirement ages or for others in the worker's family are expressed as percentages of the PIA. (*See also: Social Security.*)

principal: The applicant for or subject of insurance. An individual or company charged with the performance of certain obligations. The money due under a policy. The party to a transaction, as distinguished from a broker or agent. The person who designates another as his or her agent. A sum lent or employed as a fund or investment, as distinguished from its income or profits. The capital sum as distinguished from interest or profits. The original amount (as of a loan) of the total due and payable at a certain date. The capital sum of a mortgage loan.

principal sum: In an AD&D (accidental death and dismemberment) health insurance policy, the lump sum death benefit for accidental loss of life. (*See also: capital sum.*)

principle of indemnity: A fundamental insurance concept that is based on the assumption that an insured should not profit from a loss. To indemnify is to make financially whole again. In cases of overinsurance or double coverage, the insurance company will only pay once and for no more than the actual amount of loss.

prior death benefit: Under a retirement plan, the death benefit payable as a result of the death of a participant before he or she retires from employment.

prior insurance: Insurance written prior to the policy currently being contemplated on a given risk.

prior service: (*See: past service.*)

prior service benefit: (*See: past service benefit.*)

private annuity: (*See: annuity, private.*)

private placement: (*See: direct placement.*)

private trust: A trust created for the benefit of a certain designated individual or individuals or a known person or class of persons clearly identified or capable of identification by the terms of the instrument creating the trust, as distinguished from trusts for public institutions or charitable uses.

privilege of estate transfer: The right of an estate owner to transfer his or her estate at death to another person or legal entity.

privity: The legal status of being a party to a contract or a third party beneficiary of a contract.

probability: The likelihood or relative frequency of an event or the truth value of a statement. The mathematics of chance. (*See also: odds.*)

probable life curve: Primarily with respect to life insurance, a statistical curve used to plot future probable mortality based on past experience.

probable lifetime: Based on actuarial statistics, the average expected longevity of any given individual at a particular age.

probate: Proofs of a will before the proper court. The official copy of the will with a certificate validating its authenticity. It typically refers to the legal process of transferring an estate to one's heirs.

probate court: A court of law having jurisdiction over probating wills, administering estates, and the guardianship of children.

probate estate: The estate over which a probate court has jurisdiction. When an individual dies, his or her estate is said to go into probate, where a determination is made as to distribution of assets.

probationary period: In health insurance, a specified number of days after policy issue during which time coverage is not provided for certain sicknesses. This period protects the insurance company against preexisting conditions. Also called incubation period.

probationary provision: A provision in health insurance policies to exclude benefits for sickness beginning within a specified number of days, such as 15 or 30, following the policy date. Its purpose is to reduce the number of claims for sickness that may have had their inception prior to the policy date and to prevent antiselection on the part of persons who know they are in ill health. (*See also: probationary period.*)

proceeds: In life insurance, the net amount of money payable by the insurance company at the death of an insured or at the maturity of a policy.

process: With respect to an insurance application, to submit it for underwriter. With respect to a policy, to issue it.

producer: A term commonly applied to an agent, broker, personal producing general agent, solicitor, or other person who sells insurance, producing business for the insurer.

product: The merchandise marketed. In life and health insurance, the policies sold by a company.

production: In insurance, the sales volume of a company, an agency, or a producer, measured in face amount of protection or in premium dollars.

production club: In life and health insurance, an organization within a particular insurance company and bearing a company-oriented name, composed of agents who meet or exceed specified production standards set by the club or the company. Club conferences or conventions constitute the primary activity resulting from qualification.

production office: In insurance, an office having the necessary underwriting staff and supporting clerical personnel for the production of business. (*See also: general agency* and *branch office.*)

productivity: The number and volume or amount of sales made by an insurance agent or broker within a specified period of time.

professional association insurance: (*See: wholesale insurance.*)

professional partnership: A partnership of professionals (such as physicians or lawyers) that derives its income primarily from the personal services rendered by the partners, with capital investment being almost incidental.

professional reinsurer: A term sometimes used to designate an organization whose business is confined solely to reinsurance and adjunct services, as contrasted with other insurance organizations that exchange reinsurance or operate reinsurance departments as adjuncts to their basic business of issuing primary insurance.

professional service employer: Any proprietorship, partnership, corporation or other association or organization owned or controlled by professional individuals or by the executors or administrators of such professional individuals, such as doctors, dentists, attorneys, etc.

profit commission: (*See: commission, contingent.*)

profit-sharing plan: Any plan whereby a portion of the profits of a company is set aside for distribution to employees who qualify under the plan. The plan may provide for immediate, quarterly, or annual distribution of the profits to employees as an incentive to more efficient production. Profit-sharing distributions may also be set aside in a trust fund for eventual distribution to employees—usually upon death, disability, termination, or attainment of a specified retirement age. Such plans are known as profit-sharing trusts and are subject to special tax exemptions if certain qualifications, set down in the Internal Revenue Code, are met.

profit-sharing trust: (*See: profit-sharing plan.*)

programmed instruction: A self-instruction method utilizing the read-response-reinforcement format, whereby individuals study and respond to questions as they go along, receiving constant feedback on their answers.

programming: An obsolete term previously used to describe the activity of outlining a plan of coverage for a prospect, whereby a plan is designed to meet the complete life insurance needs of the prospect and dependents. (*See also: total needs selling, estate planning* and *capital needs analysis.*)

progressive vesting: (*See: graded vesting.*)

prohibited provisions: Life insurance policy provisions that are not allowed in the contract, such as a provision eliminating the insured's right to sue the insurance company.

prohibited risk: In insurance, any class of business that an insurance company will not insure under any conditions.

project budget: A separate budget in an insurance company, set aside for the development of new products, the appointment of new agencies, the development of new territories, etc.

projected benefit cost method: A pension cost method under which the actuarial costs are based upon total prospective benefits, whether or not they are attributed to specific periods of service. The actuarial cost determination assumes regular future accruals of normal cost, generally level in amount or as a percentage of earnings, whose actuarial present value is equal to the present value of prospective benefits, less the value of the plan assets and unfunded supplemental liability. (*See also: target benefit plan.*)

projection: In statistics, an estimate of future numbers based upon the extension of present relationships, but, which may also incorporate expected changes in such relationships. In insurance, an estimate of future conditions, such as mortality, morbidity, sales, lapse rate, etc.

promise to pay: As specified in a policy, the insurance company's stated agreement to make payment of all stipulated sums to designated beneficiaries in the event of certain, specified occurrences.

proof of loss: A mandatory health insurance policy provision stating that the insured must provide a signed and completed claim form to the insurance company within 90 days of the date of loss.

property, personal: (*See: personal property.*)

property, real: (*See: real property.*)

property tax: A tax imposed upon those who own property for the right and privilege of owning property.

proposal: A sales presentation or illustration of facts and figures pertaining to a plan of insurance, as shown to a prospect by an agent.

pro rata: According to a calculated share or portion; in proportion. For example, if an estate is distributed on a pro rata basis, it is divided proportionately to all legal heirs, claimants and creditors.

pro rata cancellation: The termination of an insurance contract or bond, with the premium charge being adjusted in proportion to the exact time the protection has been in force. (*See also: short rate.*)

pro rata premium: (*See: fractional premium.*)

pro rata rate: In insurance, a short-term premium rate proportionate to the rate for a longer term.

pro rata unearned premium reserve: In health insurance, a reserve calculated to represent the unearned portion of the liability to policyowners to be discharged in the future with future protection, by return to the policyowner in event of cancellation, or by reinsuring the business with another insurer.

prorating: In insurance, the proportionate reduction in the amount of benefits payable as provided in the contract; for example, because the insured has changed to a more hazardous occupation since the issuance of medical policy, or because benefits payable by all the insured's disability insurance exceed his or her current or average earnings over the preceding two years, or because he or she is actually older than stated in a life insurance application, etc.

proration: In health insurance, the modification of policy benefits because of a change in the insured person's occupation or the existence of other insurance.

prospect: In insurance, a potential purchaser; an individual or business meeting the following qualifications: (1) has a need for insurance; (2) can afford the coverage; (3) qualifies as an insurable risk; (4) can be approached by the agent under favorable circumstances. A potential purchaser about whom too little is known to determine if these four qualifications are met is called a suspect. (*See also: suspect.*)

prospect file: In life and health insurance, the agent's card of computerized listing of present clients, prospects and suspects, usually arranged according to alphabet and by date to contact. (*See also: tickler.*)

prospecting: In insurance, the process of identifying and contacting people and businesses to discuss their insurance needs.

prospecting, endless chain: (*See: endless chain prospecting.*)

prospecting rating plan: The formula in a reinsurance contract for determining reinsurance premium for a specified period on the basis, in whole or in part, of the loss experience of a prior period.

prospective future service benefit: In a pension plan, that portion of a participant's retirement benefit relating to his or her period of credited service to be rendered after a specified current date.

prospective rating: A method used to arrive at the reinsurance rate and premium for a specified period, based in whole or in part on the loss experience of a prior period. (*See also: self-rating* and *experience rating.*)

prospective reserve: A life or health insurance reserve computed as the present value of assumed future claims minus the present value of net premiums, both values computed on the basis of assumed rates of interest. (*See also: retrospective reserve.*)

prospectus: A registered, two-part document describing both the insurance portion and the investment portion of a variable life insurance product. A copy of the prospectus must be provided to the prospect at some time during the selling process.

protection: In insurance, a term used interchangeably with the word "coverage" to denote the insurance provided under the terms of a policy.

protection to age 100: In life insurance, a characteristic of the traditional whole life policy in that premium payments and insurance protection continue to age 100, at which time the policy endows for the face amount.

protective service: A period of time that may or may not be counted for pension benefit accruals or for minimum service requirements, but that is recognized under the provisions of a plan or an agreement for purposes of preventing a break in continuous service.

prototype plan: A standardized IRS-approved employee retirement plan document, with or without a trust, made available by the sponsoring organization to use without charge to an employer who wishes to adopt such a plan. The plan is not administered by the sponsoring organization; the employer administers the plan. (*See also: master plan.*)

Provincial Superintendents' Association: (*See: Association of Superintendents of Insurance of the Provinces of Canada.*)

provisional commission: In insurance, the tentatively established commission rate, subject to subsequent adjustment.

provisional premium: (*See: deposit premium.*)

provision rate: In insurance, the tentative rate, subject to subsequent adjustment.

provisions: The terms or conditions of an insurance policy as contained in the policy clauses.

provisions, general: (*See: additional provisions.*)

proximate cause: A cause that—in a natural and continuous sequence, unbroken by any intervening efficient cause—brings about the injury or death, and without which the result would not have happened.

prudent man rule: A rule requiring anyone acting for another, in a fiduciary or trust capacity, to make judgments and act as would a prudent person. For example, it permits a trustee to step outside the sanctioned legal list for investment of trust assets, provided the trustee acts prudently. Most prudent man rules limit the percentage of trust assets permitted outside the legal list.

P.S. 58 Tables: U.S. government tables of premium rates for individual one-year term insurance policies.

public assistance: The federal-state system for providing welfare payments to the aged, blind, and disabled and to families with dependent children.

public conveyance benefit: In insurance, an additional benefit for accidental death, or loss of sight or limbs, occurring as the result of an accident while the insured was a passenger on a public conveyance.

Public Law 15: Congressional Act of 1945 exempting insurance from federal antitrust laws to the extent that it is regulated by the states.

public trust: One constituted for the benefit either of the public at large or of some considerable portion of it answering a particular description; public trusts and charitable trusts may be considered in general as synonymous expressions.

purchase payment: The consideration given for an annuity contract.

purchaser insurance: *(See: payor insurance.)*

pure endowment: A life insurance contract that provides for payment only upon survival of a certain person to a certain date and not in event of that person's prior death. A pure endowment contains no insurance elements. This type of contract is the opposite of a term contract, which provides for payment only in event the insured person dies within the term period specified.

pure insurance risk: *(See: mortality risk.)*

pure premium: In life and health insurance, the premium necessary to cover the morbidity cost only, without expense loading.

pure risk: Uncertainty as to whether a gain or loss will occur, either being possible. Fifty-fifty is a pure risk situation.

Q

Q schedule: A schedule of business expenses required of all life insurance companies operating in New York State, used to determine degree of compliance with the state's limitation on total expenses, which has the effect of setting a ceiling on commissions. (Inasmuch as New York law required that any company doing business in the state comply substantially with the New York code in all its operations, the New York limitations on business expense have an extraterritorial effect for any insurance company operating there.

quadruple indemnity: In insurance, multiple indemnity to the fourth power, but otherwise corresponding to double and triple indemnity. (*See also: double indemnity.*)

qualification laws: Rules governing the license of insurance agents and brokers as stipulated from state to state and detailing such matters as license fee and methods of revoking and suspending an agent's license.

qualified deferred compensation plan: A deferred compensation plan meeting all the requirements set forth in Section 401(k) of the Internal Revenue Code of 1954. (*See also: deferred compensation.*)

qualified joint and survivor annuity: The retirement benefit resulting from a qualified pension plan, that provides for benefits for life at retirement to the participant, with a continuing annuity thereafter for life to his or her surviving spouse.

qualified pension plan: A pension plan within the meaning of Section 401(a) of the Internal Revenue Code, established and maintained by an employer primarily to provide for the payment of benefits to employees over a period of years, usually for life, after retirement. The major requirements are that the plan be in writing, be permanent, be for the exclusive benefit of employees or their beneficiaries, and not be discriminatory in favor of officers, stockholders, supervisors or higher paid employees. A qualified plan (meaning it has been approved by the IRS) will receive favorable tax treatment. Employer contributions constitute a business deduction in determining the employer's taxable income; employer contributions are not regarded as employee earnings and are, therefore, not taxable to the employee; and the earnings of the pension fund are not subject to current income tax.

qualified plan: (*See: qualified trust* and *qualified pension plan.*)

qualified profit-sharing plan: A plan established and maintained by an employer to provide for the participation by employees in the company's profits. The plan must provide a definite, predetermined formula for allocating the contributions made to the plan among the participants and for distributing funds accumulated under the plan after a fixed number of years, the attainment of a stated age, or upon the prior occurrence of some event, such as hardship.

qualified prospect: In insurance, one who meets the four qualifications of a prospect, as opposed to a suspect, who may or may not be qualified. (*See also: prospect* and *suspect.*)

qualified trust: A pension, deferred compensation, or bonus plan that meets the standards established by the Internal Revenue Service, thus providing tax advantages for both the employer and employee.

qualifying prospects: In insurance, the process of discovering vital information about a prospect, such as need, ability to pay, etc. Until a prospect has been qualified, he or she is a suspect. (*See also: suspect.*)

quality business: In life insurance, a term used to describe the staying power of an agent's business. It is characterized by good persistency, satisfactory mortality, and low acquisition and maintenance costs.

quantity discount: In life insurance, a per thousand discount allowed when the policy face amount is in excess of a certain amount designated by the insurance company. The discount is based on the concept that the acquisition cost for a small policy is the same as that for a larger one, so that in the larger policy, the cost per thousand to issue the policy is less, thus justifying the discount.

quarantine indemnity: An insurance benefit paid for loss of time while an insured is quarantined by health authorities because of exposure to a contagious disease.

quarter of coverage: With regard to eligibility for Social Security benefits, a unit of coverage is credited to an individual worker for each portion of a calendar year's covered wages or self-employment income that equals or exceeds the amount per quarter specified by law for the year. Not more than one may be credited to a calendar quarter not more than four in a calendar year. Exception: No quarter that (1) began after his or her death; (2) lay within a period of disability (other than the first or last quarter of such period); or (3) has not yet begun can ever be a quarter of coverage.

quasi contract: An obligation similar in nature to a contract, arising not from an agreement of the parties but from some relation between them or from a voluntary act of one of them. Also, a situation imposed by law to prevent unjust enrichment or injustice and not dependent on agreement of the parties to the contract.

quasi-insurance institutions: A term referring to social insurance plans under government authority and direct supervision that have some but not all of the characteristics of insurance. Examples are Social Security's old-age and survivors benefits, unemployment insurance, Medicare, Medicaid, etc. (*See also: social insurance.*)

quasijudicial bodies: Some federal agencies, such as the Federal Trade Commission that have powers similar to a judicial body, thus permitting them to enforce their regulations and rules.

quasi-public corporation: An incorporated organization, privately operated but in which some general interest of the public is evident. The line of demarcation is not clear when a private company comes into this classification. Charitable and religious companies are quasi-public.

quick asset ratio: The ratio of cash, accounts receivable and marketable securities to current liabilities. Also called *acid test.*

quick assets: Cash or those assets that can quickly be converted into cash.

quid pro quo: Latin for *this for that* or *one thing for another,* such as the consideration in an insurance contract, which requires the exchange of something of value by both parties for there to be a valid contract.

qui facit per alium, facit per se: He who acts through another acts himself—that is, the acts of the agent are the acts of the principal.

quota sample: The separation of a given population into groups on the basis of a common characteristic, such as age or sex, and the formation of a sample by selecting from each group the same proportion of the sample as that group bears to the total aggregate.

quota share reinsurance: That type of reinsurance contract in which a quota or percentage of every risk falling under terms of the agreement is ceded.

R

ratable charge method: In life insurance, a method of accounting for policy cash values, policy loans and premiums. This method calls for amortization of *cost of life insurance* on a straight-line basis over the policy life.

rate: The cost of a given unit of insurance. In life insurance, for example, it is generally the price per $1,000 of coverage. In disability income insurance, it is usually the price of a $100 per month benefit. The premium is the rate multiplied by the number of units of insurance purchased, plus a policy fee (if any) added to the initial premium payment. Also, the percent or factor applied to the ceding company's subject premium to produce the reinsurance premium or the percent applied to the reinsurer's premium to produce the commission. (*See also: premium.*)

rate basis: In insurance, the factors taken into account for the calculation of a premium rate or the formula used to arrive at the rate.

rate book: (*See: rate manual.*)

rate card: In insurance, a quick reference brochure or card giving rates for various types of insurance coverage issued by a given insurance company. A convenient adaptation summary of the rate manual.

rate discrimination: The practice of using different rates for insureds or risks of the same class and general characteristics. Prohibited by state insurance laws. (*See also: discrimination.*)

rate, flat: (*See: flat rate.*)

rate manual: A book containing rates for various types of insurance coverage issued by a given insurance company and usually containing information and instructions on field underwriting, rules for guidance of agents, and, in the case of life insurance rate manuals, cash and nonforfeiture values and dividend scales (if participating coverage is issued).

rate of death: (*See: death rate.*)

rate of interest: With respect to a loan or loan type of investment (mortgage, bond, savings account, etc.), the percentage of principal charged to a borrower by a lender for use of the latter's money, usually expressed in terms of an annual rate unless otherwise stated.

rate of natural increase (decrease):   With respect to a population of a nation or geographical area, birth rate minus death rate. If there were no migration, this would equal the rate of population increase (decrease).

rated: A term used to describe insurance issued to a person who is a substandard risk and is charged a premium rate that is higher than that charged for a standard risk.

rate of return method: A means of estimating the potential economic loss that a person's family would suffer if he or she died prematurely. It involves calculating the human life value lost to the family by capitalizing, at an appropriate rate of return, that portion of his or her average annual earnings that go to the family.

rates, contract: (*See: contract rates.*)

rates, current: (*See: contract rates.*)

rates, gross: (*See: gross rates.*)

rating: The making of insurance rates. Also, the premium classification given an individual who makes application for life or health insurance and, most commonly, when the applicant is designated as a substandard risk. A higher premium reflects the increased risk.

rating bureau: An organization that classifies and promulgates insurance rates and, in some cases, compiles data and measures hazards of individual risks in terms of rates in given geographical areas.

rating class: In insurance, the rate class into which a risk, especially an impaired risk, has been placed.

rating experience: In group insurance, the determination or adjustment of the premium rate for an individual group, partially or wholly on the basis of that group's own previous experience.

rating in age: In life insurance, when an applicant is a substandard risk, he or she may be offered a policy with a premium elevated to that of one who is older.

rating, merit: The determination of an insurance rate for an individual risk based on its variation in hazard from the average or standard for its class.

rating, retrospective: *(See: prospective rating.)*

readjustment income: *(See: adjustment income.)*

real estate: *(See: real property.)*

realization: The disposal or liquidation of assets for cash. This has tax significance in that it is upon realization of a capital gain on the disposition of assets, and not before, that the gain is subject to income or capital gains tax.

real property: Land and generally whatever is erected or growing upon or affixed to the land. That which is not of a personal and movable nature. *(See also: personal property.)*

realty: A term often used to designate real estate. *(See also: real property.)*

reasonable charges: Under Medicare or a major medical policy, the customary charges for similar services made by physicians. The range of prevailing charges for physicians engaged in specialty practices may be different from one locale to another.

rebate: In insurance, a controversial practice whereby a portion of the agent's commission, or anything of value is given to the prospective insured as an inducement to buy. Rebates are illegal in most states.

rebating: In insurance, granting any form of inducement, favor, or advantage to the purchaser of a policy that is not available to all under the standard policy terms. Rebating in some states is a penal offense for which both the agent and the person accepting the rebate can be punished by fine or imprisonment, and in virtually all states the agent is subject to revocation of license.

recapture: With respect to reinsurance, the action of a ceding company in taking back insurance previously ceded to a reinsurer.

receipt: A written acknowledgment of a payment.

receipt, conditional: (*See: conditional receipt.*)

receipt, conditional premium: (*See: conditional premium receipt.*)

receipt, premium: (*See: premium receipt.*)

receivership: The condition a person or firm is said to be in when a court appoints someone (the receiver) to administer the affairs of that person or firm because he, she or it is unable to meet debts as they mature. The receiver administers matters until a decision is made to reorganize or to liquidate. If the decision by the court or by the owners is to liquidate, the receiver carries out the liquidation, although his or her title is changed to trustee in bankruptcy.

recession: A receding of something that has been previously ceded. In reinsurance, for example, the recession of coverage to the original insurer (the ceding company) by the reinsurer. Also, a withdrawal or a period of reduced economic activity.

reciprocal insurance: Insurance resulting from an interchange among persons (subscribers) of reciprocal agreements of indemnity, the exchange being made through an attorney-in-fact common to all such persons, the group of such subscribers being a reciprocal insurer or reciprocal exchange.

reciprocal law: With reference to insurance, a law by which State A grants the same privileges to State B's insurers and producers operating in State A that State B grants State A's insurers and producers operating in State B; or for regulating its domestic insurers or producers in their relations with the other state according to a specified standard if that other state regulates its domestic insurers or producers according to the same standards.

reciprocity: In insurance, the practice whereby a company places reinsurance only with a reinsurer who is able to offer reinsurance in return.

reciprocity agreement: An agreement between two or more employee benefit plans, under which service with any signatory to the agreement will be recognized for such purposes as (1) satisfying minimum service requirements for plan participation; (2) fulfilling minimum service requirements for benefit entitlement; (3) preventing a break in continuous service; or (4) accumulating benefit credits

recruiting: Under the agency system of marketing insurance, the process and all the activities involved in looking for, attracting, interviewing and/or preparing to contract prospective agents. It is not unusual for the term to refer only to the processes of looking for and attracting prospective agents, while all interviewing (including testing and pre-contract training) is referred to as selection. (*See also: selection.*)

recruitment ratio: In an insurance agency operation, the number of people who must be interviewed and evaluated in order to obtain one new agent.

recurrent disability: In health insurance, a disability resulting from the same or related cause of a prior disability.

recurrent disability provision: In health insurance, a provision that specifies a period of time during which the recurrence of a disability from the same accident or sickness is considered to be a continuation of the prior disability, thereby eliminating the need for a second deductible period.

recurrent hospitalization provision: A health insurance provision that specifies a period of time (usually six months) during which the recurrence of a disability from an accident or sickness is considered a continuation of the prior disability, thereby eliminating a new deductible charge.

reduced benefits for early retirement: Under Social Security, a monthly retirement income benefit paid for life, but at a reduced benefit level because it is taken starting between age 62 and 65 (rather than at age 65, in which case, the worker would receive full retirement benefits).

reduced moral hazard: A condition or provision that discourages an insured from trying to make a profit through his or her insurance. The suicide clause and the duplication of benefits clause are examples.

reduced paid-up option: In life insurance, a nonforfeiture option contained in permanent policies, providing that the insured may elect to have the cash surrender value of his or her policy used to purchase a paid-up policy for a proportionate amount of insurance.

reduction of benefits: In disability income insurance, a provision sometimes included for automatic reduction in coverage under certain specified conditions, e.g., after the insured has reached age 60, 65, etc.

reductions: Decreases in benefits from an insurance policy as a result of specified conditions.

referral: (*See: referred lead.*)

referred lead: A prospect obtained when a client, prospect or friend personally refers the insurance agent to someone else, often with an introductory phone call, letter, or brief note on the back of the agent's card. The term can also apply to a referral given to an agency head or supervisor engaged in agent recruiting activity.

refund annuity: (*See: annuity, refund.*)

refund, experience: (*See: experience refund.*)

refund life income option: Similar to the life income settlement option, except that if the sum of the payments made to the primary payee during his or her lifetime is less than the proceeds of the insurance policy, the difference is paid in a lump sum to a secondary payee. (*See also: life income option.*)

register: In combination or home service insurance, a record of all policies charged to a debit.

Registered Retirement Savings Plan: In Canada, an individual retirement savings plan similar to Individual Retirement Accounts in the U.S. Plans are established in accordance with the Canadian Income Tax Act. Their primary purpose is to provide income tax incentives to save money for retirement income in the case of those taxpayers whose access to a registered pension plan is either insufficient or nonexistent. RRSPs are issued by life insurance companies and trust companies.

regular annuity: (*See: fixed annuity.*)

regular medical benefit: Under a health insurance plan, the stipulated benefit for physician's services, usually a per diem allowance for a physician's call.

regular medical expense insurance: Provides benefits for payment of doctor fees for nonsurgical care, commonly in a hospital, but also at home or at a physician's office. Frequently contained in hospital and surgical expense policies.

rehabilitation: The return of a disabled person to a recognized acceptable and attainable physical, mental, emotional, social, and economic usefulness and, if employable, to gainful employment.

rehabilitation clause: Any clause in a health insurance policy (particularly a disability income policy) describing benefits intended to assist a disabled policyowner in vocational rehabilitation.

reimbursement: In insurance, payment to the insured for a covered expense or loss incurred by or on behalf of the insured.

reimbursement allowance, expense: (*See: expense reimbursement allowance.*)

reimbursement benefits: In health insurance, provisions under which the actual expense incurred by the insured (usually for medical, nursing, and hospital treatment) is paid.

reinstatement: Policyowners' rights, by the terms of most life insurance policies, to reinstate lapsed policies within a reasonable time after lapse, provided they present satisfactory evidence of insurability and pay back premiums and interest. The right is usually denied if a policy has been surrendered for its cash value.

reinsurance: The sharing or spreading of a risk too large for one insurer by ceding part of the risk to another company or reinsurer. For example, most companies place a limit on the amount of insurance they will risk on a single life; therefore, when issuing policies for larger amounts than their own limit, they cede the excess over that limit with a reinsurance company for a portion of the premium.

reinsurance assumed: The portion of risk that the reinsurer accepts from the original reinsurer; the premium for an assumption of reinsurance.

reinsurance, automatic: An agreement between the ceding company and the reinsurer whereby the latter agrees to automatically cover all amounts above the original company's retention limit, up to an agreed maximum.

reinsurance broker: An individual or organization that places reinsurance through a reinsurance underwriter.

reinsurance ceded: The portion of risk that the original insurer transfers to the reinsurer. The premium for a cession of reinsurance.

reinsurance, coinsurance plan: An arrangement whereby the original insuring company cedes to a reinsurer the amount of the original contract that exceeds its retention limits and continues that amount of reinsurance in force throughout the life of the contract.

reinsurance credit: Credit taken on its annual statement by a ceding insurance company for reinsurance premiums ceded and losses recoverable.

reinsurance, disaster: Reinsurance coverage designed to limit losses to insurance companies under individual as well as group policies in cases of multiple-person accidents. It supplements the basic, underlying reinsurance plan. The ceding company purchases an amount of reinsurance per accident in excess of a per accident retention limit.

reinsurance excess: Reinsurance coverage in excess of a stipulated primary amount.

reinsurance, facultative: Reinsurance of individual risks at the option of the reinsurer and the reinsured, whether under a treaty of reinsurance or by negotiation in respect of an individual risk. The reinsuring company is free to accept or reject the offerings of the originating or ceding company.

reinsurance, modified, coinsurance plan: A plan whereby a company wishing to reinsure on a coinsurance basis with a carrier not licensed in its state can in effect retain the entire reserve under the contract. Reserves held by reinsurance companies not licensed in the state usually are not allowable as deductions from the reserve liability of the direct writer. Also, the plan permits the ceding company to hold and invest the money it collects. The modified coinsurance plan differs from the yearly renewable term plan in that the amount at risk decreases each year for both the ceding company and the reinsurer, rather than initially for the reinsurer only.

reinsurance, nonproportional: Castastrophe and stop-loss reinsurance.

reinsurance, obligatory: (*See: reinsurance, automatic.*)

reinsurance premium: The consideration paid by the ceding insurance company to the reinsurer for the reinsurance provided by the latter.

reinsurance, proportional: Under a reinsurance contract, the sharing of each claim for each risk in a proportion determined in advance.

reinsurance, quota-share: (*See: reinsurance, share.*)

reinsurance reserve: (*See: reserve, unearned premium.*)

reinsurance, share: Acceptance of a portion of the risk or risks of the reinsured by the reinsurer, the two sharing all losses and expenses as agreed.

reinsurance, stop-loss: Excess reinsurance covering all losses incurred after the reinsured's aggregate loss on a line reaches a specified amount or after the loss ratio reaches a specified figure.

reinsurance, surplus share: Reinsurance of amounts above a specified amount retained by the primary insurer, the reinsurer contributing to the payment of losses in proportion to its share of the total amount of the insurance. A type of reinsurance in which the writing company cedes all of the coverage in a given policy above a certain retention limit. (*See also: reinsurance, share.*)

reinsurance treaty: An agreement existing between two or more insurance companies whereby they agree to share large insurance risks. A contract between two insurers under which one, the insurer, agrees to reinsure risks written by the other, subject to the conditions of the contract.

reinsurance, yearly renewable term plan: A plan whereby a company reinsures only the net amount-at-risk in excess of its retention amount. The net amount-at-risk on any life policy is the difference between its face amount and the amount of its terminal reserve.

reinsured: An insurer that has ceded a portion of its risks to a reinsurer. Also, that portion of a risk that has been ceded to a reinsurer.

reinsurer: A special type of insurer that assumes all or a part of the insurance or reinsurance written by another insurer.

rejection: Refusal by an insurance company to underwrite a risk; or denial of a claim by an insurer. (*See also: declination.*)

related company: (*See: affiliated company.*)

relation of earnings to insurance: In disability income, a provision that limits an insured's total disability income benefits to the amount of his or her earnings (or a portion thereof) prior to disability. Typically, if at the time disability begins the total benefits payable under all coverages owned by the insured exceed the average earnings of the insured over the preceding two years, the benefits will be reduced pro rata to such amount.

relationship of mortality to quality business: *(See: quality business.)*

relinquishment of power in contemplation of death: *(See: three year rule.)*

remainder: With respect to reinsurance, that part of a risk to be reinsured after deducting the amount the ceding company keeps in its own account. Also, the estate in property created simultaneously with one or more other estates by a single grant and consisting of the rights and interest contingent upon and remaining after the termination of the other estate (such as the remainder following a life estate, both created simultaneously).

remarriage clause: In life insurance, a settlement provision specifying that, where payments are not contingent on the life of the beneficiary, all further payments are to be made to a contingent beneficiary if the beneficiary should remarry.

removal, extra premium: *(See: extra premium removal.)*

renewable and convertible term: In life insurance, term insurance offering the policyowner both the option to renew the coverage at the end of the term period and the option (within the term period) to convert it to a permanent basis.

renewable term insurance: Term life insurance under which the insured has the right, at the end of the term, to elect to continue the insurance for another term of the same length (at the premium for his or her then attained age) without submitting evidence of insurability. The policy may give the right to several successive renewals.

renewable term insurance, group: *(See: group life insurance.)*

renewal: Continuance of coverage under an insurance policy beyond its original term. Also, especially with respect to life insurance, the payment of premiums after the first year of a policy or the agent's commissions on such second and subsequent years' premiums.

renewal agreement: A provision stating the conditions under which the insurance company will or will not renew a policy.

renewal commission: In life and health insurance, the commission paid or credited to an agent after the first policy year for premiums received by the company or business written by the agent.

renewal premium: In life and health insurance, any premium due after the first policy year. Also called renewal.

renewals: In life and health insurance, the premiums paid for renewed policies. Also, the commissions paid on renewal premiums.

rent continuation insurance: In life insurance, a form of home assurance whereby proceeds are intended for the purpose of providing monthly rent payments to the beneficiaries of the insured.

replacement: In life insurance, the act of substituting a new policy for another policy already in force. In situations where replacement is not warranted, it is sometimes called twisting. (*See also: twisting.*)

representations: In life and health insurance, statements made by an applicant on the application that he or she represents as being substantially true to the best of his or her knowledge and belief, but which are not warranted as exact in every detail, as compared to warranties. (*See also: warranties and representations.*)

representative: (*See: agent.*)

representative, field: (*See: agent.*)

required provisions: With respect to state insurance laws, those provisions expressly required to be included in an insurance policy, such as the incontestability clause, misstatement of age clause, and provision for a grace period.

requirements for eligibility: In an employee benefit plan, those rules to determine which employees may enter into the plan.

rescind: To recall an insurance policy, usually for misrepresentation.

rescission: Repudiation of a contract for cause, such as for fraud, misrepresentation, or duress. The rescission of an insurance policy is its recall and voiding, usually for misrepresentation.

reserve: With respect to level premium life insurance, the combined funds held by the company for all policies which, together with future premiums and interest earnings, are sufficient to meet all future claims. (*See also: active life reserve.*)

reserve basis: In life insurance, the mortality table and the assumed interest rate used in the computation of rates. All companies were required to change to the 1980 CSO table by 1989.

reserve, contingency: *(See: contingency reserve.)*

reserve, expense: A liability for incurred but not yet unpaid expense.

reserve, initial: In life insurance, that amount of the reserve existing at the beginning of the policy year immediately after payment of the current premium. The net premiums are the initial reserve of the first year.

reserve, mean: In life insurance, the average of the reserve at the beginning of the policy year and the reserve at the end of the policy year.

reserves, deficiency: *(See: deficiency reserves.)*

reserves, expense: *(See: expense reserve.)*

reserves, funding of: *(See: funding of reserves.)*

reserves, loss: *(See: loss reserve.)*

reserves, premium: *(See: premium reserves.)*

reserves, surplus: *(See: surplus reserves.)*

reserve, terminal: In life insurance, that reserve at the end of a full policy year after the cost of insurance has been deducted and before the renewal premium, if any, has been paid.

reserve, unearned premium: In certain forms of health insurance, a reserve approximately equal to the total of the unearned premiums on insurance in force with an insurance company.

reserve valuation, full preliminary term: *(See: full preliminary term reserve valuation.)*

reserve value: In life insurance, the net accumulations in a policy to date, and equal to the present value of future obligations less the present value of future net premiums under the policy, based on the actuarial assumptions underlying the policy.

reserve, voluntary: *(See: voluntary reserve.)*

resident agent: An agent domiciled in the state in which he or she sells insurance.

residual benefit: Relates to the part of anything remaining or the residue. In health insurance, a generally variable, long-term partial disability benefit tied to the insured's actual income loss. The percentage amount of loss is often measured on a monthly basis.

residual disability: In health insurance, a disability that limits an insured's earning ability even though he or she may be able to work full time. Many insurance companies are replacing the partial disability benefit with the residual disability benefit because it improves coverage with a longer benefit period and with benefits that are based on lost income instead of loss of time at work. (*See also: partial disability* and *total disability.*)

residuary: Refers to the residue or remainder.

residuary legacy: A gift by will of part or all of the personal property of an estate remaining after specific legacies have been met. (*See also: specific legacy.*)

residuary legatee: The person receiving "all the rest, residue, and remainder" of the personal property left by the testator after payment of debts and particular legacies.

respite care: Care provided either by paid workers who come to the home for short periods of time or by a nursing facility when a patient stays for a short period of time to give family members a rest.

respondeat superior: A general rule in law that a principal or employer is liable for an agent's or representative's acts performed on behalf of the principal's business.

restrictions: In life or health insurance, limitations or exclusions in a policy.

retained earnings: Earnings of an incorporated business that are accumulated in the business rather than distributed to owners in the form of salary or dividends.

retainer: An ongoing fee paid to a professional person to engage his or her services.

retaliatory law: A state law providing that the treatment accorded insurers or agents of its state by a *foreign state* (referring to a state within the United States in which a company does business) will be the treatment that the state will provide insurers or agents of the foreign state when they apply to operate in the retaliatory state.

retention: In insurance, the amount of liability for coverage retained by the writing company and not reinsured.

retention limit: In life insurance, the maximum amount of coverage a company will retain on one life at its own risk. (*See also: reinsurance.*)

retired lives reserve: Under Section 79 (IRC) group benefit plans, an employee benefit concept that enables an employer to prefund with tax-deductible dollars the cost of providing post-retirement life insurance for all or certain of its employees. Pre-funding is done by making contributions to a reserve fund used to continue the premiums on an individual's insurance after a stated retirement age.

retirement: The period after a person has withdrawn from active working life, often beginning at age 65—although retirement may commence earlier or later in life.

retirement allowance: An annuity or pension paid to an employee upon retirement. (*See also: retirement annuity; pension annuity; income bond; retirement policy.*)

retirement annuity; pension annuity; income bond; retirement policy: Deferred annuity and life insurance contract whose primary purpose is to supply annuity income at a selected retirement age. Excepting the retirement policy, the only "insurance" involved is either return of premiums or cash value, whichever may be higher. The usual settlement and annuity options are available for income purposes at retirement age.

retirement, automatic: (*See: retirement, compulsory.*)

retirement benefit: (*See: benefit, retirement.*)

retirement benefits, disability: (*See: disability retirement benefits.*)

retirement, compulsory: A rule in many businesses requiring employees to retire when they reach a specified age.

retirement, deferred: An arrangement whereby an employee is permitted to work after normal retirement on a year-by-year basis. If the employee works beyond the age of normal retirement, he or she does not usually receive a larger pension.

retirement, early: A retirement option whereby the employee may choose to retire before the normal retirement age, often with full benefits or an incentive bonus.

retirement endowment: (*See: retirement income policy and retirement annuity.*)

retirement income: One of the basic uses of life insurance. Life income beginning at a selected retirement age, derived by applying contractual settlement options to policy or annuity cash values. The definition may apply to individual or to joint lives. (*See also: annuity, joint life* and *annuity, joint and survivor.*)

retirement income bond: (*See: retirement income policy* and *retirement annuity.*)

retirement income contract: A type of life insurance policy which matures at a predetermined retirement age for an amount sufficient to provide an annuity of a specified amount for the life of the recipient, and sometimes beyond.

retirement income insurance, group: (*See: group retirement income insurance.*)

retirement income policy: A life insurance contract designed to provide old-age security, emphasizing a guaranteed monthly income for life, beginning at a certain age, usually 65. Such policies are generally sold in units of monthly life income. Unlike annuities, they also provide a death benefit. (*See also: retirement annuity* and *retirement income contract.*)

retirement, normal date: The accepted, specified or usual retirement date upon which retirement of an employee from a company occurs. It is the basis of all retirement benefits.

retirement plan: (*See: pension plan.*)

retirement plan, contributory: (*See: contributory retirement plan.*)

retirement plan, defined contribution: (*See: defined contribution plan.*)

retirement plan, fixed benefit: (*See: fixed benefit retirement plan.*)

retirement test: (*See: earnings limitation.*)

retroactive conversion: Conversion of a term life insurance policy to a permanent plan as of age of issue rather than as of attained age.

retroactive disapproval: With respect to pension plans, disqualification of a plan by the IRS for a given year and for any open taxable years following its adoption.

retrocession: In insurance, the act of a reinsuring company that has accepted a particular risk in ceding the risk to still another company. A cession of reinsurance by a reinsurer to another reinsurer.

retrocessionaire: The term applies to a reinsurer that has accepted a retrocession. (*See also: retrocession.*)

retrospective rating: (*See: prospective rating.*)

retrospective reserve: A life or health insurance reserve computed as the past value of assumed claims and past premiums, both accumulated at an assumed rate of interest. (*See also: prospective reserve.*)

return commission: That percentage of a commission paid to an agent by an insurance company that must be returned in the event a policy is canceled.

return for no claim: A provision in some health policies stating that if no claims have been paid during the term of the policy (or after the policy has been in force for a specified time), the insurance company will refund a portion of the premium.

return of cash value: A life insurance policy provision or rider in which the insurance company agrees to pay, upon the death of the insured, an amount equal to the cash value. This agreement is generally limited to a specific number of years from policy issue.

return of premium rider: A life insurance policy rider that provides that in event of the death of the insured within a specified period of time, the policy will pay, in addition to the face amount, an amount equal to the sum of all premiums paid to date. Also, a health insurance policy rider agreeing to pay a benefit equal to the sum of all premiums paid, minus claims paid, if claims over a stated period of time do not exceed a fixed percentage of the premiums paid.

return premium: The amount due the policyowner if an insurance policy is canceled, reduced in amount, or reduced in rate.

return premium policy: A life insurance policy that not only provides for payment of the face amount upon maturity, but also for the return of all or a portion of the premiums paid.

reversionary annuity: (*See: survivorship annuity.*)

reversionary basis: The beneficiary designation used when a beneficiary is named on an irrevocable basis. It returns to the policyowner the right to name a new beneficiary in the event that the original beneficiary predeceases the insured.

reversionary interest: The interest that a person has in the reversion of lands or other property. A right to the future enjoyment of property that is at present in the possession of another.

reversionary trust: One in which the trust property reverts back to the original holder after a certain period of time. For instance, one individual may place stocks in a reversionary trust for another person (perhaps as an education fund for a grandchild). All earnings from the stock accrue to the trust recipient. After a certain number of years, the stock returns to the possession of the owner, while the earnings remain in trust for the trust recipient.

revival: *(See: reinstatement.)*

revocable beneficiary: In life insurance, a beneficiary whose rights in a policy are subject to the insured's right to revoke or change the beneficiary designation and the right to surrender or make a loan on the policy without the consent of the beneficiary.

revocable trust: A trust in which the donor retains income rights, as well as the right to terminate the trust and recover the property. Such trusts will eliminate probate costs and may also qualify for estate tax marital deduction.

revocation: The act of cancelling a power or authority previously conferred.

rewritten: In insurance, a revised policy or a new policy issued on an insured who has previously let his or her coverage lapse.

rider: In insurance, an attachment to a policy that adds something to or deletes something from the contract. The term generally refers to any supplemental agreement attached to and made a part of a policy, whether the conditions or coverage of the policy are expanded or some coverage or conditions are waived.

rider, family: *(See: family rider.)*

right of assignment: In insurance, the right of a policyowner to legally transfer all or some of the policy benefits or rights to another party.

right of representation: *(See: per stirpes.)*

right to renew: A written guarantee in an insurance policy that enables the policyowner to continue coverage for another policy term.

risk: The degree or percentage of chance that a given contingency will occur. In life and health insurance, an individual or group of individuals being considered for, or covered by, a policy.

Risk and Insurance Management Society: A professional society of individuals involved in insurance buying and risk management. Formerly called the American Society of Insurance Management.

risk appraisal: In insurance, the underwriting process.

risk appraisal factors: The major risk appraisal factors for life or health insurance are age, sex, build, habits, physical impairments, medical history, occupation, family history, and finances.

risk, borderline: *(See: borderline risk.)*

risk, degree of: The probable deviation of actual experience from expected experience.

risk factor: The estimated cost of future claims, based on the mortality and morbidity tables for life and health insurance respectively. The factors that determine chance of loss are age, sex, physical impairments, medical history, habits, occupation, and finances. The risk factor is one element of the gross premium. *(See also: gross premium.)*

risk, poor: *(See: substandard risk.)*

risk, pure: The possibility of economic loss without any possibility of gain.

risk, pure insurance: *(See: mortality risk.)*

risk selection: The method used by a home office underwriter in choosing applicants that the insurance company will accept. The underwriter must determine whether risks are standard, substandard or preferred and set the premium rates accordingly.

risk, special class: *(See: special class.)*

risk, speculative: A questionable *gambling* sort of risk involving uncertainty with respect to a given event that may produce a loss, but that may, on the other hand, produce a gain.

risk, standard: *(See: standard risk.)*

risk, substandard: *(See: substandard risk.)*

rollover IRA: An Individual Retirement Account that an owner establishes by transferring to it a distribution from another IRA or
from another qualified retirement plan, which has terminated or
from which he or she has terminated. *(See also: Individual Retirement Account.)*

room and board benefits: In medical expense health insurance policies, benefits covering the daily cost of hospital room and food.
These benefits are usually expressed in terms of the dollar
amount allowed per day. Also referred to as DBR (daily board
and room) benefits.

route card: In home service insurance, the form an agent uses to
outline in detail the production, collection and servicing calls he
or she makes each day.

run-off: A reinsurance policy termination provision under which
the reinsurer remains liable for losses occurring after the date of
termination on policies in force on that date.

S

salaried professionals: Highly trained individuals who work as employees of corporations, hospitals or other medical facilities, government agencies, scientific and educational institutions, or other organizations.

salary allotment insurance: A life or health insurance plan arrangement for employees with an employer whereby regular forms of insurance are sold individually to employees on a payroll allotment basis, with premiums deducted from the wages of insured employees by the employer, who remits all premiums, generally in one monthly check, to the insurance company. Also called payroll deduction insurance, salary savings insurance, or payroll allotment plan.

salary continuation: An arrangement whereby an income, usually related to the salary or compensation of an employee, is continued upon his or her death or disability often paid to the employee's beneficiary.

salary deduction insurance: *(See: salary allotment insurance.)*

salary funding: With respect to business life insurance, a cross-purchase, buy-sell funding technique where the shareholders authorize the corporation to pay the insurance premiums and charge the premiums as additional income to the shareholders as employees.

salary savings: *(See: salary allotment insurance.)* (Note: consumer protection movements have included efforts to disassociate the word savings from life insurance.)

sales guides: Training and educational booklets used to aid insurance agents in understanding specific knowledge and skill-oriented material and to inform prospects of their potential insurance needs.

sales interview: *(See: selling interview.)*

sales kit: *(See: visual sales kit.)*

sales manager: The home office or field management person responsible for managing those persons and activities that generate sales. *(See also: supervisor, manager, general agent and superintendent of agencies.)*

sales quota: A set goal or requirement, expressed in terms of dollars or units of sales for a specified period of use in supervision of selling efforts.

sales visuals: *(See: visual sales kit.)*

savings bank life insurance: Life insurance sold over-the-counter by mutual savings banks in New York, Connecticut, and Massachusetts.

Savings Bank Life Insurance Council: A voluntary association of savings banks, formed in 1938 in Massachusetts for the purpose of furnishing mutual savings banks and their policyowners with various services.

savings element: The part of a life insurance product used as an investment vehicle for an IRA. Also previously used to designate the cash value or reserve accrual (and dividend accumulation, if any) element in life insurance, as contrasted with the protection element.

schedule: In health insurance, a list of specified amounts payable, usually for surgical operations, dismemberment, fractures, etc.

scheduled premium: The recommended or ideal premium in variable and universal life policies.

schedule of insurance: The list of individual terms, conditions and provisions covered under one policy. Also, an inventory listing an insured's policies, for example, in estate planning or total needs selling.

schedule policy: An insurance policy that covers, under separate insuring agreements in one policy, several hazards that are frequently handled under separate policies.

Schedule Q: (*See: Q Schedule.*)

schedule type policy: An insurance policy that includes a listing and a complete text of the provisions of each of several benefits, most of which are optional, and some of which may be omitted at the election of the applicant.

secondary beneficiary: (*See: contingent beneficiary.*)

second death estate shrinkage: The estate transfer taxes, costs, and other shrinkage factors that occur when a surviving spouse dies. It is noteworthy that any property transferred to a surviving spouse by a marital deduction is subject to taxation—again—in the spouse's estate at his or her death.

second preliminary notice: (*See: intermediate notice.*)

second selling interview: In life insurance, that selling or closing interview in a two-interview sales method, the first interview being the fact-finding interview. Also refers to the job of reselling the value of a policy that has been written without payment of initial premium. During the delivery, the buyer must sometimes be reminded of the reasons for purchasing the coverage and the benefits it provides.

second surplus reinsurance: That insurance amount that exceeds the total of the reinsured's original insurer's net retention, plus the full limit of the first surplus treaty.

secretary: The term, when used in connection with an employee welfare benefit plan or an employee pension benefit plan, refers to the Secretary of Labor.

secret trust: A situation in which a testator gives property to a person on a verbal promise that it will be held in trust for another person.

Section 79 plan: A group term life insurance plan under Section 79 of the Internal Revenue Code, whereby the employer pays the premiums. The employee must report as gross income only the cost of insurance over $50,000. When properly arranged, the cost of the premiums is also fully deductible by the employer.

Section 162: Section 162 of the Internal Revenue Code provides that employer-paid premiums for group term life insurance are deductible to the firm as an employee benefit expense.

Section 303: Section 303 of the Internal Revenue Code permits an estate to sell stock of a family corporation to the corporation on an income tax-free basis when the proceeds of such sale are to be used to pay taxes and other costs of estate administration and settlement.

Section 401(a)(3)(A): *(See: arbitrary rule.)*

Section 403(b) plan: Under Section 403(b) of the Internal Revenue Code, a qualified retirement plan for employees of 501(c) organizations and educational institutions, whereby contributions are used to purchase annuities or mutual fund shares by employers for employees. The plan must not be part of another qualified pension or profit-sharing plan, must be nonforfeitable to the employee, and contributions must not exceed a specified limit. The funds in the plan are nontaxable until they are taken as income in retirement. *(See also: Section 501(c)(3) organizations.)*

Section 501(c)(3) organization: Under Internal Revenue Code Section 501(c)(3), organizations operated exclusively for religious, charitable, scientific, literary, or educational purposes. No organization qualifies if it carries on propaganda or if its net earnings benefit any private individual.

secured creditor: A creditor whose claim against a debtor has been secured by the pledge of, or a lien on, property as collateral.

secured loan: A loan secured by the pledge of, or a lien on, property as collateral; for example, a mortgage loan on real estate property.

selection: Under the agency system of marketing insurance, the process of looking for, attracting, interviewing, testing and preparing to hire prospective agents. Pre-contract training or pre-contract orientation often constitutes an important aspect of agent selection. *(See also: recruiting and selection of risk.)*

selection, adverse: *(See: adverse selection.)*

selection against the company: *(See: adverse selection.)*

selection, benefit of: *(See: benefit of selection.)*

selection of risk: In insurance, the process of determining upon what terms coverage will be issued on applications received. This is commonly referred to as underwriting. *(See also: underwriting and risk selection.)*

select mortality table: A mortality table, based on life insurance experience, showing the rates of mortality according to both age at issue and duration of insurance. A mortality table (by attained age) for each age at issue.

self-administered plan: With respect to employee retirement plans, any uninsured plan. A plan administered by the employer. Pay-as-you-go, balance sheet reserve plans and trusteed plans in which personnel of the employing company serve as trustees are self-administered plans.

self-administered trusteed plan: An employee retirement plan under which contributions to purchase pension benefits are paid to a trustee, who invests the money, accumulates the earnings and interest, and pays benefits to eligible employees under the terms of the retirement plan and trust agreement. This type of plan is administered by the employer alone, or by a committee appointed by him or her under the terms of the plan, and the trustee.

self-employed individual: For purposes of taxation and qualified retirement plans, a person who has an ownership interest in an unincorporated business, trade or profession, which may be either a sole proprietorship or a partnership.

Self-Employed Individuals Retirement Act: (*See: Keogh Act plan.*)

self-employed professionals: Independent practitioners, such as doctors, lawyers, accountants, architects and others, who earn income by rendering personalized services. They may operate as sole proprietors or in a partnership.

self-inflicted injury: In insurance, bodily injury that is deliberately inflicted by the insured to himself or herself.

self-insurance: An individual's or business's financial preparation for meeting pure risks by setting aside funds to meet projected losses and absorb the difference between actual and calculated probable losses. (*See also: noninsurance.*)

self-insured pension plan: A self-administered pension plan under which a designated trustee or a pension committee manages the plan and its benefits, and the trustee (as fiduciary) administers the fund and handles the investments.

self-rating: In insurance, especially group, a form of rating in which a large risk's premium is determined entirely by its own losses in a given period, plus an allowance for the insured's expenses. (*See also: prospective rating.*)

self-reinsurance: In insurance, creation of a fund by an insurer to absorb losses beyond the insurer's normal retention.

selling interview: A meeting between a salesperson and a prospective buyer that has the objective of closing the sale. In life insurance, an organized presentation of an insurance plan by an agent to a prospect. It usually includes a review of the prospect's personal situation, the sales presentation and the close.

seminar: In insurance, a group study course in which several students under a supervisor or trainer do advance study.

senior citizen policy: *(See: older age policy.)*

separate account: In insurance, an account established or maintained by an insurance company, under which the income, the gains and the losses of that specific account or fund are credited or charged to the account without consideration of the income and investment results of the other assets of the insurance company. In variable universal life products, the cash value investment has subaccounts, so named because the funds within each account are managed and invested separately.

separate accounts funding: A pension plan funding technique whereby an insurance company establishes and maintains one or more special accounts, entirely independent of the general investment account, for the sole purpose of investing funds of pension plans.

separation of accounts: In a stock insurance company, an accounting division of the company into two branches, or a dual line stock company into three branches.

service: Relating to an agreement by the insurance company to pay certain providers of health care services, under arrangements with them, for rendering such services to covered persons. These arrangements may preclude or limit any additional charges for the defined services. Also, the practice of tending to the insurance needs of a client by an agent, as in servicing an account.

service benefit: A contract benefit paid directly to the provider of hospital or medical care for services rendered.

service benefit, current: *(See: current service benefit.)*

service benefit, future: *(See: future service benefit.)*

service cost, current: *(See: current service cost.)*

service cost, future: (*See: future service cost.*)

service, credited: (*See: credited service.*)

service, current: (*See: current service.*)

Service Employees Group Life Insurance: Term life insurance coverage issued to members of the armed forces while in service, convertible after separation to individual policies in participating or eligible private insurance companies.

service fees: With reference to agent commissions paid as compensation for the sale of life insurance, the smaller percentage commission paid beyond the first few years—often 1, 2, or 3 percent. These service fees are paid to the writing or servicing agent so long as the policy and the agent's contract are both in force, and are intended to compensate the agent for providing policyowner service.

service, future: (*See: future service.*)

service insurance: A type of insurance or prepayment plan that pays benefits in medical or hospital services rather than in dollars. Best known examples of such coverages are the Blue Cross and Blue Shield plans. (*See also: prepayment plans.*)

Servicemen's Group Life Insurance (SGLI): Group term life insurance under which all members of the armed forces on active duty are automatically covered for a specified amount, unless they elect no coverage or lesser amounts. The insurance is written by commercial companies and premiums are deducted from the pay of those who are insured. After separation this coverage is convertible to individual coverage in participating private insurance companies.

settlement: In insurance, a term that is synonymous with the payment of a claim. It implies that both the policyowner and the insurance company are satisfied with the amount and the method of payment.

settlement certificate: In life insurance, a contract issued in conjunction with a policy that sets out in detail the disposition of the proceeds of the policy.

settlement dividend: In life insurance, a special or extra dividend payable at the time of termination of a policy by death, surrender or maturity as an endowment.

settlement options: The various methods by which the beneficiary or the insured may have life insurance policy proceeds paid. The usual options are: (1) cash; (2) interest; (3) installments for a fixed period; (4) life income; and (5) fixed income as long as proceeds and interest will last.

settlement provisions: *(See: settlement options.)*

settlor: One who creates a trust.

severance benefits: Regarding pension plans, the benefits, if any that are payable on termination of employment prior to retirement for reasons other than death. Usually consists of a refund of employee contributions with or without interest or the granting of certain vested rights.

share reinsurance: *(See: reinsurance, share.)*

shifting trust: An express trust that may, upon specified contingencies, operate in favor of beneficiaries additional to, or substituted for, those first named.

shock loss: An insurance claim or loss that is so large as to materially affect the underwriting averages, such as that that might occur through a major natural disaster.

short period insurance: Insurance issued for terms of less than one year.

short rate: The rate charged for insurance taken for a period of less than one year. Also, the earned premium retained by the insurance company for insurance canceled by the insured before the end of the policy period.

short-term disability income policy: A disability income policy with benefits payable for a limited period of time, and often with a waiting period as short as 30 days before benefits become payable. *(For contrast, see: long-term disability income policy.)*

short-term policy: An insurance contract in effect for less than one year.

short-term trust: A kind of reversionary trust under which the income or principal of the trust reverts to the grantor after a specific event or period. *(See also: reversionary trust.)*

shrinkage, estate: *(See: estate shrinkage.)*

sickness: In health insurance, an illness or a disease that results in an economic loss to the insured. (Pregnancy is considered a sickness.) Sickness is one of the two perils covered by health insurance. (Accident is the other.).

sickness and accident insurance: *(See: accident and health insurance.)*

sickness, confining: *(See: confining sickness.)*

sickness insurance: A form of health insurance providing coverage against loss by illness or disease.

side fund: In pension plans, an unallocated fund of assets.

simple interest: Interest earned on the principal sum only, with no interest computed on interest past due.

simple trust: Arises where property is simply vested in one person for the use of another, and the nature of the trust, not being qualified by the settlor, is left to the construction of law.

simultaneous death: *(See: Uniform Simultaneous Death Act.)*

sine prole: Died without issue.

single dismemberment: In health insurance, loss of one hand, one foot, or sight in one eye.

single extra: In life insurance, refers to an extra premium, charged as a single amount, for an impairment or extra risk.

single interest policy: Insurance protecting the interest of only one of the parties having an insurable interest in certain property, such as insurance protecting a mortgagee but not the mortgagor, or protecting the seller but not the buyer.

single payment: *(See: single premium.)*

single-payment annuity: An annuity created by the payment, at its inception, of the entire consideration in one sum.

single-payment life: A form of permanent, cash-value life insurance, purchased with an initial premium and requiring no further premiums. It is paid up for life with the first premium payment. *(See also: limited payment policy.)*

single premium: The lump-sum premium payment required to cover the entire cost of a life insurance or annuity contract.

single-premium deferred annuity: Annuity purchased with one premium, well in advance of the time the income period is to begin.

single-premium funding method: In employee retirement plans, a method of accumulating money for future payment of benefits under which the money required to pay for each year's accumulated benefits is paid to an insurance company or paid to the trust fund annually without any further contribution requirements.

single-premium immediate annuity: Annuity purchased with one lump-sum payment, with the annuity income to begin immediately.

single-premium insurance (annuity): Life insurance or annuity contract paid for in full at its inception by one premium, with no further premiums due during the term of the contract.

single-premium policy: With respect to life insurance and annuities, any of a number of kinds of policies in which the entire premium is paid in one sum at the beginning of the contract period. Seldom used in connection with term contracts, but required for immediate annuities and sometimes used for the purchase of deferred annuities, as well as whole life and endowment contracts.

single taxpayer: For federal income tax purposes, a person who is not entitled to file a joint return or a return as a head of household. Generally, the tax rates or individual incomes are higher for single taxpayers than for other classifications.

sinking fund: Money accumulated to pay for losses. Some businesses and individuals choose this form of self-insurance to cover a portion of certain losses.

sinking fund approach: In a business buy-sell arrangement, a funding technique that involves setting aside a fixed amount of money each year, usually beginning when the agreement is signed.

skilled nursing care: Daily nursing and rehabilitative care, ordered by a doctor and performed by, or under the supervision of, trained medical personnel.

skilled nursing facility: A medical institution, licensed by the state and often certified by Medicare and Medicaid to provide skilled medical care.

sliding scale commission: In insurance, a commission adjustment on earned premiums under a formula whereby the actual commission (paid by a reinsurer to a ceding insurer) varies inversely with the loss ratio, subject to a maximum and minimum. Also refers to a group insurance commission schedule that declines as the volume of a case increases.

Social/Health Maintenance Organization (SHMO): A prepaid, Congressionally mandated plan that provides consolidated healthcare and support services (such as long-term care benefits) to its members.

social insurance: Compulsory plan under which participants are entitled to certain benefits as a matter of right. The plan is administered by a state or federal government agency aimed at providing a minimum standard of living for lower and middle wage groups. Social Security, unemployment compensation, etc., are social insurance programs.

social insurance programs: Encompasses all the insurance benefit (pecuniary or service) programs provided for the public, or large segments of it, by federal, state, and/or local governments, including: old-age, survivors and disability insurance; Medicare and Medicaid; unemployment compensation; workers' compensation; compulsory temporary disability insurance; railroad retirement; railroad unemployment and temporary disability insurance; assistance to the blind and to dependent children, etc.

Social Security: Programs provided under the United States Social Security Act, originally passed in 1935 and now including Medicare, Medicaid, OASDI and a variety of grants-in-aid. Government programs that provide economic security to the public. For example, social insurance, public assistance, family allowances, grants-in-aid, maternity benefits, etc.

Social Security Act: Federal legislation providing social insurance on a national scale.

Social Security benefit, primary: Retirement income for life, payable to a worker without dependents under the old-age, survivors, and disability insurance section of the Federal Social Security Act.

Social Security benefits: Benefits provided for eligible workers and their families under Social Security programs; can be placed in three general categories: survivor benefits, retirement benefits, and disability benefits.

Social Security, integration under Section 401: Regulations in accordance with Section 401 of the Internal Revenue Code regarding the manner in which benefits under a private employee retirement plan and benefits under Social Security must be related so that the private plan does not discriminate in favor of higher paid employees.

society, foreign: (*See: foreign society.*)

Society of Actuaries: An association of actuaries, organized in 1948 as successor to the Actuarial Society of America and the American Institute of Actuaries. Grants the designations of Fellow of the Society of Actuaries (FSA) on completion of ten examinations in mathematical and statistical disciplines and of Associate of the Society of Actuaries (ASA) on completion of the first five of the ten examinations.

sole proprietorship: The simplest form of business organization, whereby one individual owns and controls the entire company. All the personal assets of the owner are subject to the indebtedness of the business. Legally there is no distinction between personal assets and business assets.

sole proprietorship insurance: Life and health insurance purchased for the purpose of handling the business continuity problems arising in a sole proprietorship.

solicitor: In general, one who solicits, as business or charitable donations, etc. In insurance, one who acts for an agent in soliciting risks, but who has no authority to bind those risks. The solicitor may seek prospects and collect premiums on behalf of the agent.

sound health clause: A clause sometimes included in a policy that states that the policy will not take effect on delivery unless the applicant is alive and in good health.

Southeastern Underwriters Association Case: A famous court case resulting in a 1944 landmark decision by the Supreme Court of the United States, in which insurance was declared to be interstate commerce and, therefore, capable of regulation by the U.S. Congress.

special acceptance: In reinsurance, the specific agreement by a reinsurer to include under a reinsurance contract a risk that is not automatically included within the terms thereof.

special agent: In insurance, an agent representing his or her company in an exclusive territory.

special class: In insurance, the status of an applicant who cannot qualify for a standard policy, but may secure one with a rider waiving the payment for a loss involving certain existing health impairments. He or she may be required to pay a higher premium, or the policy may be issued with lesser benefits than those requested.

special class insurance: *(See: substandard insurance.)*

special contract: *(See: combination policy* and *guaranteed dividend policy.)*

special features: In a health insurance policy, the benefits paid with respect to losses other than those covered by principal sum and loss of time. Hospital and surgical benefits are among these.

special hazard: In insurance, a risk of more than average size, duration or danger.

special indemnities: In a health insurance policy, provisions that extend the coverage of the policy or more clearly define the risks covered. *(See also: optional benefits.)*

special risk: *(See: special class.)*

special risk policies: Insurance agreements providing benefits for losses sustained because of unusual risks or providing benefits in unusual amounts.

special services benefits: *(See: hospital miscellaneous benefits.)*

special trust: One in which a trustee is interposed for the execution of some purpose particularly pointed out, and is not, as in case of a simple trust, a mere passive depositary of the estate, but is required to exert himself or herself actively in the execution of the settlor's intention.

specialty risk: *(See: special class.)*

specific legacy: A gift of personal property provided for by will, the gift being limited to a particular asset or fund of the decedent's.

specific market: As a market for insurance, a group of people or businesses with common needs, usually of the same occupation. Grocers, surgeons, etc., constitute specific markets. This is compared to general markets, such as merchants, medical people, etc. *(See also: general market.)*

specified amount: The initial death benefit selected under a variable universal life policy.

specified disease insurance: Insurance that provides certain benefits for the treatment of a disease named in the policy, often a rare disease with very high benefits payable if it occurs.

speculative risk: In insurance, uncertainty as to whether a loss will occur, no gain being possible.

spendthrift provision: A policy provision stipulating that, to the extent permitted by law, the policy proceeds shall not be subject to the claims of creditors of any beneficiary or contingent beneficiary or to any legal process against any beneficiary or contingent beneficiary.

spendthrift trust: A trust established to provide a fund for an individual that includes a provision intended to secure it against that person's improvidence and protect it against the claims of creditors.

split-dollar insurance: An arrangement between two people (often employer and employee or parent and grown child) where life insurance is written on the life of one, who also names the beneficiary of the net death benefits (death benefits less cash value), and the other is assigned the cash value (or equivalent amount of death benefits), with both sharing the premium payments (usually the noninsured paying a portion equal to the increase in cash value each year and the insured paying the balance of the annual premium). Upon termination of the plan while the insured is living, the cash value generally would go to the noninsured to compensate for the portion of premiums paid. Upon death of the insured, an amount of proceeds equal to the cash value generally would go to the noninsured, and the balance of proceeds would go to the insured's beneficiary. This method permits a financially able person (an employer or parent), at only the cost of the interest lost on the money tied up in the portion of premiums paid, to help another person (a favored employee or child) to obtain substantial amounts of needed life insurance with a very low premium outlay on his or her part.

split-dollar plan: (*See: basic split-dollar plan* and *split-dollar insurance.*)

split-dollar plan, family: (*See: family split-dollar life insurance plan* and *split-dollar insurance.*)

split funded plan: A pension plan in which part of the employer's contribution is used as premiums for insurance and part of the contribution is placed with a trustee to invest. The policies provide death benefits prior to retirement, while the cash value of the policies, together with the money in the side fund, is earmarked to provide retirement benefits.

split funding: In pension plans, the practice of funding one portion of the plan benefits through a group annuity contract or life insurance policies and the other portion through a trust fund.

split-gift provision: A provision in the Internal Revenue Code that allows a husband and wife to treat transfers of property made by one of them to a third party as if made one-half by each. This results in doubling the applicable annual exclusion and gift tax credit.

split lift insurance: A combination of installment annuity and term insurance under which the amount of annuity consideration paid determines the amount of one-year renewable term the annuitant can purchase and place on the life of anyone designated.

spoliation: The alteration of an insurance policy by a party other than the insurer or insured and without their consent and approval. It does not render the policy void and will not affect the insurance if the original words can be restored with certainty.

spousal IRA: A trust or custodial account or subaccount created for the exclusive benefit of an individual who is not otherwise covered by a qualified employee retirement plan, or an eligible individual and his or her nonworking spouse. Such account or subaccount may also be established by purchasing individual retirement annuities from an insurance company or by purchasing individual retirement bonds issued by the federal government.

spousal IRA combination: Refers to the combination of a regular IRA and a spousal IRA as provided for in Section 220 of the Internal Revenue Code.

spread loss agreement: In reinsurance, a type of agreement designed to spread mortality fluctuations from year to year, thereby concealing a high (or particularly low) mortality experience in any single year. This is an illegal practice in almost all states.

staff manager: Unit manager in an agency. (*See also: supervisor.*)

stamping office: In insurance, a central office or bureau to which agents and companies send certain daily reports and endorsements for auditing before transmittal to the insurance company. If incorrect, notice is sent to the writing office and company requesting correction.

standard: In life insurance, coverage written or issued on a basis of the regular mortality and underwriting assumption used by the insurance company.

standard account, funding: (*See: funding standard account.*)

Standard Annuity Table: The 1937 Standard Annuity Table; a mortality table widely used for annuities.

standard exceptions: In workers' compensation insurance, certain classes of employees who are classified separately for rating.

standard form: (*See: standard policy.*)

Standard Industrial Table, 1941:   A mortality table developed for use in weekly premium insurance; sometimes referred to as the 1941 SI Table.

standard issue: An insurance policy written on a basis of the regular mortality or morbidity standards used by the company. It is insurance issued at normal rates.

standardized death rate: That ratio between the total number of deaths in a year and the total number living, after proportional adjustment has been made in the numbers living and dying in each age group to fit some standard distribution of lives by age, thus permitting comparison of overall mortality rates of different groups free from the distortions that arise from different distributions by age.

standard policy: An insurance contract in common use and complying with state laws as to form and content. Also, a policy issued with standard provisions and at standard rates; not rated or with special restrictions.

standard provisions: In life insurance, provisions stating certain policyowner rights, such as grace periods and reinstatement, etc., and the rules of doing business, such as claims notification. In health insurance, the same result is accomplished by the Uniform Provisions Law, an NAIC model bill enacted by virtually all jurisdictions. (*See also: Uniform Provision Law.*)

standard risk: In life and health insurance, a person entitled to insurance protection without extra rating or special restrictions; a risk meeting the same conditions as the tabular risks on which rates are based.

state agent: In insurance, senior to a special agent, given authority in an exclusive territory, generally a state, by a company. The state agent supervises the agents and the business of that company in the assigned territory.

state death taxes: Taxes, usually of the inheritance type, levied by the state (or states) against the shares received by the heirs or beneficiaries of an estate. But in some states death taxes are of the estate type, levied against the estate of the deceased; and some states levy both types of death tax.

stated value benefit: (*See: fixed benefit.*)

stated value policy: An insurance contract that pays a certain, specified amount regardless of the size of the loss actually sustained. These are face value policies that have a stated or known amount that will be paid in the event of loss.

state fund: A fund set up by a state government to finance a mandatory insurance system, such as workers' compensation or nonoccupational disability benefits. Such a fund may be monopolistic (purchasers of the type of insurance required must place it with the state fund) or it may be merely an alternative to private insurance if the purchaser desires to use it. In some cases, it may provide the only source of coverage for certain risks (usually poor ones).

state fund, competitive: A state fund writing insurance in competition with private insurance companies.

state fund, monopolistic: A state fund with which competition has been prohibited by statute.

state insurance department: A department of a state government, created and maintained for the purpose of regulating the business of insurance, establishing licensing and continuing education standards, and disseminating information on insurance.

state license: In insurance, that document issued by the department of insurance of a state, to an insurance agent, authorizing the agent to engage in the selling of insurance for an insurance company authorized to do business in that state. Also, the document issued by such department, to an insurance company, authorizing it to do business in the state.

statement blank: A multi-page form that insurance companies must, by law, file annually in each state in which they do business.

statement of changes in financial position: One of the three major kinds of financial statements used by businesses. It is primarily a flow report that explains changes over one accounting period in the cash account of the balance sheet.

static impairment: In health insurance, a physical condition in which the body has suffered some loss or injury, but further loss or worsening of the condition is not expected. Permanent loss of sight and the amputation of a limb are two examples of static impairment.

statistics, vital: (*See: vital statistics.*)

status request: A request for the status of an insurance policy, as shown on the insurer's records.

statutory: Required by state or federal statute. Insurance is subject primarily to the laws of the state or states having jurisdiction where it is issued and sold.

statutory conditions: With respect to insurance in Canada, uniform conditions required by the Insurance Act to be part of each and every individual accident and sickness policy. Certain conditions may be omitted from the policy if the contract does not contain any provisions respecting the matters dealt with therein. Statutory conditions are for the protection of both the insured and the insuring company.

statutory disability insurance: Compulsory disability income insurance that provides specified benefits for nonoccupational disabilities. Presently only some states require such coverage.

statutory reserve: In insurance, especially life, a reserve, either specific or general, required by law.

stepped-up basis: The value of an asset for taxation purposes, generally equal to the value of estate assets at the time of a decedent's death. Appreciated property passing from a decedent to beneficiaries receives an appreciated basis for purposes of determining capital gains tax. It is equal to the fair market value of the property at the date of the decedent's death, or at an alternative valuation date.

step-rate plan: An insurance plan that has a lower premium than usual during the initial years of coverage. Premiums are stepped up over time as the contract stipulates. The overpayment in the later years offsets the earlier underpayment. Often called modified life.

stipulated payment: (*See: purchase payment.*)

stipulated premium company: (*See: assessment insurance.*)

stipulated premium insurance: A form of assessment insurance whereby a standard rate is charged. However, under certain conditions the company may require additional payment.

stock bonus plan: A plan under which bonuses are paid to corporation executives and employers in shares of stock.

stock company: In insurance, a company that is owned and controlled by a group of stockholders whose investment in the company provides the capital necessary for the issuance of guaranteed, fixed premium, nonparticipating policies. The stockholders share in the profits and losses of the company. Some stock companies also issue participating policies.

stockholder: An individual who owns some part or share of an incorporated stock company. The stock shares represent proof of ownership. The stockholders select a board of directors and share in the company's profits and losses.

stockholders' equity: In a stock insurance company selling participating life insurance, the sum of the net worth accounts allocated to the nonparticipating stockholders' branch.

stockholders' fund: In a stock insurance company marketing participating life insurance, that portion of the company's assets equal to the sum of the liabilities in the stockholders' branch and the net worth accounts allocated to the stockholders' branch.

stockholders' fund ratio: The ratio of the stockholders' fund to the total funds of a stock company selling participating insurance.

stockholders' surplus: The portion of a company's surplus allocated to the stockholders' branch in a stock company selling participating life insurance.

stock life insurance company: (*See: stock company.*)

stock purchase agreement: *(See: buy-sell agreement.)*

stock redemption: A buy-sell agreement where the business assumes the obligations of purchasing (retiring or redeeming) a deceased owner's interest in the business.

stop and go provision: In some group permanent pension plans, a clause under which the employer may temporarily discontinue payments for the insurance, and later reinstate it.

stop loss: Any insurance policy provision designed to stop the company's loss at a given point, as an aggregate payable under a policy, a maximum payable for any one disability, or the like.

straight life: *(See: ordinary life insurance.)*

straight life annuity: *(See: annuity, life.)*

straight life insurance: *(See: ordinary insurance.)*

straight life policy: A whole life policy that allows an insured to pay premiums until death or age 100. As with all whole life policies, the protection lasts throughout the insured's lifetime. *(For contrast, see: limited life policy.)*

straight line rule: One of the three statutory limitations on pension funding, permitting the employer to deduct any amount in excess of 5 percent of compensation necessary to provide, with respect to all employees under the trust, the remaining unfunded cost of their past and current service credits distributed as a level amount, or as a level percentage of compensation, over the remaining future service of each such employee.

straight term: A basic form of term life insurance, written for a specific number of years, having a level premium and automatically terminating at the end of the period.

student insurance: Insurance policies issued to students, usually college students.

subaccount: One of the separate investment accounts within a variable life policy. Each subaccount has its own investment portfolio and objectives.

subagent: An individual who reports to an insurance company through another agent.

sub-broker: In reinsurance, an intermediary from whom another intermediary obtains reinsurance business to be placed.

Subchapter S: Subchapter S of the Internal Revenue Code providing, among other things, that a corporation meeting certain conditions can elect to be taxed like a partnership. Thus, corporate profits would be taxed only once, instead of twice as in a regular corporation.

Subchapter S corporation: A corporation electing not to pay the corporate tax, having its income taxed to each stockholder in proportion to his or her interest in the corporation.

subject premium: In reinsurance, the ceding company's premium (written or earned) to which the reinsurance premium rate is applied to produce the reinsurance premium.

submitted business: Applications for coverage submitted to the insurance company, but not yet acted upon by it.

subscriber: The name given to a policyowner of a health plan that is underwritten by a service insurance carrier, such as Blue Cross/Blue Shield.

subscription policy: An insurance policy to which two or more insurance companies may subscribe, indicating on the policy the share of the risk to be borne by each company.

substandard: *(See: substandard risk.)*

substandard insurance: Life insurance issued, at premium rates higher than standard, to applicants who do not meet the underwriting requirements set for standard life insurance coverage.

substandard risk: In life and health insurance, a risk that is below the standard or average. Substandard risks, if covered at all, are usually underwritten in health insurance by the use of a waiver; in life insurance, substandard risks are charged additional premium.

succession duty: In Canada, a tax levied by some provinces on the value (subject to exemptions) received by a beneficiary of an estate at the estate owner's death. Under certain conditions, life insurance proceeds are includible in the estate.

succession tax: *(See: inheritance tax.)*

sufficiency of notice: In insurance, a written statement sent to the insurance company or its authorized agent with sufficient information to identify the insured in event of a claim.

suicide provision: Most life insurance policies provide that if the insured commits suicide within a specified period, usually one or two years after date of issue, the company's liability will be limited to a return of premiums paid.

sui juris: An individual who may enter into a legal and binding contract, uncontrolled by another person.

suitability: Refers to the agent's legal responsibility under Securities and Exchange Commission requirements to determine, within reason, the suitability of a variable life product for a given prospect or client.

sum insured: In life insurance, that amount paid as a death claim, or at maturity of the contract, as stated on the face of the policy.

superannuated: Antiquated; incapacitated or disqualified for active work by advanced age; retired. In employee retirement planning, the condition of an employee who has reached or passed the age of retirement.

superannuation: To become antiquated; to become incapacitated or disqualified for active work because of old age or infirmity. With respect to employee retirement plans, having reached or passed the age of retirement.

superimposed plans: In insurance, plans designed to supplement plans already in existence, for the purpose of extending and broadening benefits.

superintendent of agencies: The title used by many insurance companies to designate an executive in the home office agency department responsible for supervising agency heads and for sales generated in the assigned agencies. Common titles include director of agencies, regional director and field vice president.

supervised study: A method of agent training whereby the agent studies instructional material (text or other media), then answers questionnaires, which are submitted to a grading service for evaluation.

supervisor: In a life insurance branch office or agency, the second line management person immediately responsible for the supervision of agents. He or she reports directly to the agency head. Some common titles include assistant general agent, associate general agent, district manager, sales manager, unit supervisor, staff manager or staff assistant.

supplemental contract: (*See: supplementary agreement.*)

supplemental conversion fund: (*See also: conversion fund (supplemental).*)

supplemental cost: In employee benefit plans, a separate element of actuarial cost that appears when the actuarial cost method establishes future normal cost accruals whose actuarial present value is less than the actuarial present value of the total prospective benefits of the plan. Such supplemental cost is generally, but not always, the result of applying the actuarial cost method on the assumption (explicit or implicit) that the actuarial cost accrual began before (1) the establishment of the plan or (2) the commencement of funding (or other recognition of cost accruals). A supplemental cost may also arise after inception of the plan because of plan changes in actuarial assumptions, actuarial losses, or failure to fund or otherwise recognize normal cost accruals or interest on the supplemental cost.

supplemental payments: With respect to some pension plans, additional amounts of money usually provided out of the employer's current income and paid to retired employees to supplement their pensions.

supplemental retirement income: All unearned income in excess of Social Security benefits, such excess income stemming from retirement plans, life insurance, annuities, investments, etc.

supplemental term insurance: In life insurance, a supplemental agreement available in some policies, providing for the payment of an additional specified sum in event the insured dies during the given term period. In general, any coverage purchased in addition to ongoing, base plans.

supplementary agreement: A document or rider attached to an insurance policy and made a part of it, providing for an additional benefit or some modification of a benefit already contained in the policy.

supplementary contract: With respect to life insurance, an agreement between an insurance company and the beneficiary whereby the company retains the lump-sum proceeds payable under an insurance policy and makes payments in accordance with the settlement options chosen. It specifies the amounts and times of the payments to be made, the payee or payees, and all other pertinent factors in connection with the settlement.

surgical expense insurance: A basic health insurance policy (or coverage added to, or included in, a policy) that provides benefits to pay for surgical costs including fees for the surgeon, the anesthesiologist and the operating room.

surgical indemnities: In health insurance, fixed indemnities for certain surgical operations specified in the policy or in provisions attached to the policy.

surgical schedule: In a basic medical expense health insurance policy, the list of cash allowances that are payable for various types of surgery, with the respective maximum amounts payable based upon the severity of the medical procedure. The stipulated maximum usually covers all professional fees involved (e.g., surgeon, anesthesiologist).

surplus: The amount by which assets exceed liabilities. Also, with respect to reinsurance, the portion of a ceding company's gross amount of insurance on a risk remaining after deducting the retention established by the ceding company.

surplus account: The difference between a company's assets and liabilities. Net surplus includes contingency reserves and unassigned funds, while gross surplus also includes surplus assigned for distribution as dividends.

surplus business: In life and health insurance, business placed by agents who are not full-time, regular representatives of the insurance company to which they are directing the business.

surplus, contingency: *(See: contingency reserve.)*

surplus, divisible: *(See: divisible surplus.)*

surplus line broker: *(See: excess line broker.)*

surplus reserves: Surplus accounts set up by insurance companies to cover possible unfavorable future developments. They represent portions of surplus appropriated to special accounts, so that the balancing assets will not be distributed as profits, but retained as margins of safety for the protection of the companies and their policyowners.

surplus share reinsurance: *(See: reinsurance, surplus share.)*

surplus to policyowners: With respect to insurance, the capital of the insurer, all unassigned funds, including general and special reserve funds (providing such funds are not liabilities).

surrender a policy: In life insurance, the policyowner's return of a policy to the insurance company in exchange for the policy's cash surrender value or other equivalent nonforfeiture values. (*See also: nonforfeiture values.*)

surrender charge: Under a group plan, the charge for the cancellation of an insurance or annuity policy. When an employee in good health withdraws from a group annuity plan, the total contributions are returned or credited back with interest, but minus a surrender charge. If the plan is contributory, the employer almost invariably absorbs this cost. In traditional individual life insurance, there is no direct charge for surrendering a policy. Cash values are disassociated from the reserve and calculated directly. In a variable or universal life policy, however, a charge may be deducted from the available cash value to cover the expense of a policy surrender. Also called a back-end load.

surrender dividend: In life insurance, a special, or extra, dividend payable by some companies at the time of the termination of a policy by surrender for cash. Usually, there is a minimum number of years that premiums must be paid to be eligible for this dividend. (*See also: maturity dividend.*)

surrendered policy: A life insurance policy that has been returned to the insurance company and terminated, generally under the nonforfeiture provisions of the policy after surrender values have become available.

surrender options: (*See: nonforfeiture options and provisions.*)

surrender value: (*See: cash value* and *nonforfeiture options and provisions.*)

surrogate court: (*See: probate court.*)

survivor—monthly income for dependent child: Under Social Security, a monthly benefit paid to each eligible child of a fully or currently insured deceased individual until the child reaches the age of 18 (age 22 if a full-time student in a public or accredited school or college) or beyond if the child is disabled—unless the child marries.

survivor—monthly income for widow or widower: Under Social Security, a monthly benefit paid to an eligible widow or widower (age 60 or over) of a deceased covered individual.

survivor—monthly income for widow or widower with child (children) in his or her care: Under Social Security, a monthly benefit paid to an eligible widow or widower of a deceased fully insured or currently insured individual, who has in his or her care a child (or children) of the deceased under age 16 (or disabled) and eligible for a child's benefit. Such benefits are in addition to those payable to the child. (They do not continue to the widow or widower beyond the child's age 16, by virtue of the child's receiving a benefit beyond 18, as a student.)

survivorship annuity: A life insurance policy, rather than an annuity contract, providing a set amount of income for life to the beneficiary, beginning at the death of the insured. The actual amount of insurance required depends upon the age of the beneficiary, as well as the age of the insured, since the sum required to provide a life annuity of a given amount decreases with the advancing age of the beneficiary. If the beneficiary predeceases the insured, the policy is terminated and no benefits are paid. Survivorship annuities are sometimes called reversionary annuities.

survivorship life annuity: (*See: annuity, joint life and survivorship.*)

suspect: In an insurance agent's prospecting activities, a potential prospect whose name has been obtained, but about whom there is not presently enough information regarding needs, ability to pay, etc., to determine if he or she is, in fact, a qualified, legitimate prospect.

suspension: With respect to some contributory employee retirement plans that do not permit employees to withdraw from the plan while continuing in employment, the temporary discontinuance of contributions by a participant (generally permitted upon application). The term also refers to a temporary interruption of employer contributions that may sometimes be permitted by an insurance company and/or the Secretary of the Treasury without terminating the plan.

swap maternity: In some group health insurance plans, a provision allowing immediate maternity coverage under a plan, but terminating coverage on pregnancies in progress upon termination of the plan.

switching: Changing insurance (usually life) to another form or to another company more for the purpose of obtaining commissions than for the benefit of the client. This is an illegal practice. (*See also: twisting.*)

switch maternity: In group health insurance, a provision for maternity coverage on female employees only when their husbands are included in the plan as dependents.

T

tabular: Of or pertaining to a table. Tabular cost, the cost of mortality, morbidity, or other claims according to the valuation tables and assumptions used by the insurance company. Tabular mortality, mortality as shown on a mortality table. Tabular morbidity, morbidity as shown on a morbidity table.

tabular cost: In insurance, the mortality or morbidity cost from a table, based on the valuation assumption used.

tabular mortality or morbidity: Mortality or morbidity as indicated on the mortality or morbidity table in use; expected mortality or morbidity.

take-home pay: A worker's net income; the money received after all deductions, including taxes.

tangible asset: An asset having physical, material substance, such as gold or machinery with an actual value.

tangible net worth: An organization's or individual's net financial worth, not including such assets as goodwill and patents.

tangible personal property: Physical assets in the form of movable wealth (household furniture, farm machinery, automobiles, farm animals, jewelry, etc.), as compared to real property. (*See also: real property.*)

target benefit: In some pension plans, the goal as to the result of the retirement benefit. However, it is not a promised retirement income and, therefore, the plan is not a defined benefit plan, but a defined contribution plan, called an individual account plan under ERISA.

target benefit plan: A plan under which an amount of pension benefit is determined by applying some formula to the current compensation of each participant. Having determined the pension benefit, an annual contribution is then computed for each participant. This contribution may be the premium necessary to buy an insurance contract that will normally produce the desired pension benefit.

target premium: Periodic premium that will provide a schedule of benefits using a specific set of assumptions; usually in reference to universal life policies.

target risks: Policyowners or prospects whose insurance coverage calls for large premiums, making these persons targets for competing insurance agents and brokers. Also used to describe risks of large value or limits, and severe hazards that are difficult to insure or for companies to reinsure.

taxable estate: The gross estate, less funeral and administration expenses, debts of the decedent, claims against the estate, losses during administration (the adjusted gross estate), less the marital deduction (if the estate qualifies for the marital deduction), less charitable deductions and orphan's exclusion.

taxable gift: A voluntary and complete lifetime transfer of property by an individual to another individual or private organization for less than adequate and full consideration; not a bona fide business transaction.

taxable income: Gross income minus certain deductions and exemptions, from which the income tax due is determined.

taxable year: A period of time for which a report is to be made by a person or business, of income received, allowable deductions, etc., for income tax purposes. This is generally a calendar year for individuals, but may be another acceptable 12-month period (fiscal year) for businesses. A taxpayer on the cash basis is required to include items in gross income in the taxable year received; a taxpayer on the accrual basis is required to include items in gross income in the taxable year they accrue.

tax and board: In insurance, the percentages of paid premiums going for state and local taxes and for the support of the various rating offices, bureaus, and rating boards.

tax carryback and carryover: A provision in the income tax laws that states that, within defined limits, losses can be carried back or forward to apply against a preceding or following year's income. The effect is to level income over the years for tax purposes.

tax credit: An amount that may be applied directly to reduce a tax liability, as in the case of the unified credit against estate taxes and the unified credit against gift taxes.

tax-deferred annuity: A retirement plan, not necessarily an annuity, for employees of non-profit organizations, such as schools and churches. Those who qualify can elect to have a specific percentage of their income set aside for retirement and delay income taxes until the money is withdrawn. Sometimes called tax-sheltered annuity or TSA. (*See also: tax-sheltered annuity.*)

tax-deferred 403(b) plan: A retirement plan provided for employees of Section 501(c)(3) organizations and public schools only, under Section 403(b) of the Internal Revenue Code, purchased by the employer with increases in salary or salary reductions continued by the employees.

tax, estate: (*See: estate tax.*)

tax-exempt securities: Securities of state and local governments—usually called municipals—the interest on which is generally exempt from federal income taxation. Capital gains on state and local securities, however, are subject to federal income (capital gains) tax, except when the initial issue is at less than par. The interest on federal government securities is not exempt from state and local taxation.

tax-favored retirement plans: Retirement plans in which (1) deposits are tax deductible; (2) the deductible deposits are not currently taxed, but taxes are paid when benefits are actually received; and (3) income realized on invested retirement funds accumulates on a tax-deferred basis.

tax, federal estate: (*See: federal estate tax.*)

tax, federal gift: (*See: federal gift tax.*)

tax free: Anything upon which no tax is imposed; proceeds from a life insurance policy are generally received on a tax-free basis.

tax-free rollover: The tax-free transfer of accumulated assets from one qualified retirement plan to another, such as from an IRA or annuity.

tax insurance: Insurance coverage, the proceeds from which are used to pay the insured's estate taxes upon his or her death.

tax-option corporation: (*See: Subchapter S corporation.*)

tax-sheltered annuity: A tax-deferred retirement plan available to employees of Code Section 501(c)(3) institutions and public school teachers. Although the word annuity is used descriptively, mutual funds and life insurance policies where the insurance amount is incidental may be used, along with annuities, as funding mechanisms. More and more, the term "tax-deferred annuity" is replacing this term, as the word "deferred" is more accurate. (*See also: tax-deferred annuity.*)

temporary and conditional receipt: (*See: temporary receipt.*)

temporary disability benefits (TDB):   Benefits payable to employees for nonoccupational disabilities, especially under TDB laws in several states.

temporary level extra premiums: In life insurance, a type of rating most frequently used with physical impairments where the risk is considered to be of a temporary nature.

temporary license: In insurance, an agent's license issued by some states, permitting an individual to operate as an agent, usually for six months or less, prior to complying fully with licensing requirements. After that time, the individual must comply with the state's licensing requirements and obtain a regular license or cease operating as an agent.

temporary life annuity: A contract providing for the payment of an annuity for a limited period only, or until the annuitant's death within the specified period.

temporary partial disability: A disability that causes some loss of activity and income-earning ability, and from which full recovery is expected. Used mainly in workers' compensation insurance.

temporary receipt: In life insurance, a form given by an agent to the policyowner paying a premium when the premium receipt book or the official premium receipt is not available or when the premium cannot be officially receipted because the grace period has expired.

temporary total disability: A disability that causes complete loss of income-earning ability, from which full recovery is expected. Used mainly in workers' compensation insurance.

tenancy by the entirety: Joint ownership by husband and wife, with right of survivorship, as usually expressed in titles to real property. In most states today, equated (by statute) to joint tenancy. (*See also: joint tenancy.*)

tenancy in common: A form of estate ownership held in common by two or more persons, each of whom is considered as being possessed of the whole of an undivided part. Under this form of ownership, when one dies, the interest of the one dying passes to the heirs of the deceased and not to the co-tenants.

ten-day free look provision: A life and health insurance policy provision (often required by law) giving the policyowner ten days to review a new policy. If the policyowner is not satisfied with the policy, it can be returned to the insurance company for a 100 percent refund of premium paid. Coverage is then cancelled from the date of issue and the insurance company is not liable for any claims. Some state laws require a twenty-day free look provision.

tender: An offer of money or property.

ten percent rule: With respect to employee retirement plans, one of three statutory limitations on pension funding, stating that the employer may deduct, in lieu of the amounts allowed under the two funding limitation rules, a sum equal to the normal cost of the plan, plus (as long as an unfunded amount remains) ten percent of the initial past service liability adjusted for past experience.

ten-year funding: In employee retirement plans, a type of funding, primarily for superannuated people, requiring that premiums be payable for ten years, even though retirement may occur sooner.

term: In insurance, that period of time during which a policy is in force. Also, a clause in a contract of health insurance that makes no provision for renewal or termination other than by expiration of the policy term. (*See also: term contract or policy.*)

term contract or policy: Life insurance issued for a specified number of years, normally building up no cash value and expiring without value. Also, the period of time during which a policy runs. In health insurance, a contract that makes no provision for renewal. The policy terminates at the end of the policy term.

term, convertible: (*See: convertible term insurance.*)

term, decreasing: (*See: decreasing term insurance.*)

terminable interest: One that may terminate or fail upon the lapse of time, the occurrence of an event or contingency, or the failure of an event or contingency to occur. Life estates, leasehold interests, annuities, patents, and copyrights are examples of terminable interests.

terminal dividend: In life insurance, dividends (mortuary, maturity, and surrender) that may be payable upon termination of a policy at death, maturity, or surrender for its cash value, usually after the policy has been in force for at least a specified number of years. Some companies provide for such dividends; many companies do not.

terminal funding: A pension plan funding method under which benefits are funded in full as each participant reaches retirement, but in which no money is set aside for active participants.

terminal reserve: *(See: reserve, terminal.)*

terminated policy: An insurance policy that is no longer in effect.

termination: In insurance, refers to a policy's becoming of no effect. No more premiums are payable on the policy after termination, and it no longer has any value. Termination can occur in a number of ways, including failure to pay premiums as required, surrendering the policy for its cash value, etc.

termination date: The date on which the coverage under an insurance policy ends.

termination insurance: *(See: Pension Benefit Guaranty Corporation.)*

term insurance: Life insurance protection for a limited number of years and expiring without value if the insured survives the stated period. The protection period may be as short as 30 days (as in temporary insurance agreements) or as long as 20 years or more. *(For contrast, see: whole life insurance.)*

term insurance, convertible: *(See: convertible term insurance.)*

term insurance, decreasing: *(See: decreasing term insurance.)*

term insurance, deposit: *(See: deposit term life insurance.)*

term insurance, extended: *(See: extended term option.)*

term insurance, family: *(See: family term insurance.)*

term insurance, group renewable: *(See: group life insurance.)*

term insurance rider: A form providing term life insurance that is attached and added to a permanent life insurance policy, with the purpose of increasing the total amount of protection during the term period. The premium-paying period of the permanent policy must be as long as, or longer than, the premium-paying period of the term rider.

term, level: (*See: level term insurance.*)

term loan: A loan, generally for a period longer than five years, usually made by insurance companies or banks to businesses that typically agree to restrict their activities to specified areas.

term, long: (*See: long term.*)

term, monthly reducing: (*See: mortgage protection insurance.*)

term, mortgage protection: (*See: mortgage protection insurance.*)

term of policy: The period for which a policy runs. In life insurance, this is to the end of the term period for term insurance, to the maturity date for endowments, and to the insured's death (or age 100) for whole life policies. In most other kinds of insurance, it is usually the period for which the premium has been paid.

term, renewable: (*See: renewable term insurance.*)

term, renewable and convertible: (*See: renewable and convertible term.*)

term reserve valuation, full preliminary: (*See: full preliminary term reserve valuation.*)

term rider: (*See: term insurance rider.*)

term, straight: (*See: straight term.*)

term to age ( ): A form of long-term life insurance continuing to the designated age of the policyowner. (*See: long term.*)

territorial limits: (*See: geographical limitations.*)

tertiary beneficiary: In life insurance, a beneficiary designated as third in line to receive the proceeds or benefits if the primary and secondary beneficiaries do not survive the insured.

testamentary disposition: A disposition of a person's property at death by will or testament. A transfer of property ownership without consideration (gift) that is not to take effect until the death of the grantor, and that is specified and described by a will or testament made by the grantor.

testamentary trust: A trust created by provision in the grantor's will and therefore not to become effective until his or her death.

testate: Having left a will. Also, disposing of one's property by will.

testator: The person making a will.

theory of probability: An area of mathematics from which comes the law of large numbers (also called law of simple probability and Poisson's law), that is the mathematical principal that insurance is based upon. (*See also: law of large numbers.*)

Thiasoi: Ancient Greek benevolent societies considered a step in the evolution of life and health insurance.

thin market: A volatile stock or securities market where bid and asked prices are usually well below or above the price at the last sale.

third party beneficiary: A person not a party to a contract, yet who has legally enforceable rights under the contract. Such a person might be a life insurance beneficiary, a mortgagee holding an assignment, or a member of a group insurance plan.

three-year rule: The three-year rule that required gifts made within three years of death to be included in the gross estate, was largely eliminated by the 1981 Economic Recovery Tax Act. However, the three-year rule is retained where the decedent made a gift within three years of death of one or more of the following property interests: transfers with a retained life interest; reversionary interests; revocable transfers; general powers of appointment; and incidents of ownership in life insurance policies. (*See also: contemplation of death, gift in.*)

thrift plan: Any type of retirement plan, pension or profit sharing, in which an employee savings feature is added. Usually, the employer's contributions or the plan's allocations (if profit sharing) are based upon the amount the individual employee elects to save.

ticket insurance: Accident-only protection issued in conjunction with the purchase of a ticket for transportation on a common carrier. (*See also: travel-accident policies.*)

tickler: A file designed to jog one's memory and call attention to something at a certain time. In life insurance, birthday and call-back tickler files are common examples. In other kinds of insurance, the policy-expiration and premium-due tickets are examples of this device.

time deposit: A bank savings deposit account subject to at least 30 days' notice before withdrawal of funds. Thirty days' notice is the dividing line, used by the Federal Reserve System, between time and demand deposits.

time limit: In health insurance, the period of time within which a notice of claim or proof of loss must be filed.

time limit on certain defenses: A provision required by state law to be included in every individual health policy issued stating that after a certain number of years (usually two or three) no statements other than fraudulent misrepresentations made in the application shall be used by the insurance company to deny a claim for life insurance. (*See also: incontestable clause.*)

time of endowment: In life insurance, the time when a cash value policy endows for its face amount. In a whole life policy, the time of endowment is age 100. Under an endowment policy, this is the date on which the endowment matures, as stated in the policy.

time of no risk: In life insurance, the time at which the cash value of a policy equals or exceeds its face amount. From this point on, there is no longer any insurance risk involved in the policy.

time of payment of claims provision: A mandatory, health insurance provision specifying how long an insurance company has to pay claims.

title: The ownership of anything of value. Property and rights of great value require written evidence of title, such as a deed to real estate or a stock certificate for ownership of an interest in a corporation. It is also often the name used to refer to the document itself, which really is not the title, but is the evidence of ownership.

tontine: A financial arrangement in which a group of participants share advantages on such terms that upon the default or death of any participant, his or her advantages are distributed among the remaining participants until only one remains, whereupon the whole goes to that person; or on the expiration of an agreed period, the whole goes to those participants remaining at that time.

tort: A wrongful act (or failure to act) by one person that gives another person the right to sue for damages.

total anticipated earnings method: A means of estimating the potential economic loss that a person's family would suffer if he or she died prematurely. It calculates the total projected earnings (to age 65) that would be denied the family by the person's premature death.

total asset turnover: A business evaluation ratio arrived at by dividing the total operating assets of a business into its sales. It tells how many times operating assets are turned over, in terms of sales, during a given period (usually a year).

total cash available: With respect to a life insurance policy, the guaranteed cash value, plus dividend accumulations or the cash value of paid-up additions, if any, plus terminal dividend, when payable.

total disability: There are many definitions of this term in health insurance. The most common states that the totally disabled person is not able to perform any of the duties and responsibilities of his or her occupation. The actual definition, however, will depend upon the wording in the insured's policy. (*See also: partial disability.*)

total equity, estimated: (*See: adjusted net worth.*)

total funds: In a stock life insurance company that sells participating life insurance, the total assets of the company, made up of a combination of the participating fund, the nonparticipating fund, and the stockholders' fund.

total needs selling: In life insurance, a combined service and marketing system designed to satisfy virtually all of a family's cash and income needs, if the earnings of the family's income producer(s) are cut off by death or retirement, with one coordinated plan and with one sale of any additional insurance needed on the income producer(s).

total service: With respect to employee retirement plans, the period of time beginning with the date an employee was hired, and ending with the date of his or her retirement.

traditional net cost comparison method: The determination of the actual cost of life insurance has been widely discussed. Traditional net cost method (that adds a policy's premiums and subtracts dividends and cash value) does not consider time value of money. A remedy for this was the Linton yield method which compares a cash value policy with a combination of decreasing term and the yield of side fund of bonds. Presently many states require prospective insured's to be given interest-adjusted cost figures that take into consideration the time value of money.

traditional product: A life insurance product with fixed premiums, death benefit and cash value growth. Contrasts to such *new generation* products as universal and variable life.

trainee: A new agent or prospective agent undergoing training and education on the facts of insurance, the pertinent laws of the state, company procedures, and insurance sales and service skills.

trainer: A general term applied to an agency supervisor or other person in charge of training and educating a new agent regarding the facts of insurance, the pertinent laws of the state, company procedures, and insurance sales and service skills.

training module: A learning unit or component covering a specific aspect of a given subject. A module is designed to be a self-contained learning unit. (*See also: module.*)

transaction: Any business exchange. With respect to stocks and bonds, the purchase and the sale of a security; it makes no difference which is made first.

transaction in contemplation of death: (*See: three-year rule.*)

transfer: The act of changing policies from one insurance account to another. In variable products, refers to the changing of cash values from one or more such-accounts to others within the policy.

transferability: The right or relative ease in transferring ownership or title.

transfer, conditional: (*See: conditional transfer.*)

transfer, estate: (*See: estate transfer.*)

transfer income: A form of unearned income received without service currently rendered by the person receiving it, such as old-age pensions, unemployment relief, and Social Security.

transfers in contemplation of death: (*See: three-year rule.*)

transfer tax: A tax imposed upon the right and privilege of transferring property to another person or legal entity. Gift and estate taxes are examples, as are taxes imposed on the transfer of real estate or securities.

transition register: A book listing all the weekly premium or monthly debit ordinary policies (of a home service company) in force on an account, that listing is kept current by the addition of records of business entering the account through new issue, revival or transfer and business leaving the account through lapse or transfer from the account.

transportation ticket insurance: (*See: ticket insurance.*)

traumatic injury: In general, damage of a physical nature caused by accidental means and not resulting from disease or illness.

travel-accident policies: Health insurance policies that limit the payment of benefits to losses that result while traveling, usually by common carrier. (*See also: ticket insurance.*)

treasury stock: Refers to issued stock that has been reacquired from stockholders by the corporation. Less commonly, authorized but unissued stock that is still in the treasury of the corporation.

treaty: In reinsurance, a contract between the ceding company and the reinsurer, setting forth the conditions of the reinsurance agreement between the two companies. This is also a term historically applied to reinsurance contracts in general.

treaty reinsurance: Reinsurance ceded and assumed in accordance with the terms of a treaty; sometimes used in contrast to facultative reinsurance. Note, however, that facultative reinsurance can also be treaty reinsurance.

trial application: In life insurance, an application submitted to the company so that the underwriting department can give some indication as to whether or not a policy will be issued and under what conditions, if a regular application is submitted. Trial applications are submitted normally if it is suspected that the prospect is a poor risk.

trial solutions: In insurance selling, possible solutions offered to the prospect by the agent or to problems uncovered during the interview. These are tested on the prospect throughout the interview and are summarized near the end of the interview.

triple indemnity: (*See: double indemnity.*)

triple protection: (*See: double indemnity.*)

true group: Group insurance issued under a master contract, with certificates of insurance that are not policy contracts issued to covered persons. In contrast to franchise or wholesale group under which each covered person is issued an individual policy contract.

trust: A legal arrangement in which property is held by a person or corporation (trustee) for the benefit of others (beneficiaries). The grantor (person who transfers the property to the trustee) gives legal title to the trustee, subject to the terms set forth in a trust agreement. Beneficiaries have equitable title to the trust property.

trust, active: (*See: active trust.*)

trust agreement: With respect to distribution of life insurance proceeds, a supplemental settlement agreement that distributes the proceeds in a special way, much as a regular fiduciary trust does. Insurance companies cannot enter into trust agreements, though policyowners can.

trust, cestui que: (*See: cestui que trust.*)

trust, charitable: (*See: charitable trust.*)

trust company: A corporation formed for the purpose of taking, accepting, and executing lawfully established trusts, and acting as trustee.

trust contingent: (*See: contingent trust.*)

trust deed: That document that establishes a trust conveying legal title of property to a trustee and which states his or her authority and the conditions that bind the trustee in dealing with the property held in a fiduciary capacity.

trust, direct: (*See: express trust.*)

trust, directory: (*See: directory trust.*)

trust, dry: (*See: dry trust.*)

trustee: One who holds the legal title to the property for the benefit of another. This may be either an individual or a company such as a bank or trust company.

trusteed pension plan: A pension plan in which the contributions are paid to and invested by a trustee. The duties of the trustee, as set forth in the trust agreement or indenture, may range from mere investment and conservation of the funds subject to various restrictions to complete administration of the plan.

trustee in bankruptcy: Person or persons authorized by a court to liquidate the assets of a bankrupt or to supervise reorganization, although the one performing the latter function is usually called a receiver.

trustee of moneys collected: Refers to the relationship of the agent to the insurance company, policyowner and state.

trustee, pension plan: (*See: pension plan trustee.*)

trust, employees': In employee benefit plans, a medium through which a plan is financed and given effect.

trust, employee stock ownership: (*See: employee stock ownership trust.*)

trust estate: May mean either the estate of the trustee—that is, the legal title—or the estate of the beneficiary, or the corpus of the property that is the subject of the trust.

trust, executed: (*See: executed trust.*)

trust, executory: (*See: executory trust.*)

trust, exempt pension: (*See: exempt pension trust.*)

trust, express: (*See: express trust.*)

trust, fixed: (*See: fixed trust.*)

trust fund: (*See: pension trust fund.*)

trust, funded: (*See: life insurance trust.*)

trust, general management: (*See: general management trust.*)

trust group: Small groups of individuals that need life and health insurance, but are too small to qualify for true group insurance. Under the trust laws of states, companies have banded together these very small groups for the purpose of purchasing insurance at rates close to those available for true group insurance. Sometimes referred to as multiple employer trusts.

trust, imperfect: (*See: executed trust.*)

trust, implied: (*See: implied trust.*)

trust indenture: The written document containing the terms and conditions binding the trustee and his or her conduct. The document is signed by the person or persons establishing the trust (called the settlor) and by the trustee. The term also refers to an arrangement under which a third party holds the instrument in trust as security for the payment of a debt.

Trust Indenture Act: This law, passed by Congress in 1939, regulates some of the terms and conditions of trust arrangements in connection with corporate security issues.

trust, involuntary: *(See: involuntary trust.)*

trust, naked: *(See: dry trust.)*

trust, passive: *(See: passive trust.)*

trust, pension: *(See: pension trust.)*

trust, precatory: *(See: precatory trust.)*

trust, private: *(See: private trust.)*

trust, public: *(See: public trust.)*

trust, secret: *(See: secret trust.)*

trust, shifting: *(See: shifting trust.)*

trust, simple: *(See: simple trust.)*

trust, special: *(See: special trust.)*

trust, spendthrift: *(See: spendthrift trust.)*

trust, testamentary: *(See: testamentary trust.)*

trust, voluntary: *(See: voluntary trust.)*

T Tables: With respect to employee retirement plans, a collection of factors incorporating the ideas of interest, mortality, and turnover used to properly fund retirement benefits for employees of varying types of industries.

turnover: Refers to the number of persons hired within a stated period to replace those leaving or dropped; also, the ratio of this number to the average work force maintained. In pension plans, turnover refers to the ratio of participants who leave employment through quitting, discharge, etc., to the total of participants at any age or length of service.

turnover, discount for: Under some types of pension plan funding, the anticipated cost of the plan is reduced by assuming that a certain percentage of employees will terminate employment before retirement for reasons other than death. The rate of withdrawals cannot be determined on the basis of any actuarial table, but on experience within the company or on some other assumption.

turnover rate: In pension plans, the rate at which participating employees' services are terminated, as a ratio of total participants.

For actuarial assumptions under a pension plan, turnover rate should be analyzed by age, sex, and length of service.

twenty-four-hour coverage: A provision of health insurance plans that provides benefits for loss incurred on or off the job.

twister: In life insurance, an informal term that refers to an agent who, by misrepresentation, induces an insured to lapse or surrender a policy he or she holds and to replace it with a new policy. (*See also: twisting.*)

twisting: In life insurance, inducing an insured through misrepresentation to drop an existing policy in order to take a similar policy from the selling agent. Twisting is cause for license revocation in most states and is an offense that is against the law in many states. (*See also: replacement.*)

two-income family: A family in which husband and wife both are employed and share the income-producing responsibility for the household. It is characterized by distinct life insurance needs often quite different from the traditional single-income family of the past. Also called dual-income family.

U

ultimate mortality table: A mortality table based on life insurance experience after the first few (usually five) policy years from date of issue have been excluded. The purpose is to show the rate of mortality by attained age after the effects of selection (by medical examination, etc.) have worn off.

ultimate net loss: That total sum that the insured or any company as insurer, or both, becomes legally obligated to pay, such as legal, medical and investigatory costs.

umpire clause: In some insurance policies, a provision that, in the event the insured and the insurance company cannot agree on a claim settlement, each party is to select an arbitrator, and the two arbitrators then select an umpire. The insured and the insurance company agree to abide by the decision of the majority vote of the arbitrators and umpire.

unaccrued: Most often, this describes income resulting from payments received but not yet due, as in the case of one receiving a rent payment before the due date. (*See also: unearned income.*)

unallocated benefit: A reimbursement provision in health insurance policies, usually for miscellaneous hospital and medical expenses that does not specify how much will be paid for each type of treatment, examination, or the like, but only sets a maximum that will be paid for all such treatments.

unallocated claim expense: Expenses of loss adjustment that an insurance company incurs but cannot charge specifically to any single claim, such as claim department salaries and office overhead.

unallocated funding: A pension plan funding technique whereby employer contributions to the plan are held in an undivided fund until used to meet benefit payments as they come due, or to purchase annuities for participants on retirement or on earlier termination of employment with vested benefits.

unallocated funding instruments: With respect to pension plans, group deposit administration annuity contracts and trust agreements under which all benefit payments in a trust are made from a trust fund. (*See also: unallocated funding.*)

unallocated loss expense: (*See: unallocated claim expense.*)

unauthorized insurance: Insurance written by a company not licensed to do business in the state or country in which it sold the policy.

unauthorized insurer: An insurance company not licensed to do business in a particular state. (*See also: nonadmitted company.*)

unbundled fees: Refers to the legal requirement that variable and universal life insurance policy costs and deductions be clearly stated and explained.

uncancellable: (*See: noncancellable.*)

unconditional vesting: That form of vesting in a contributory plan under which entitlement to a vested benefit is not based upon the nonwithdrawal of the participant's contributions.

underinsurance: In life and health insurance, a condition in which inadequate insurance is carried to satisfy an individual's or business's insurance needs in the event of the insured's death or illness.

underlying insurance: The amount of insurance or reinsurance on a risk that attaches before the next higher excess layer of insurance or reinsurance attaches.

underlying premium: (*See: subject premium.*)

underwrite: To examine a risk, decide on its eligibility for insurance, and determine the appropriate rate.

underwriter: Technically, the person who writes his or her name under an insurance agreement, accepting all or part of the risk. In life and health insurance, used to designate that official in the home office who reviews the facts about the risk, accepts or declines the risk and assigns the rate; the home office underwriter. In life insurance, to designate a soliciting agent, the term being somewhat more descriptive than agent, since the agent does exercise underwriting discretion in selecting the risks (prospects) he or she contacts.

underwriter, field: (*See: underwriter* and *agent.*)

underwriting: The process of selecting risks and classifying them according to their degrees of insurability so that the appropriate rates may be assigned. The process includes rejection of unacceptable risks.

underwriting department: That department or division of an insurance company that handles underwriting.

underwriting, group: (*See: group underwriting.*)

underwriting profit (or loss): The profit (or loss) received from insurance or reinsurance premiums, as contrasted to that realized from investments. Also, the excess of premiums over claims paid and expenses (profit), or the excesses of claims paid and expenses over premiums (loss).

undivided right: The property rights of an individual involving jointly owned property. Each person has a right to his or her stated portion of the total property and no exclusive right to any particular part of the property.

unearned income: An individual's income derived from investments, as opposed to salary or wages.

unearned premium: That portion of written premium applicable to the unexpired or unused part of the period for which the premium has been charged. Thus, in the case of an annual premium, at the end of the first month of the premium period, eleven-twelfths of the premium is unearned.

unearned premium reserve: (*See: reserve, unearned premium.*)

unearned reinsurance premium: That part of the reinsurance premium applicable to the unexpired portion of policies that are reinsured.

unemployment compensation: Benefit payments paid to unemployed workers who meet the qualification requirements of the law, the requirements being that the worker not be unemployed voluntarily; that the worker have worked in employment covered by the law; that the worker be willing and able to take employment if offered; and that an initial waiting period of unemployment has elapsed before compensation is paid.

unemployment compensation disability: *(See: temporary disability benefits (TDB).)*

unemployment insurance: *(See: unemployment compensation.)*

unfair competition and practices law: State law that spells out those deeds and acts of a life or health insurance agent or company that are deemed unfair competition and practices that are specifically outlawed by most states. They may include twisting, rebating, defamation of persons or companies, and committing any act tending toward monopoly of the business. *(See also: twisting, rebating* and *defamation.)*

unfunded actuarial liability: The actuarial liability less the value of plan assets as of the date of plan valuation.

unfunded pension liabilities: With respect to a pension plan, money a business will be obligated to pay at some future date, but it has not yet set aside for that purpose. Unfunded pension liabilities depend for their fulfillment upon the future profitability and success of the business or firm covered by the pension plan.

unfunded pension plan: A pension plan that has made no financial provision for payment of pensions that ordinarily must be financed out of current income.

unfunded trust: *(See: life insurance trust.)*

Uniform Gift to Minors Act: A provision in the Internal Revenue Code stipulating that a gift to a minor that satisfies certain requirements will not be taxed.

uniform policy provision: A provision that is required by state statute to be in all insurance contracts of a given type; generally taken from or patterned after the model provisions provided by the National Association of Insurance Commissioners (NAIC). *(See also: Uniform Provisions Law.)*

Uniform Premium Table: A table provided by the Internal Revenue Service (in Reg. 1.70-3) standardizing the taxability of group term insurance protection costs. Also known as Table 1. *(See also: Section 79 plan.)*

Uniform Provision Law: In health insurance, a list of standard provisions that must be included in every individual health policy.

The National Association of Insurance Commissioners (NAIC) recommended these provisions and every state has adopted them. These 23 provisions spell out the rights and obligations of the policyowner and the insurance company, such as grace periods, claim reports, misstatements, claim payments, etc. The insurance company is not required to include these provisions in group contracts.

Uniform Simultaneous Death Act: The act that states that, when an insured and beneficiary die at the same time, or when they die together and it cannot be determined who died first, it is presumed that the insured survived the beneficiary. The insurance company then pays the proceeds to the next beneficiary in line, the secondary or contingent beneficiary, or to the insured's estate if the policyowner has not named a secondary beneficiary.

unilateral contract: A distinguishing characteristic of a life or health insurance agreement in that only the insurance company pledges anything. The policyowner doesn't even promise to pay premiums and only the insurance company can be sued for breach of contract.

uninsured plan: *(See: noninsured plans.)*

unit annuity: A specified amount or unit of annuity purchased each year for each participant under a group annuity contract. The participant's total retirement benefit is the total of these yearly purchases.

unit benefit: A definite or fixed pension benefit expressed as an amount or percentage of earnings per year of participation or service.

unit benefit formula: The prescription in a unit benefit pension plan for a unit of benefit to be credited to a participant for each year of recognized service with an employer.

unit benefit plan: A type of pension plan providing retirement benefits expressed as a definite amount or percentage of a participant's earnings for each year of service with the employer. The plan usually defines the benefit as a small percentage of the employee's earnings, such as one percent for each year of service. The total of these units is the amount he or she will receive each year upon retirement. If a unit of annuity is purchased each year to fund the ultimate benefit, this may also be referred to as a unit-purchase type of plan.

United States Government Life Insurance: A form of life insurance issued to members of the armed forces during World War I and until about the time of World War II.

universal life: As in traditional policies, universal life pays a death benefit and accumulates cash value. Unlike traditional products, universal life completely separates the protection element from the accumulation element of the policy. Cash value builds and is used to buy term insurance. The flexible features are the premium, the death benefit, the payment, and the protection periods.

unlicensed insurer: (*See: unauthorized insurer* and *nonadmitted company.*)

unqualified pension plan: A special arrangement between an employer and selected employees, that provides for the payment of flexible retirement benefits (and death benefits, if desired) without the necessity of submitting the plan to the government for approval, as is the case with a qualified pension plan. These plans do not receive special tax treatment.

unreported claims: Claims in the making that have not yet been reported to the insurance company. Also, the reserve set up to meet those claims.

unsecured creditor: A creditor of a debt not secured by any collateral or mortgage.

usurious rate of interest: Interest charged in excess of the maximum rate of interest that the law allows. Not to be confused with the legal rate of interest, which is the rate applied by law when there is no agreement by the parties as to the rate of interest.

usury: Excess rate of interest over the legal rate charged to a borrower for use of money. Each state has its own definition of the exact rate and conditions that result in usury.

V

valuation: With respect to life insurance, the act of calculating a policy's reserve. The process of determining the total of policy reserves. Also, the act of determining the value of estate property in the estate settlement process.

valuation, asset: The process of determining the value of a company's investments or other assets.

valuation, full preliminary term reserve: (*See: full preliminary term reserve valuation.*)

valuation, gross premium: (*See: gross premium valuation.*)

valuation, group: (*See: group valuation.*)

valuation, policy: The process of determining an insurance company's liabilities under its policy obligations.

valuation reserve: That sum deducted from an asset to indicate by estimate that the market value of that asset is less than its book value or, in the case of a liability, to indicate the estimate that the liability may be greater (for example, income taxes) than is stated on the books.

value: The worth of anything, often expressed in terms of money, but not necessarily so. The present worth of all the rights to future benefits arising from ownership of the thing valued.

value, current: (*See: current value.*)

valued: one of the distinguishing characteristics of a traditional life insurance contract, meaning that the contract has a fixed value payable at maturity, death of the insured, or at any other time, as opposed to other insurance contracts that only reimburse actual loss.

valued basis of payment: An arrangement whereby the insurance company agrees to pay to or on behalf of the insured, upon occurrence of a defined loss, a specified amount of money, regardless of the extent of such loss.

valued benefit: (*See: fixed benefit.*)

value of all consideration: (*See: consideration.*)

value, reserve: (*See: reserve value.*)

values, commissioners: (*See: commissioners values.*)

values, convention: (*See: commissioners values.*)

vanishing point: In some cash value policies, such as variable life, the projected time that all premium payments will end permanently, based on premium amount and assumed rate of return on cash value.

vanishing premium: A feature in some cash value policies whereby the premium, which is based on premium amount and assumed interest rates, will end after a specified period of time.

variable annuity: An annuity similar to a traditional fixed annuity in that, on retirement, payments will be made periodically to the annuitant, usually over the remaining years of that person's life, but differing in that payments generally vary in amounts. With the fixed annuity, the dollar amount of each payment is guaranteed by the company. The annuitant may well receive more than the guaranteed amount through dividends, but never less. Under the variable annuity, to the contrary, there is no guarantee of the dollar amount of the payments. The payments, rather, will fluctuate up and down in accordance with the earnings of an invested account.

variable annuity accumulation unit: A unit representing a share of a contract holder's ownership in the specified and segregated assets of an insurance company selling a variable annuity, during the years prior to the contract holder's retirement. These accumulation units are purchased by the contract holder's payments made to the company. The value of the unit changes in each valuation period according to the changes in the market prices of the separate variable annuity portfolio securities owned by the insurance company and with investment income earned on these securities.

variable death benefit: A death benefit option in most variable universal life policies. Consists of a specified amount of pure protection (which remains level) plus all available cash value within the policy.

variable life insurance: Life insurance that provides a guaranteed minimum death benefit, but the actual benefit paid may be more, however, depending on the fluctuating market value of investments behind the contract at the time of the insured's death. The cash surrender value generally fluctuates with the market value of the investment portfolio. (*See also: equity linked.*)

variable universal life: The generic name for a life insurance policy, distinguished by a flexible premium and separate cash value investment accounts.

vehicles: Instruments used to carry out or fund a plan, as an insurance policy may be used as a vehicle to fulfill a plan of income security for an individual's family.

vested: A legal term identifying a right of immediate or future enjoyment that cannot be altered without the consent of the party having the right. However, such a right may be forfeited. (*See also: vested benefit.*)

vested benefit: A pension benefit, the payment of which is not contingent upon a participant's continuation in specified employment. Pension plan agreements or employee pension plan brochures generally do not differentiate the portion of vested benefits attributable to employer contributions and the portion provided by employee contributions. A right may be forfeited even after vesting if the agreement so provides. For example, the pension right of a retired person who takes employment with a competitor may be forfeited if the agreement so stipulates.

vested liability: With respect to a pension plan, the present value of a participant's immediate or deferred benefits, payable at his or her normal retirement age, which are nonforfeitable.

vested rights: A right is vested when it has become the property of some particular person or persons and cannot be denied to each vested individual without that person's consent. For instance, in a vested pension plan, the rights to benefits cannot be denied to the employees, even if they leave the plan.

vesting: The right of an employee under a retirement plan to retain part or all of the annuities purchased by the employer's contributions on the employee's behalf or, in some plans, to receive a cash payment of equivalent value on termination of employment after certain qualifying conditions have been met.

vesting, conditional: *(See: conditional vesting.)*

vesting, contingent: *(See: contingent vesting.)*

vesting, deferred: *(See: deferred vesting.)*

vesting, fractional: *(See: partial vesting.)*

vesting, full: Within a pension plan, that form of immediate or deferred vesting under which all accrued benefits of a participant become vested benefits.

vesting, graded: *(See: graded vesting.)*

vesting, graduated: *(See: graded vesting.)*

vesting, immediate: *(See: immediate vesting.)*

vesting, locked-in: *(See: locked-in vesting.)*

vesting, partial: *(See: partial vesting.)*

vesting, percentage: *(See: partial vesting.)*

vesting, progressive: *(See: graded vesting.)*

vesting rights: In a pension plan, giving the employee certain rights to the employer's contributions upon termination of employment. The amount of vesting may depend upon the employee's years of service and/or age. Under the ordinary plan, the employee does not receive the amount due him or her under the vesting rights in cash, but in an annuity payable upon retirement.

vesting, unconditional: *(See: unconditional vesting.)*

Veterans' Group Life Insurance (VGLI): A low-cost, nonrenewable but convertible five-year term insurance to which Servicemen's Group Life Insurance (SGLI) is converted automatically at the time an insured servicemember leaves active duty. At the end of the five-year period, the veteran may convert his or her VGLI to an individual policy with any company which participates in the VGLI program.

vis major: An accident for which no one is responsible; an act of God occurrence.

visual sales kit: A sales presentation package consisting of various literature, charts and other materials that are used to support the insurance salesperson's sales presentation.

vital statistics: Specific information and records pertaining to marriage, births, deaths, health and demography.

void: Used in referring to a contract, insurance or otherwise, when it is no longer valid. Also, null, ineffectual; having no legal force or binding effect; unable (in law) to support the purpose for which intended.

voidable: A policy contract that can be made void at the option of one or more parties to the agreement.

voluntary assignment: In insurance, assignment of a policy made without a valuable consideration. Also called gratuitous assignment.

voluntary compensation insurance: Coverage providing benefits similar to those of workers' compensation, used in circumstances in which workers' compensation does not apply or is not required by law.

voluntary reserve: An allocation of surplus not required by law. Such reserves are often accumulated by insurance companies to strengthen financial structure.

voluntary trust: An obligation arising out of a personal confidence reposed in, and voluntarily accepted by, one for the benefit of another, as distinguished from an involuntary trust that is created by operation of law.

W

waiting period: In general, the duration of time before a person is eligible for participation, coverage or benefits under a group insurance or retirement plan or for benefits under a health policy or disability provision. For example, the time between the beginning of an insured's disability and the commencement of the period for which benefits are payable; also called elimination period in individual health policies.

waive: A legal term meaning to surrender a right or privilege.

waiver: In insurance, an agreement contained in the policy that releases the insurance company from liability to pay for losses resulting from risks ordinarily covered in the policy, such as specified disabilities or injuries, or death from certain causes.

waiver of premium provision: A provision available in many life insurance policies and in disability income health policies that exempts the insured from the payment of premiums after he or she has been disabled for a specified period of time (usually six months in life policies and 90 days or six months in health policies).

waiver of premium with disability income rider: A life insurance rider that pays a monthly income and waives the policyowner's obligation to pay further premiums in the event he or she becomes totally and permanently disabled.

want: In insurance sales terminology, a desire for certain coverage or for a certain amount of coverage. There is a distinction between want and need. Many people want coverage of types or in amounts that are not necessities. Thus, wants may be in excess of needs, or vice versa.

war clause: A clause in an insurance contract limiting the insurance company's liability, for specified loss caused by war.

ward: A person, especially a minor, who is placed by law under the care of a guardian.

warranties and representations: Under the laws of most states, all statements made by a life or health insurance applicant, whether in the application blank or to the medical examiner, are considered, in the absence of fraud, to be representations and not warranties. A warranty must be literally true, and a breach of warranty, even by error, is sufficient to render the policy void, whether the matter warranted is material or not and whether or not it had contributed to the loss. A representation need be only substantially true. As a general rule, representations are considered fraudulent only when they relate to a matter material to the risk and were made with fraudulent intent. (*See also: representations.*)

warranty, implied: A warranty that is assumed to be a part of a contract even though not expressly included.

weekly account: In life and health insurance, a form completed to account for the premiums collected on weekly premium home service policies.

weekly premium increase: Sometimes called industrial increase. Combination companies use this phrase to measure the amount of net weekly gain in a debit's premium collection total. Where an agent adds $1.00 of new weekly premiums while 50 cents is going off the books, he or she would have a weekly premium increase of 50 cents. Usually death claims and maturities are excluded from the calculations.

weekly premium insurance: Also called industrial, debit or home service insurance. Life or health insurance issued on individual lives, usually without medical examination, at ages from birth to 70 years, in amounts less than $1,000, with premiums payable weekly or monthly to an agent who calls at the home to collect the premium. (*See also: industrial insurance.*)

weekly premium status card: A computer printout card showing the status of weekly premium policies.

weight and height table: A statistical table providing such information as average weight and height for men and women by age. Such tables may be prepared by the Actuarial Society of America and the Association of Life Insurance Medical Directors or by individual insurance companies.

welfare benefit plan, employee: (*See: employee welfare benefit plan.*)

whole life insurance: A form of life insurance offering protection for the whole of life, proceeds being payable at death. Premiums may be paid under a continuous premium arrangement or on a limited payment basis for virtually any desired period of years; e.g., ten, 20, 30, or to ages 60 or 65. (*See also: ordinary life.*)

wholesale insurance: A life or health insurance plan for covering groups of persons with individual policies having uniform provisions, although the policies may differ in benefits. Individual contracts are issued to persons in the group. This type of insurance generally is written in groups too small to qualify for regular group coverage.

widow's life income: One of the basic uses for life insurance. Life income for the widow after the children have reached maturity. If there are no children, the income is considered as starting at the death of the insured.

widow's-widower's benefit: The eligible surviving spouse of a fully insured deceased worker under Social Security is entitled, at age 65, to a life income equal to 100 percent of the worker's primary insurance amount (PIA). If preferred, the eligible survivor may choose a reduced amount as early as age 60.

wife insurance: Insurance on the life of a wife, designed to create cash in an amount sufficient to replace her economic value to the family unit in the event of her death. Even more significant since the advent of the two-income family.

wife's-husband's benefit: Under Social Security, the benefit payable to an eligible spouse of a worker entitled to a retirement or disability benefit after attaining age 62 or at any age while caring for an eligible child of the deceased worker.

will: A written legal document, executed in the form required by state law, by which a person makes a disposition of his or her property, to take effect upon the individual's death.

willful injury: (*See: intentional injury.*)

withdrawal: (*See: turnover.*)

withdrawal credits: Under a pension program, credits to the employer when an employee withdraws from the plan or terminates employment for reasons other than death; employer contributions on the employee's behalf to a fully insured pension plan—plus interest but minus a surrender charge—are credited back to the employer, but can be used only to pay future contributions. The employer usually gets no such credit when an employee dies, because, generally, the contribution rate was discounted for the probability of death. Under insured plans, withdrawal credits correspond to the discount for turnover under trusteed or deposit administration plans. Withdrawal credits are based on actual turnover when it occurs. The discount for turnover is based on an estimate of future withdrawal rates.

withdrawal rate: *(See: turnover.)*

without prejudice: A legal term meaning that an action, such as an offer to settle, is made without any admissions or waivers. Part of a nonwaiver agreement that holds that the insured who signs the agreement cannot legally construe certain actions, such as the determination of the value of a claim by the insurance company, to be an admission of liability on the company's part.

work clause: Under Social Security, a provision that all or part of a recipient's benefits will be lost if he or she earns over a certain amount of money in a given year. However, there are no restrictions on earnings after age 70. *(See also: earnings limitation.)*

workers' compensation benefits: Life and health insurance coverage for employees while they are on the job. Premiums are paid by the employer. Each state sets the benefit schedule and requirements. Coverage includes medical expenses, disability income, dismemberment and death benefits. By providing workers' compensation benefits, the employer's liability for injuries and sickness on the job is usually eliminated.

workers' compensation catastrophe covers: Excess of loss reinsurance purchased by primary insurance companies to cover their unlimited medical and compensation liability under the workers' compensation laws.

working capital, gross: *(See. current assets.)*

working capital, net: Current assets minus current liabilities.

working spouse: Designation given to a spouse who is an employee or is self-employed and who receives earned income

worldwide: Insurance coverage that remains in effect regardless of the geographical location in which loss occurs.

write: In insurance, to insure, to underwrite or to take an application.

written: Insurance for which an application has been taken, but that is not yet delivered and/or the first premium settled. Also, written premium, the entire amount of insurance premium on contracts issued by the insurer. The amount of premium for insurance recorded by the insurer during a specified period of time.

written business: In insurance, business for which applications have been signed by the applicant, but for that policies are not yet in force and that are classified as paid business.

written premium: That entire amount of premium on policy contracts that has been issued by an insurance company.

X: An unknown factor or amount. In an illustration, any factor or amount to be filled in when the general illustration is applied to a specific case.

X Table: A designation sometimes used for an experimental table or a draft of a table that has not yet developed to a point of satisfaction or for actual use in rating.

Y

yearly renewable term insurance: Renewable term insurance under which the successive terms are for one year. The right of renewal may extend to ten years or more or to an age such as 60 or 65. (*See also: renewable term insurance.*)

yearly renewable term plan reinsurance: (*See: reinsurance, yearly renewable term plan.*)

year of service: For pension, profit-sharing and qualified plans in general, employment of at least 1,000 hours in a 12-month period. In the case of an employee working on other than an hourly basis, 25 weeks of 40 hours each or 125 days of eight hours each are considered to be equal to 1,000 hours per year.

years certain annuity: (*See: annuity certain.*)

yield test: A measurement applied to bond investments in the portfolios of insurance companies. It is the relationship of the yield of bonds the insurance company has in its portfolio individually to the yield of fully taxable United States government bonds of the same maturity.

yield to maturity: The rate of return that is expressed in a percentage that will be obtained on an investment if the investment is held to maturity, taking into consideration that few investments are bought exactly at par and thus have a capital gain or loss in addition to the rate of return stated on the face of the instrument.

Z

zone system: A system developed by the NAIC for the triennial examination of insurers, under which teams of examiners are formed from the staffs of several states in each of several geographical zones. The results of their examinations are then accepted by all states in which the insurance company is licensed, without the necessity of each such state having to conduct its own examination.

Z Table: A mortality table showing ultimate experience on insured lives and computed from the experienced mortality on life policies issued by major companies from 1925 to 1934. The Z Table was a step in the development of the Commissioners Standard Ordinary Table of Mortality.

ABBREVIATIONS

AAA: American Academy of Actuaries

AABD: Aid to the Aged, Blind and Disabled (*See: public assistance.*)

AALU: Association of Advanced Life Underwriting

A & H: accident and health insurance

A & I: accident and indemnity

A & S: accident and sickness insurance

ABA: American Bar Association

ACLI: American Council of Life Insurance

ACLU: American College of Life Underwriters

ACV: actual cash value

AD & D: accidental death and dismemberment

ADB: accidental death benefit

AFDC: Aid to Families with Dependent Children

AI: accident insurance

AICPA: American Institute of Certified Public Accountants

AIME: average indexed monthly earnings (under Social Security)

ALC: American Life Convention

ALI—ABA: American Law Institute—American Bar Association

ALIC: Association of Life Insurance Counsel

ALIMD: Association of Life Insurance Medical Directors

AMA: American Medical Association

AMW: average monthly wage (under Social Security)

AO: at occupation

AP: additional premium

APL: automatic premium loan

APP (or app): application

APTD: Aid to the Permanently and Totally Disabled (*See: public assistance.*)

ARIA: American Risk and Insurance Association

ART: annual renewable term

ASA: Association of the Society of Actuaries (*See: Society of Actuaries.*)

ASCLU: American Society of chartered Life Underwriters

ASIM: American Society of Insurance Management

BCA: Blue Cross Association

BI: bodily injury

CA: current assets

CBT: computer based training

CDT: Commissioners Disability Table

CEBS: certified employee benefit specialist

CFA: Chartered Financial Analyst

CFC: Certified Financial Consultant

CFO: Chief Financial Officer

CFP: Chartered Financial Planner

ChFC: Chartered Financial Consultant

CIET, 1961: Commissioners Industrial Extended Term Mortality Table, 1961

CLU: Chartered Life Underwriter

COB: coordination of benefits

COBRA: Consolidated Omnibus Reconciliation Act

COL: cost of living

COLA: cost-of-living adjustment

CPA: Certified Public Accountant

CPCU: Chartered Property and Casualty Underwriter

CPI: consumer price index

CPP: Canada Pension Plan

CREF: College Retirement Equities Fund

CSI, 1961:   Commissioners Standard Industrial Mortality Table, 1961

CSO Table: Commissioners' Standard Ordinary Table

CSV: cash surrender value

CUNA: Credit Union National Association

CVLI: cash value life insurance

DA plan: deposit administration plan

D & B: Dunn and Bradstreet

DB: death benefit, direct broker

DBL: disability benefit law

DBO: death benefit only

DBR: daily board and room hospital benefit

Def. Comp.:   Deferred Compensation

DEFRA: Deficit Reduction Act of 1984

DI: double indemnity, disability income

DITC: Disability Insurance Training Council

DLP: date of last payment

DNR: do not renew

DOB: date of birth

DPP: deferred payment plan

DSP: (demisit-sine-prole) died without issue

EP: earned premium

ERA: expense reimbursement allowance

ERISA: Employee Retirement Income Security Act of 1974

ERTA: The Economic Recovery Tax Act of 1981

ESOP: employee stock ownership plan

ESOT: employee stock ownership trust

FALU: Fellow, Academy of Life Underwriters

FCII: Fellow of the Chartered Insurance Institute

FDIC: Federal Deposit Insurance Corporation

FEGLI: Federal Employee Group Life Insurance

FHA: Federal Housing Administration

FIA: Fellow of the Institute of Actuaries

FIC: fraternal insurance counsellor

FICA: Federal Insurance Contributions Act

FLMI: Fellow of the Life Management Institute

FMDF: Five Million Dollar Forum

FNA: financial needs analysis

FNMA: Federal National Mortgage Association (Fannie Mae)

FO: foreign to occupation

FOAB: federal old-age benefits

FSA: Fellow of the Society of Actuaries (*see: Society of Actuaries*) and Federal Security Agency

FSLIC: Federal Savings and Loan Insurance Corporation

FTC: Federal Trade Commission

FUTA: Federal Unemployment Tax Act

GA: general agent

GAMA: General Agents and Managers Association

GAMC: General Agents and Managers Conference of NALU

GAO: General Accounting Office

GNP: Gross National Product

GPO: guaranteed purchase option

HI: health insurance

HIAA: Health Insurance Association of America

HII: Health Insurance Institute

HIQA: Health Insurance Quality Award

HMO: health maintenance organization

HOLUA: Home Office Life Underwriters Association

HSA: Health Systems Agencies

IAAHU: International Association of Accident and Health Underwriters

IAFP: International Association for Financial Planning

IAHU: International Association of Health Underwriters

IASS: Insurance Accounting and Statistical Society

IBNR: incurred but not reported

ICA: International Claim Association

ICPI: Insurance Crime Prevention Institute

IHOU: Institute of Home Office Underwriters

IIA: Insurance Institute of America, Inc.

IIAA: Independent Insurance Agents Association

III: Insurance Information Institute

IIS: International Insurance Seminars, Inc.

IPA: individual practice association

IPRC: Insurers Public Relations Council

IRA: Individual Retirement Account, Individual Retirement Annuity

IRC: Internal Revenue Code

IRS: Internal Revenue Service

ISO: Insurance Services Office

IYM: investment year method

J & S: joint and survivorship annuity

LAMP: Life Agency Management Program of GAMC

LCA: Life Communicators Association

LIAA: Life Insurance Association of America and Life Insurance Advertisers Association

LIAMA: Life Insurance Agency Management Association

LIC: Life Insurers Conference

LIMRA: Life Insurance Management Research Association

LIMRF: Life Insurance Medical Research Fund

LLB: Bachelor of Laws

LOMA: Life Office Management Association

LPRT: Leading Producers Round Table

LTD: long-term disability

LUAC: Life Underwriters Association of Canada

LUATC: Life Underwriters Association Training Course

LUPAC: Life Underwriters Political Action Committee

LUTC: Life Underwriter, Training Council

MAAA: Member, American Academy of Actuaries

MDO: monthly debit ordinary

MDRT: Million Dollar Round Table

MET: multiple employer trust

MIB: Medical Information Bureau

MLS: maximum loss expectancy

MP: minimum premium; also, multi-peril

NAIA: National Association of Insurance Agents

NAIB: National Association of Insurance Brokers, Incorporated

NAIC: National Association of Insurance Commissioners

NAII: National Association of Independent Insurers

NAIW: National Association of Insurance Women

NALC: National Association of Life Companies

NALU: National Association of Life Underwriters

NASD: National Association of Securities Dealers

NFC: National Fraternal Congress

NHI: national health insurance

NIA: National Insurance Association, Inc.

NIDA: National Institute on Drug Abuse

NOL: not officially lapsed

NQA: National Quality Award

NSAA: National Sales Achievement Award

NSLI: National Service Life Insurance

NTO: not taken out

NW: net worth

OAA: Old-Age Assistance (*See: public assistance.*)

OAS: Old-Age Security (Canada)

OASDHI: Old-Age, Survivors, Disability, and Health Insurance program (known as Social Security and Medicare)

OASDI: Old-Age, Survivors, and Disability Insurance (commonly known as Social Security)

OASI: Old-Age and Survivors Insurance (known as Social Security)

OCA: outstanding claims account

Occ: occupation

OSHA: Occupational Safety and Health Act and Occupational Safety and Health Administration

OTI: over-the-counter

P/A: power of attorney

PAP: pension administration plan

PGP: prepaid group practice

PIA: Primary Insurance Amount (Social Security)

PLR: primary loss retention

PNO: premium notice ordinary

PPGA: personal producing general agent

PPO: Preferred Provider Organization

PR: pro rata

PRB: premium receipt book

PRD: pro rata distribution

REIT: Real Estate Investment Trust

RIA: Registered Investment Advisor

RIMS: Risk and Insurance Management Society

RHU: Registered Health Underwriter

RLR: retired lives reserve

RP: return premium

RPU: reduced paid up

RRSP: Registered Retirement Savings Plan

SA: Society of Actuaries

SBLI: savings bank life insurance

SDB: survivor's death benefit

SEC: Securities and Exchange Commission

SEGLI: Service Employee Group Life Insurance

SEP: Simplified Employee Pension

SGLI: Servicemen's Group Life Insurance

SI Table: Standard Industrial Table, 1941

SP: sine prole (died without issue), single premium.

SPVL: single premium variable life

SPWL: single premium whole life

SS: Social Security, salary savings

SSA: Social Security Administration and Social Security Act

STD: short-term disability

TDA: tax-deferred annuity

TDB: temporary disability benefits

TEFRA: Tax Equity and Fiscal Responsibility Act of 1982

TIAA: Teachers Insurance Annuity Association

TRA: Tax Reform Act of 1986

TSA: tax-sheltered annuity

UCD: unemployment compensation disability

UL: universal life

USES: United States Employment Service

USGLI: United States Government Life Insurance

VA: Veterans Administration

VGLI: Veterans' Group Life Insurance

VLI: variable life insurance

VUL: variable universal life

WC: worker's compensation

WL: whole life

WLRT: Women Leaders Round Table

WP: waiting period, waiver of premium

WWPD Act: Welfare and Pension Disclosure Act

YRT: yearly renewable term

YTD: year to date